New Ways of
Looking at Old Texts, III

Papers of the Renaissance
English Text Society, 1997–2001

edited by

W. SPEED HILL

Arizona Center for Medieval and Renaissance Studies
in conjunction with
Renaissance English Text Society
Tempe, Arizona
2004

Library of Congress Cataloging-in-Publication Data
New ways of looking at old texts. III : papers of the Renaissance English Text
Society, 1997–2001 / edited by W. Speed Hill.
     p. cm. — (Medieval & Renaissance texts & studies ; v. 270) (Renaissance
English Text Society special publication)
    Includes index.
    ISBN 0-86698-313-9 (alk. paper)
    1. English literature — Early modern, 1500–1700 — Criticism, Textual.
2. Transmission of texts — England — History — 16th century. 3. Transmission of texts — England — History — 17th century. 4. Manuscripts, Renaissance — England — Editing. 5. Manuscripts, English — Editing. 6. Renaissance — England. 7. Paleography, English. I. Hill, W. Speed (William Speed),
1935– . II. Series. III. Medieval & Renaissance Texts & Studies (Series) ; v.
270.
PR418.T48N494 2004
820.9 '003—dc22   2004054427

New Ways of
Looking at Old Texts, III

Papers of the Renaissance
English Text Society, 1997–2001

Medieval and Renaissance Texts and Studies

Volume 270

Renaissance English Text Society
Special Publication

Contents

Preface   ix

The Josephine A. Roberts Forums, MLA

1997: *Editing Renaissance Manuscripts*
    chair, David Freeman

Queen Elizabeth's "Future Foes": Editing Manuscripts
with the First-Line Index of Elizabethan Verse
(a Future Friend)
    STEVEN W. MAY   1

Words, Artifacts, and the Editing of Donne's Elegies
    GARY A. STRINGER   13

1998: *Electronic Editing and Publication*
    chair, A. R. Braunmuller

Eclectic Circulation: The Functional Dynamics of
Manuscript and Electronic Literary Cultures
    MARGARET J. M. EZELL   27

"What Two Crownes Shall They Be?": "Lower"
Criticism, "Higher" Criticism, and the Impact of
the Electronic Scholarly Edition
    R. G. SIEMENS   37

1999: *Editing Early Modern Commonplace Books*
    chair, W. Speed Hill

Julia Palmer's "Centuries": The Politics of Editing and
    Anthologizing Early Modern Women's Manuscript
    Compilations
        VICTORIA E. BURKE & ELIZABETH CLARKE   47

Editing a Renaissance Commonplace Book:
    The Holgate Miscellany
        MICHAEL ROY DENBO   65

2000: *Forms and Formats of Renaissance Historiography*
    chair, David Scott Kastan

Richard Hooker and the Rhetoric of History
        W. SPEED HILL   75

2001: *Editing Early Modern Women Writers*
    chair, Margaret Hannay

Treacherous Accidents and the Abominable Printing
    of Katherine Philips's *1664 Poems*
        ELIZABETH H. HAGEMAN   85

A Family Affair: The Life and Letters of
    Elizabeth Cary, Lady Falkland
        HEATHER WOLFE   97

"But a Copie": Textual Authority and Gender in Editions
    of "The Life of John Hutchinson"
        DAVID NORBROOK   109

Open Business Meetings, MLA

1998: Editing Ralegh's Poetry Historically
        MICHAEL RUDICK   133

A Response to Michael Rudick
        ARTHUR F. MAROTTI   143

1999: The Ethics of Post-Mortem Editing
        SUZANNE GOSSETT   147

2000: Notes on Editing *The Verse Miscellany of
        Constance Aston Fowler: A Diplomatic Edition*
        DEBORAH ALDRICH–WATSON   157

The Medieval Congress at Kalamazoo

1998: *Editing Women Writers of the English Renaissance*
        chair, David Freeman

        Working with a Complex Document:
        The Southwell–Sibthorpe Commonplace Book
        JEAN KLENE   169

        Towards a Textual History of the 1680 Folio *The History
        of the Life, Reign, and Death of Edward II* (attributed to
        Elizabeth Cary, Lady Falkland): Understanding the
        Collateral 1680 Octavo *The History of the Most
        Unfortunate Prince*
        JESSE G. SWAN   177

2001: *Forms and Formats of Early Modern Historiography*

        The Ulster Plantation and the Colonial Archive
        MARK NETZLOFF   191

Preface

With the publication of *New Ways of Looking at Old Texts, III,* reprinting papers given at panels sponsored by the Renaissance English Text Society at the MLA's annual conference as well as selected papers delivered at the Medieval Conference held annually at Kalamazoo, 1997–2001, the present editor hands on *New Ways*'s editorial baton to Michael Denbo, who is gathering copy for *New Ways, IV* (2002–2006). Michael is currently preparing an edition of the Holgate manuscript, now at the Morgan Library, New York City, for publication by RETS. Members in good standing receive copies of each: *New Ways, IV,* compliments of the Society; the Holgate Miscellany, as part of RETS's on-going publication program.

The claim was made that these collections were a convenient way to insert these essays into the bibliographic mainstream, serving as proxies for important work being done in editing (and un-editing) Renaissance texts. They did this — and more. The earlier volumes were more widely reviewed (or 'noticed') than their editor anticipated, and the initial *New Ways,* especially, turns up on graduate reading lists, there being no alternatives.

Finally, the series title, *New Ways,* should be credited to Arthur Marotti.

W. SPEED HILL

The Josephine A. Roberts Forums, MLA

Queen Elizabeth's "Future Foes": Editing Manuscripts with the First-Line Index of Elizabethan Verse (a Future Friend)

STEVEN W. MAY

EDITORS OF ENGLISH MANUSCRIPT POETRY ENJOY FAIRLY THOR-
ough control over the pre-Elizabethan canon. *The Index of Middle English Verse* and its *Supplement* locate the texts transcribed from roughly
the twelfth through the fifteenth centuries.[1] The late William A. Ringler's
Index of English Verse in Manuscript, 1501–1558, as prepared and completed by
Michael Rudick and Susan Ringler, extends our coverage up to Elizabeth's
reign.[2] The capstone to Ringler's Tudor Verse Index is the Elizabethan Index
now in progress. It covers all poetry transcribed or printed from 1559 to
1603. It is fully computerized and has been sponsored by major grants from
the National Endowment for the Humanities. The Index is under contract with

---

[1] Carleton Brown and Rossell Hope Robbins, eds., *Index of Middle English Verse*
(New York: Columbia Univ. Press, 1943); Rossell Hope Robbins and John L. Cutler,
eds., *Supplement to the Index of Middle English Verse* (Lexington: Univ. of Kentucky
Press, 1965).

[2] William A. Ringler, Jr., ed., *Bibliography and Index of English Verse in Manuscript,
1501–1558*, prepared and completed by Michael Rudick and Susan J. Ringler (London: Mansell, 1992).

Continuum Press for publication in both hard-bound and electronic formats.

As users of Ringler's early Tudor indexes know, the Elizabethan Index is far more than a bibliography and compilation of first lines. It records up to eighteen types of information about each record, including authors and titles, the number of lines, forms and meters, refrains, subscriptions, dates of printing or transcription, and scholarship on each poem as applicable. Moreover, each entry is subject indexed in as many categories as possible: by literary genre, as a translation, in dialect, and under the chief subjects treated. Illustrations with verse are indexed by the subject of the illustration. Poems set to music are recorded with tune titles and names of composers. The Index offers a comprehensive analysis of basic information about every record, with more than thirty-two thousand entries on the database as of December 1997.

This afternoon I will concentrate on the research potential of the more than nine thousand poems from manuscripts within this total. I will offer some examples of how modern editions of Elizabethan texts might have benefited from access to the Index. I will outline its usefulness in the editing of author-centered as well as topical or genre-centered editions, and finally I will demonstrate how its manuscript holdings can be used to upgrade a standard edition.

Let me say at the outset that my remarks about the following editions are not meant as negative criticism; each of these works is a valuable scholarly contribution to our discipline. I wish only to illustrate what enormous leverage the Index provides over a wealth of Elizabethan manuscript material that scholars otherwise find very difficult to control. With the Index future editors will locate in minutes every poem attributed to a given author and every poem in the author's received canon. A separate search of the database will yield every poem attributed to someone with the poet's initials, just for good measure.

Let me begin with Professor Ringler's Clarendon Press edition of Sir Philip Sidney's *Poems*.[3] With access to the Elizabethan Index, Bill could have located all of Sidney's Elizabethan manuscript texts in two minutes instead of the two full years of work he estimated to have spent in the search. Moreover, he would have found another Elizabethan text of "Certain Sonnets" 32 plus the fragment of an unrecorded manuscript of the *Old Arcadia* which includes two of its poems.[4]

---

[3] William A. Ringler, Jr., ed., *The Poems of Sir Philip Sidney* (Oxford: Clarendon Press, 1962).

[4] The *Old Arcadia* leaf is described and its scribe identified by H. R. Woudhuysen, "A New Manuscript Fragment of Sidney's *Old Arcadia*: The Huddleston Manuscript," *English Manuscript Studies* 11 (2002): 52–69.

For his edition of *Richard Barnfield: The Complete Poems*,[5] George Klawitter was unable to locate the "Isham Manuscript." He therefore relied on Alexander Grosart's transcription of seven of its poems doubtfully ascribed to Barnfield. The manuscript is not, in fact, Elizabethan, but several of its texts are, and since the Index often cites later manuscript sources for poems it records, it reveals that Isham is now Folger MS. V.a.161.

As a final example, Dana F. Sutton edited British Library Add. MS. 22583 as volume three of *William Gager: The Complete Works*.[6] Sutton concluded that, "Save for one item (CLV) all the material in the manuscript is composed by Gager himself" (xviii). In addition to this one Latin poem, however, the Index shows that item 189 ("Mine eye why didst thou light") is attributed to William Hunnis in the *Paradise of Dainty Devices*, item 190 ("As I remember, Aeliea") appears in Timothy Kendall's *Flowers of Epigrammes*, 1577, and item 193 ("Were I a king") occurs in several other manuscripts where it is attributed to Edward DeVere, seventeenth Earl of Oxford. The contamination of Gager's anthology with three more poems demonstrably by other authors calls into question his responsibility for all of the 197 entries in the manuscript, English and Latin. Again, I am not faulting the work of these fine editors, only demonstrating one kind of contribution the Index will make to future editing of manuscript texts.

Along with authorial editions, the Index will greatly facilitate the editing of anthologies of verse organized on generic or topical principles. Sample literary genres from the manuscript verse subject fields include several types analyzed by Arthur Marotti in his *Manuscript, Print, and the English Renaissance Lyric* as particularly indigenous to manuscript environments.[7] These include satire, libel, flyting, and bawdy; and there are many more, such as verse drama, narrative, epithalamion, beast fable, riddle, street cry, prophecy, and royal entertainment. Topics include social class and social conditions, tobacco, lawyers, marriage, cuckoldry, music, poetry, Flodden Field, calendar reform, the Dissolution of the Monasteries, and the Spanish Armada. There are poems about historical figures such as Lady Catherine Grey, Esmé Stuart, Cardinal Wolsey, Mary Herbert, Countess of Pembroke, William the Conqueror, and John the Baptist. Among the fictional characters treated in manuscript verse

---

[5] George Klawitter, *Richard Barnfield: The Complete Poems* (Selinsgrove, London, and Toronto: Associated Univ. Presses, 1990), 43–45, 189–92.

[6] Dana F. Sutton, ed., *William Gager: The Complete Works*, vol. 3 (New York and London: Garland, 1994), xviii.

[7] Arthur F. Marotti, *Manuscript, Print, and the English Renaissance Lyric* (Ithaca and London: Cornell Univ. Press, 1995), chap. 2.

are Robin Hood, Paris, Cupid, and King Arthur. With the Index it will be easy to collect a wide variety of texts on these and many other subjects and literary genres.

The Index will also greatly simplify the updating of editions I shall term "fixer-uppers." They are basically sound, but would benefit from some degree of updating. An example is Leicester Bradner's edition of *The Poems of Queen Elizabeth I*. A state-of-the-art publication in 1964, it has become outmoded as the world's manuscript archives have yielded five completely new poems of the Queen's composition plus more than a dozen new versions of poems that Bradner edited.[8] This afternoon I wish to show how the text of Queen Elizabeth's lyric beginning "The doubt of future foes" can be revised using manuscript evidence collected in the course of preparing the Index of Elizabethan Verse.

"The doubt of future foes" is among the Queen's most certainly datable compositions. She wrote it very late in 1569 or early in 1570 after it became clear that the Northern Rebellion had been crushed.[9] Her armies had quickly suppressed the Catholic uprising aimed at freeing Mary, Queen of Scots, and placing her on the throne. Elizabeth knew, however, that the captive queen's presence in England would necessarily spark further rebellion among her Catholic subjects.

Most of the scribes who copied this poem had trouble preserving its dominant horticultural metaphors. As reconstructed in the critical text below, Elizabeth anticipates the gardeners' scene in *Richard II* by comparing her realm to a garden where clouds of untried joys in line 6 turn to a rain of late repent as the (military) wind shifts direction. The "top of hope supposde" in line 7 refers to the part of the plant that grows above ground (OED, sb. 5), opposite to the root which it will ironically turn out to be in this instance, a "root of rue." The rebels' "grafted guile" shall be "fruitless," nor shall "The daughter of Debate" (line 11) "reap" any gain from her continual sowing of discord. Rather, Elizabeth's "rusti sworde" will double as a scythe to poll the tops,

---

[8] Leicester Bradner, *The Poems of Queen Elizabeth I* (Providence: Brown Univ. Press, 1964). I provide critical texts of the Queen's verse reply to Sir Walter Ralegh, "Ah silly pugg," along with her Latin quatrain and English translation in Steven W. May, *The Elizabethan Courtier Poets* (Columbia, MO: Univ. of Missouri Press, 1991), 319, 342. With Anne Lake Prescott I edited a 220-line holograph poem preserved at Hatfield House, "The French Verses of Elizabeth I," *ELR* 24 (1994): 9–43.

[9] It was reported on 25 December 1569 that the Earl of Northumberland had been captured; on 30 December, field commanders wrote the Privy Council that they had discharged seven thousand men and retained the rest of the army only until their pay arrived (*CSPD*, 60/51, 59).

now ambiguously heads and the visible tops of the plants, in a political pruning that insures the stability of her reign.

Sir John Harington probably wrote the cover letter that circulated with a text of Elizabeth's poem reprinted in the 1769 *Nugae Antiquae*. The letter states that the queen's holograph draft was copied without royal permission by Lady Willoughby. The poem circulated in manuscript a good deal more widely than Bradner's edition would indicate. Lady Willoughby's copy was, presumably, Π in the stemma below, and both its descendants were originally Harington family manuscripts transcribed and published by later editors. Bradner worked from three other Elizabethan texts (identified in the collations below): *P*, George Puttenham's version published in 1589, *H*, Humfrey Coningsby's anthology,[10] and *R*, the Rawlinson manuscript, which dates from the 1570s.

The Index widens the contemporary manuscript circulation of the poem by adding four texts to those used by Bradner. The Folger copy, which descends with *R* from β, a lost intermediary in the stemma, also dates from the 1570s. The Egerton and Ottley anthologies, descendants of Δ, were compiled in Shropshire, probably within twenty miles of each other. The Harleian manuscript, *H*, is a third Salopian text but one, surprisingly, derived from an independent branch of the stemma that also gave rise to the Inner Temple text. Ancestral to Φ and both of these manuscripts is Σ, the source as well of Puttenham's version of the poem.

Bradner dismissed the Digby and both the Harleian versions of the poem on the grounds that they "have the Puttenham text with minor variations" (72). *Ha* was, indeed, copied from *P* in the eighteenth century, but *H* is a much superior independent witness. Digby is as well an Elizabethan copy of the poem unrelated to Puttenham's version. In both its states, *D* and *D2*, this manuscript provides a textbook case of conflation. It agrees in error with descendants of both Δ and Φ/Σ while avoiding all but one of the erroneous readings that allow us to reconstruct these hypothetical ancestors.

Facing fewer choices, Bradner selected *R* as his copy text although it badly distorts the Queen's metaphors in lines 5–7 where the "vntyed" clouds turn to "raige," while the top of hope is "supprest" and its root "vpreard" instead. Bradner's sensitivity to Elizabeth's metaphors rescued all but one of these readings, yet his editorial procedure left the text ultimately at the mercy of one of its most corrupt witnesses, *P*. He emended six of eight definite errors

---

[10] Henry Woudhuysen provides the fullest account to date of Coningsby's anthology and identifies the compiler of the Rawlinson anthology as Edward Gunter of Lincoln's Inn in *Sir Philip Sidney and the Circulation of Manuscripts 1558–1640* (Oxford: Clarendon Press, 1996), 278–86, 165–66.

in *R* (among the underlined readings in the critical text) with readings from Puttenham's text, from which Bradner also took "ye" in line 8.

The additional readings of *I*, the Inner Temple manuscript, allow us to reconstruct the lost intermediary, Σ, while bringing into focus the descent of *H* and *I* from another hypothetical ancestor, Φ. The Egerton and Ottley texts, however corrupt, point to the existence of Δ with only two certain errors at lines 5 and 7. The readings of β and Δ, as reconstructed from *F–R* and *E–O* respectively, define Elizabeth's text as closely, I believe, as the available evidence will permit. Their testimony allows for a substantial upgrading of Elizabeth's poem. The Folger version, as emended in four readings taken from β or Δ, also deviates in five readings from Bradner's critical text. These changes are underlined in the critical text printed below. They amount to a three percent change in the wording of this 168-word poem. Thus, if Bradner's version was ninety-seven percent correct, then the present text restores the Queen's work to its original substantive form.

The manuscript sources discovered in the course of preparing the Index bring the text of the Queen's lyric into sharper focus, while they reveal how widely the poem circulated. With access to more than double the number of contemporary texts known to Bradner, we can posit widespread copying and recopying of this poem as the Throckmorton, Parry, and Babington plots showed that the "doubts" (fears) she expressed in it were prophetic rather than paranoid. Of even greater interest in understanding the transmission of verse in manuscript, it is noteworthy that this highly author-centered text, attributed to the Queen in every one of its surviving witnesses, deteriorated in quality about as rapidly as any anonymous poem that circulated widely in the manuscript network. But why? That is matter for another essay.

A Critical Text of Queen Elizabeth's
"The Doubt of Future Foes"

Copy text: Folger MS. V.b.317, fol. 20v (lightly punctuated, with contractions expanded, i/j, u/v normalized, and variations from Bradner's text underlined.)

Verses made by the Queen's Majestie

The doubt of future foes
   exiles my present joye,
And wit me warnes to shun such snares
   as threaten myne anoy.

For falshod nowe dooth flowe
    and subjectes' faith dooth ebb,
Which should not be if reason rulde
    or wisdom weavde the web.

But cloudes of joies untride
    doe clook aspiring myndes   [5]
Which turn to rain of late repent
    by changed course of windes.

The top of hope supposde
    the root of rue shalbe,
And fruitles all theire grafted guile
    as shortli you shall see.

Their dazlde eies with pride
    which great ambition blindes
Shalbe unsealed by worthi wightes
    whose forsight falshod findes.   [10]

The daughter of Debate
    that discord ay dooth sowe
Shal reap no gayne wher former rule
    stil peace hath taught to knowe.

No forein, banisht wight
    shall ancre in this porte;
Our realm brookes no sedicious sects,
    let them els where resorte.

My rusti sworde through rest
    shal first his edge employ   [15]
To poll their tops who seke such chaunge
    or gape for future joy.

    Vivat Regina

Collations

Sigla (in collation order; asterisks indicate sources from the Index of Elizabethan Verse unknown to Bradner):

Lemma   F   *Folger MS. V.b.317, fol. 20v
        R   Rawlinson Poet. MS. 108, fol. 44v
        E   *Egerton MS. 2642, fol. 237v
        D   Digby MS. 138, fol. 159 (original readings)
        D2   Digby MS. 138, fol. 159 (as emended)
        H   Harleian MS. 7392(2), fol. 27v
        AH   Arundel Harington Manuscript (fol. 164v), ed. Ruth Hughey
              (Columbus, OH, 1960).
        I   *Inner Temple, Petyt MS. 538.10, fol. 3v
        P   George Puttenham, The Arte of English Poesie, 1589, sig.
              2E2v
        Ha   Harleian MS. 6933, fol. 8
        NA   Nugae Antiquae ... By Sir John Harington (London, 1769), v.
              1.58–59.
        O   *National Library of Wales, Ottley MS., fol. 5v

Title] verses made by the Quenes Matie R, Certen verses made by the
Queenes moste excellent Matie against the Rebells in the North partes of
England and in Norfolke & other places of the Realme Ao Dni 1569 & 1570.
E, E Reg D, Reginam left margin, I; The following Ditty ... was composed
by Q Elizabeth and was printed not long after, if not before, the beheading of
the said Scots Queen Ha; Om. AH P NA O.

1   doubt] dread AH NA; future] futures E; foes] force D; exiles] exyle
        AH.
2   threatins] threaten R E D H AH NA I P Ha O; myne] my Ha.
3   subjectes] subiect P Ha.
4   should] woud Ha; weavde] wove AH NA.
5   joies untride] ioyes vntyed R, Ioye vntried E O, toyes vntryed H Ha
        D, toie vntride I P; doe] doth AH I NA; aspiring] aspired E.
6   turns to rage] storme to reigne E, turne to ende D2, turne to Rayne H
        I P Ha; turne to rage AH NA; turnes the raigne O.
        repent] report AH NA; by] bee E; chaunged course of] course of
        changed P Ha NA; windes] minds AH; kindes NA.
7   top] topps AH NA; hope] happe O, Ioy D2; supposde] supprest R,
        suppose AH NA; root of rue] roote vpreard R, Roote of ruyne E O,
        roote of Rule D, Roote of Ruthe H I P Ha; shalbe] will be Ha.
8   all] of AH NA; theire grafted guile] the grafted guiles H Ha, their
        graffed guile AH, their guiles I, their graffed guiles P; you] ye P Ha.
9   Their] the R AH NA, Then P Ha; with] which H; which] with AH,
        And NA, that O; blindes] blynde AH NA.

10   unsealed] vnsold *I*; by worthi wightes] by woorthye wyttes *D*, of worthy wittes *H*, of worthie wites I, through worthy wittes *O*; forsight] presight *E*, foresightes *I*.

11   discord ay] discord eake *H I*, eke discord *P Ha*; dooth] dyd *R*; sowe] showe *I*

12   gayne] reigne *O*; stil] till *E*; stil ... knowe] hath taught stil peace to growe *P*, hath taught Peace still to grow *Ha*, Still Peace hathe taughte to flowe *NA*.

13   wight] wyeghtes *D*.

14   realm] Calmes *O*, Callme *D*; no] not *R E D*; sectes] sect *I*; brookes .. sectes] it brookes no strangers force *P Ha*, brooke no seditious sectes *O*.

15   My] Owr *D H I P Ha*; sworde] swordes *D I*; through] with *P Ha*; rest] ruste *I*; his] theire *I*.

16   pul] povle *R E H AH I P Ha NA O*; their] the *AH I NA*; who seke] that sekes *R E D AH*, that seeke *H Ha NA O*, which seke *P*; gape] gapes *E D AH*; for future joy] for further Ioy *AH*, and gape for ioy *P*, and gape for lawless Ioy *Ha*, for such like joye *NA*.

Sub. FINIS E. Reg *D*, EL *H*, ffinis Elizabetha Regina *AH*, Elizabetha Regina *O*.

Abbreviated Stemma

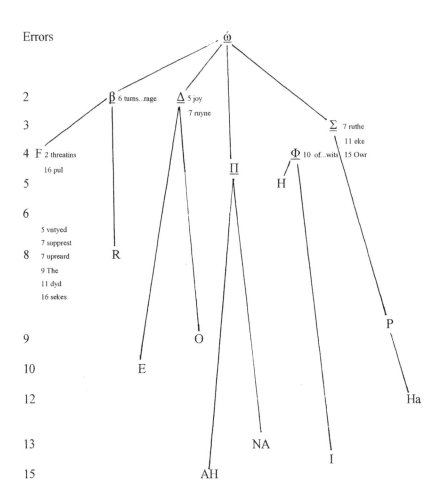

Commentary

Where the readings of β and Δ with two errors and Σ with three can be re-constructed, these hypothetical intermediaries approximate the Queen's holo-graph more closely than any extant text. Only three of the manuscripts carry real weight in constructing the critical text of Elizabeth's poem: *F* with four errors, *H* with five, and *R* with eight. Bradner saw only the last of these manuscripts, which he correctly chose as copy text. Given this version of the poem, however, and the tangle of corrupt readings in the other texts he knew at lines 5 through 7, he can hardly be blamed for not reconstructing the Queen's metaphors in this passage.

Folger is the obvious choice for copy text. It shares with *R* the faulty "turns to rage" that derives from their common ancestor, β, but avoids *R*'s mistakes in lines 5, 7, 9, 11, and 16. Two of the Folger manuscript's three errors concern subject–verb agreement that could reflect Elizabeth's grammatical practice: "snares ... threatins" in line 2 and "turns" in line 6, subject of the preceding "which" that must have as its antecedent the "cloudes," "ioyes," or "myndes" of line 5. The occurrence of the singular verb "turns" in *R* as well as *F* suggests that this could be the correct reading, but I hesitate to adopt it without systematic study of the Queen's grammatical habits with regard to subject–verb agreement. Supporting the emendation "Turn to rain" is its occurrence in Σ, as corroborated by the readings of *H*, *I*, and *P*. *E* and *O* indicate, moreover, that Δ preserves "rain" at line 6 rather than "rage." Folger's "pul" in line 16 could likewise be merely a variant spelling of the correct word, "poll," but since the OED does not record the variant "pul" I have classified it as an error.

As I read the metaphor in lines 5–6, the clouds of untried joys turn to a rain of late repent due to a shift in wind direction (the "changed course of windes"). In terms of the political realities surrounding the Northern Rebellion of 1569–70, the shifting winds are winds of fortune adumbrating the success of the Queen's forces and collapse of the Catholic opposition. As a result, the joys anticipated by the supporters of Mary, Queen of Scots, turn to a rain of repentance, a rain of repentant tears, perhaps. Elizabeth's "joye," line 1, is obviously recent ("late"), as she writes the poem, while here she considers the equally recent regret suffered by her foes. *R*'s unusual spelling of rage, "raige," likewise suggests that β merely overlooked the macron which converts this spelling to "raigne." These scribes no doubt felt that the metaphor made sense if clouds of joys turned to rage or aspiring minds turned to rage by the shifting winds, but the metaphor, it seems to me, works more consistently if the shifting winds turn the clouds to rain.

The second hypothetical ancestor, Σ, transmitted three errors to its descendants, *H*, Humphrey Coningsby's anthology, *P*, Puttenham's *Arte of English Poesy*, and *I*, the Inner Temple anthology which also preserves a unique text of Elizabeth's verse response to a poem by Sir Walter Ralegh. The agreement of *H* and *I* at line 10, "of ... wittes / wites" for "by ... wights" likewise points to a lost intermediary (Φ) between Σ and these two texts. It is possible as well that agreement in error at line 16, "sekes/gapes," suggests a

connection between the Arundel Harington version of the poem and that in
Robert Commander's collection, the Egerton manuscript. Or, *AH* could be
connected with *I* through conjunctive error at line 5, "doth," and line 16,
"the," but I think it more likely that these readings represent independent
variation rather than textual affinity.

With four emendations, *F* provides a critical text of Elizabeth's poem that
improves on Bradner's text considerably, for just three mistaken words in *R*
at lines 5 and 7 wholly obscure Elizabeth's metaphors of the clouds of untried
joys that cloak aspiring minds, and the top of a supposed hope that will turn
out to be the root of rue, the tree metaphor that is extended in line 8 to condemn its proponents' "grafted guile" to fruitlessness (top OED 4, the head;
5 the part of a plant growing above ground as opposed to the root).

Words, Artifacts, and the
Editing of Donne's Elegies

GARY A. STRINGER

B EFORE PROCEEDING TO TALK SPECIFICALLY ABOUT EDITING
Donne's elegies, I should like briefly to outline the textual circumstances that a Donne scholar faces. With the exceptions of the Anniversaries — the long commendatory poems on the death of Elizabeth Drury
— and a scattering of shorter pieces, Donne "published" his poems only in
manuscript, circulating copies (sometimes of single poems, sometimes of
groups) among members of a coterie of friends, patrons, and prospective patrons, who in turn circulated them to others. The first collected edition of
Donne's poetry, the 1633 *Poems*, was not published until two years after the
author's death, and virtually none of Donne's holographs survive: of poetic
materials in the poet's own hand, we have only four brief inscriptions, a Latin
epitaph on his wife, and a single, sixty-three-line verse epistle. The remaining
scribal copies of Donne's poems, however, total over five thousand exempla
in about two hundred and forty different manuscripts, and many poems survive in over fifty separate copies. Before reaching the relative stability of print,
of course, these texts were vulnerable to virtually infinite alteration, not only
by Donne himself, but also by inattentive, officious, or censorious copyists,
some of whom mangled poems that came into their hands almost beyond recognition. Filiation — my particular focus in this paper — really consists in the
process of trying to unravel the tangled threads of transmission extant in these
numerous and diverse transcriptions so as to retreat as far as possible upstream
toward the head — which, as Donne reminds us in the Holy Sonnet "Since
she whom I lovd," "streames do shew." Only when this has been done can

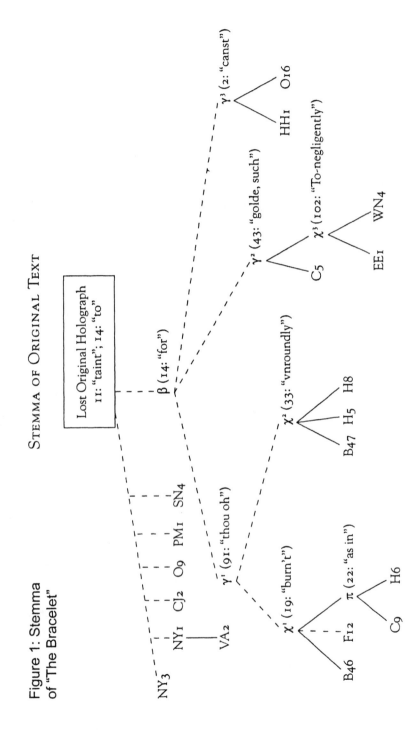

Figure 1: Stemma
of "The Bracelet"

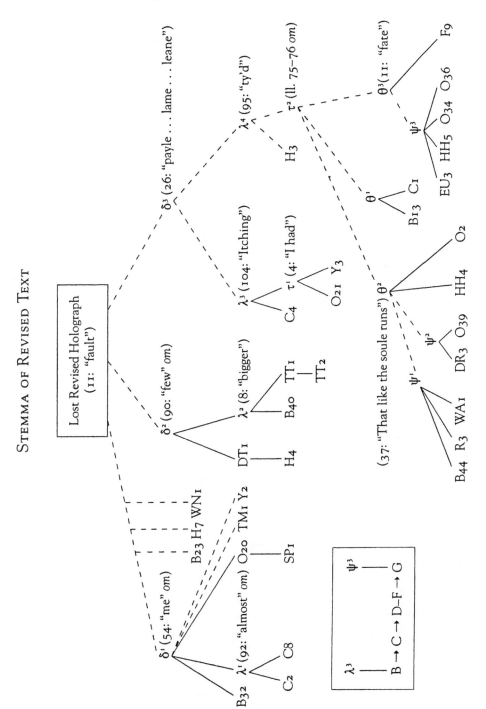

STEMMA OF REVISED TEXT

we be assured of a safe and pollution-free site upon which to erect an interpretive edifice.

Among the seventeenth-century artifacts, texts of Donne's elegies are em-
phatically as plentiful and as variegated in form as most of his other poems.
Containing 982 lines of Donne poetry — roughly one-tenth of the canon —
the eighteen authentic poems (including the generically indistinct "Sapho to
Philaenis") plus two dubious items that appear in the Variorum volume on
the elegies[1] exist in 823 individual copies totalling 48,656 lines of raw material. Among these poems, "The Bracelet," which appears as the first elegy in
the most authoritative arrangements, exhibits perhaps the single most complicated history of transmission; and in the following remarks I shall briefly
sketch in that history, with particular reference to the technical and evaluative
procedures employed in bringing it to light.

Appearing in some sixty-two manuscript and seven seventeenth-century
print sources, "The Bracelet" is one of the Donne poems most widely circulated amongst the poet's contemporaries. Fifty-two of the manuscripts and six
of the collected editions record full transcriptions of this 114-line poem.
Interestingly, it was one of five elegies officially excepted from the 1633
edition (designated A in our listing), and when John Marriot incorporated it
as the twelfth of seventeen numbered elegies in the edition of 1635 (B), government authorization had not yet been obtained. Further, as is shown in *figure 1*, when the poem entered print in 1635, it was set from a manuscript far
down the family tree from the Group-I text that had been disallowed two
years previously; and this corrupt redaction became the basis for all subsequent
editions of the poem, from the 1639 resetting of the 1635 text up to the Oxford University Press issue of Donne's *Selected Poetry* in 1996. If we do not
have a full bill of the licenser's particular objections to the text originally
rejected, the text as printed in 1635 points clearly to his general concern that
the poem trafficked in politico-theological contraband, and the omission of
certain blocks of lines in, especially, some of the later, more derivative texts
suggests that even in the relatively private sphere of scribal transmission some
copyists recognized troublesome material in the poem and practiced a self-
imposed censorship. Indeed, identification of this ideologically sensitive material is one of the major benefits to be derived from the study of the poem's
transmissional history and the development of a comprehensive stemma.

After one prepares accurate transcriptions of all seventeenth-century copies
of the elegy and turns them into computer files, the beginning step in

---

[1] Gary A. Stringer et al., eds., *The Elegies* (Bloomington: Indiana Univ. Press,
2000). Vol. 2 of *The Variorum Edition of the Poetry of John Donne*. 8 vols. 1995– .

analyzing the textual data is to run a collation in order to see how the artifacts begin to sort themselves out into families. In the Donne Variorum project we do this by means of the Donne Variorum Textual Collation Program, a sample page of output from which is shown in *figure 2*. The entire collation of "The Bracelet," of course, contains such a page for each of the poem's 114 lines plus heading and subscription, but I have selected the collation of line eleven for presentation because, as it happens, this is the single most important line in the poem for dividing the manuscript texts into the two discrete lines of textual transmission shown on the Stemma.

The elements of the collation shown in *figure 2* are as follows:

(1)   in the leftmost column appears an ordered series of eleven-character identification tags, each of which lists the work siglum for "The Bracelet" (008), the source siglum for a given artifact (from NY3 at the top to AF1 at the bottom), and the line number (011) — items which are assigned at a prior stage of the editorial process and which, along with the periods inserted for ease of reading, are entered when the transcription is turned into a computer file. This ID tag stays with the line throughout the entire analysis and will be stripped off only during construction of the textual apparatus of the edited poem.

(2)   Following the leftmost column is a succession of other columns, each of which shows at the top of the page a word in the base text (in this case NY3) against which the other copies have been collated and, under each base word, any differences that may exist between the base text and other copies. (NY3's relationship to Donne's holograph is diagrammed in *figure 1*; any of the other sources could equally have served as base text for my present illustrative purposes, however.) Looking at the column under the base word "Nor," for instance, we notice that a dozen or so transcriptions give "nor" — with a lower-case "n" — as a variant to the capitalized "N" in NY3; and the column under "yet" shows that several copies spell the word with two "t's," that O34 spells it "yit," and that WN4 follows the word with a comma. A blank space at any line-column coordinate indicates that the word appearing in that position in the artifact in question exactly matches the base text and has been omitted from the report generated by the collation program.

The crucial column of words for our purposes here is the fifth, headed by the word "taint" in NY3. Including the recognizable permutation "constraint" in PM1, as the collation shows, some sixteen manuscripts match the base-text reading, while the remaining thirty-two give the alternative "fault," which in

Figure 2: Collation of line 11 of "The Bracelet"

ws | ss | 1n

siglum							
008.NY3.011	Nor yet	by	any	taint	haue	stray'd	or	gone
008.B13.011				fault		strayed,		
008.B23.011	yett			faulte		strayde,		
008.B32.011	yett			falt		strayd,		
008.B40.011	yett			fault,	have	straid	and	gon
008.B44.011				fault		straid,		
008.B46.011				tainte		strayde,		
008.B47.011				taynt		strayd		gonne
008.C01.011				fault		strayd,		
008.C02.011	yett			fault		strayde	and	
008.C04.011				fault		strayd,		
008.C05.011	Yett			taynte		strayde		
008.C08.011	yett		anie	falt		strayed	and	gon.
008.C09.011	nor				hau*e[Mvar:>haue<]	strayd		gon
008.CJ2.011	nor			taynte				gone,
008.DR3.011	nor			faulte		straid		
008.DT1.011	nor			fault		straid,	&	
008.EE1.011						strayde,		
008.EU3.011				fate		strayde		gon,
008.F09.011				fate	have	strayd,		gon
008.F12.011				taynt		staynd		
008.H03.011			anie	faute				
008.H04.011	nor		anie	fault		straied,	and	
008.H05.011	nor							
008.H06.011						strayd		
008.H07.011					haue	straid		
008.H08.011om				fault				gon

Siglum						
008.HH1.011	nor	(by	taynts		strayd	gon
008.HH4.011	nor yett	anny	fault		strayed	gone,
008.HH5.011	nor		fate		straied %Y&%Z>%5or%6<	gone,
008.NY1.011					strayd	
008.002.011	nor	be->by<	fault,		straid	
008.009.011	nor				straid	
008.016.011			taint,	or	plague, / have / stray'd,	
008.020.011	yett		falt		strayd	
008.021.011	nor yett		fault		strayd	
008.034.011	yit		%Yfate%Z {>tainte<,}		straid	gon
008.036.011			fate		strayd	
008.039.011	yett		fault	have	straid	gon
008.PM1.011	nor	my	constraint;	have	strayd	
008.R03.011			fault		strid,	and
008.SN4.011		anie	tainte		straid	
008.SP1.011			fault		strayde	go%Mne
008.TM1.011			fault		strayde,	gon
008.TT1.011	yett		fault	have	straid	
008.TT2.011			fault	have	strayed	
008.VA2.011			fault		strayed;	
008.WA1.011			falt,		strayd	gon
008.WN1.011			fault		strayd	
008.WN4.011	nor yett,	by,	tainet		straid,	
008.Y02.011			faulte		strayd	gon
008.Y03.011	yett		faulte		strayd	gonne
008.00B.011			way	have	straid	
008.00G.011			way	have	straid	
008.AF1.011			way	have	straid	

a handful of sources (the θ^2 family on the Stemma of the Revised Text) has degenerated to "fate." One artifact — O34 — originally read "fate" but its scribe replaced that with "tainte," no doubt after comparing his text with another manuscript; and H8, the only source I have not otherwise accounted for, omits the line and must be filiated on the basis of other readings. The artifacts included at the very bottom of *figure 2* — B, G, and AF1 — represent the print tradition, and include the apparently compositorial "way" for the "taint" or "fault" found in all the surviving manuscripts. I will come back to these later.

Since filiation is essentially a matter of elaborating a hierarchical model of multiple, interlinked parts, at every structural level one is looking for discriminators that exert their force not only horizontally — separating one parallel thread or strand of transmission from another — but vertically, downward, explaining — or at least being consistent with — changes in the text that occur further down the chain. (At the beginning of the process, of course, one doesn't necessarily know what constitutes a distinct parallel strand and what is overlapping or which way is up and which way is down on the family tree.) Upon analysis, these turn out to be features of this "taint"/"fault" variant: at the very top of the hierarchy it divides the sources into two parallel and non-overlapping trains of transmission, and in both lines of descent all subsidiary texts from the head downward exhibit the defining reading — or a recognizable corruption thereof. And all parenthetically included variants on each stemma exhibit a similar bidirectional force. WN4, for instance, at the bottom right on the Stemma of the Original Text (*figure 1*), reads "taint" (instead of "fault") in line 11, "for me" (instead of "to me") in line 14, "golde, such" (instead of "such gold") in line 43, and "To-negligently" (instead of "Which negligently") in line 102.[2]

Postulation of the texts labeled with Greek letters on both stemmata is necessary because, in all cases where they appear, no surviving artifact exhibits the configuration of readings requisite to explain the textual permutations further down the tree. To return to the WN4 family to demonstrate this point, a series of interrelated considerations point to the quondam existence of γ^2 and χ^3. It is easiest to explain this by starting at the bottom:

(1)   Though EE1 and WN4 share the distinctive "To-negligently" in line 102 (as well as the family's "gold, such"), each contains certain lines

---

[2] I should stress at this point that the variants cited on the stemma have been chosen for their succinct illustrative power and do not by any means exhaust the substantive evidence that could be adduced to support this analysis.

that are missing in the other; they thus cannot be copied one from the other (see *figure 3*). We are thus led to postulate the lost χ^3 as a parent from which these siblings derived "To-negligently."

(2)   We are prompted to postulate χ^3 rather than to suppose that EE1 and WN4 stem from C5 because of the extreme unlikelihood that both the EE1 and the WN4 scribes would independently misread C5's "Which negligently" as "To-negligently." And these artifacts contain other variants that point to the same conclusion.

(3)   We are led to see χ^3 as the sibling of C5 rather than as its offspring by certain corrupt readings present in C5 that are absent from EE1 and WN4 (see *figure 4*). In line 59, for instance, C5 gives "some deade Coniurer," but the authorial reading — "some dread Coniurer" — appears in EE1 and WN4 and must therefore have been the reading in χ^3. To think that χ^3 derived from C5, we would have to imagine that the χ^3 scribe, who made so many other errors, had independently restored C5's "deade" to "dread" — not impossible, but not very likely — as well as correcting other errors. The only credible inference is that χ^3 is the sibling, not the child, of C5, a fact that further implies the existence of γ^2 as a lost ur-text from which both C5 and χ^3 independently derive.

As is implied by *figure 3* above, *lacunae* in the text are often extremely useful in filiation. Especially when the subject matter of a given passage is politically or morally inflammatory, of course, it is possible that different scribes might independently delete the same or similar sections of text — thus one always seeks corroborative evidence for any genealogical linkages based on omissions — but missing lines often provide the earliest and clearest clue to genealogical relationships. For example, the omission of lines 75–76 — "And they are still bad Angels, myne are none / For forme giues beeing, and their forme is gone" — is the single most conspicuous feature of the fourteen extant descendants of τ^2, which appears at three removes from the Lost Revised Holograph on the δ^3 branch of the Stemma of the Revised Text. And some families and subfamilies descending from τ^2 omit far more than those two lines (see *figure 5*).

Among the artifacts listed on *figure 5*, O34, in the ψ^3 subfamily, appears to exhibit an anomalous pattern of omission. Whereas the other three members of the subfamily omit lines 97–98, O34 has these lines, and their presence might at first suggest that O34 is not correctly placed on the stemma as a sibling in the ψ^3 subfamily. There is, however, an explanation for O34's

Figure 3: Lines present/absent in EE1 and WN4

arabic numerals = lines present; *om* = lines omitted

```
EE1: 1 ——————— 36 om 43 ——— 68  om  79 ——————————— 114
WN4: 1 ————————————— 74 om 77 ——————— 96 om 99 ——— 114
```

Figure 4: Partial collation of C5, EE1, and WN4

```
008.NY3.0HE Elegia      .1.%5a%6%K
008.C05.HE1 Elegye      .7.
008.EE1.HE1 M%5r%6      {Donne}{his}{Elegy,}{/Vpon}{his}{Mistress}{Chayne.}
008.WN4.HE1 D%5r%6:     Down's {Elegy}{on}{/%Xhis}{Mistresses}{chaine.|}

008.NY3.005 Nor for y%5t%6 sely   old   moralitee
008.C05.005            that  sillye olde mortallitye,
008.EE1.005            that  silly  Morality,
008.WN4.005 nor        that  silly  ould morality

008.NY3.059 Or  let  me   creepe to some dradd Coniurer
008.C05.059     lett      Creepe          deade Coniurer,
008.EE1.059          mee  creep           dread Coniurer,
008.WN4.059 or  lett mee                  dread coniuorer
```

Figure 5: The descendants of τ²

arabic numerals = lines present; *om* = lines omitted

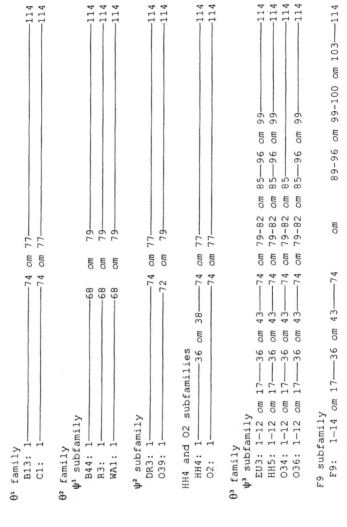

```
θ¹ family
  B13: 1——————————————74 om 77——————————————————————————114
  C1:  1——————————————74 om 77——————————————————————————114

θ² family
  ψ¹ subfamily
    B44: 1—————————68 om 79                               114
    R3:  1—————————68 om 79                               114
    WA1: 1—————————68 om 79                               114

  ψ² subfamily
    DR3: 1——————————————74 om 77——————————————————————————114
    O39: 1———————72 om 79—————————————————————————————————114

HH4 and O2 subfamilies
    HH4: 1———36 om 38——————74 om 77————————————————————————114
    O2:  1——————————————74 om 77——————————————————————————114

θ³ family
  ψ³ subfamily
    EU3: 1-12 om 17———36 om 43———74 om 79-82 om 85—96 om 99———114
    HH5: 1-12 om 17———36 om 43———74 om 79-82 om 85—96 om 99———114
    O34: 1-12 om 17———36 om 43———74 om 79-82 om 85—96 om 114
    O36: 1-12 om 17———36 om 43———74 om 79-82 om 85—96 om 99———114

  F9 subfamily
    F9:  1-14 om 17———36 om 43———74      om      89-96 om 99-100 om 103———114
```

inclusion of these lines that is consistent with the filiation exhibited in the stemma, and it arises from proper attention to the "bibliographical code" that must be interpreted along with the lexical substance embodied in the manuscript. This explanation will begin to emerge if we redirect our attention to *figure 2* for a moment, and specifically to the line recording the collation of O34, about two-thirds of the way down the page. In the "taint"-"fault" column at the O34 line, we see that O34 originally read "fate," but that the scribe canceled this word and substituted "tainte" for it (all this information was encoded in the original transcription and is signaled here by the %Y/%Z that surround the word "fate" and by the single angle brackets [> <] that surround "tainte"). This alteration tells us that the O34 scribe at some point compared his text with an artifact containing the original version — a manuscript belonging on the stemma of the Original Text (*figure 1*). And another bit of the bibliographical code — also noted in the original transcription — supplies the last piece of the puzzle: in the artifact, the anomalous lines 97–98 do not follow line 96 directly, but are instead written in the margin. We thus conclude that, while collating his corrupt θ^3 text with a descendant of the original lost holograph, the scribe of O34 also discovered that this couplet was missing from his copy and decided to include it. The ideological implications of θ^3's omissions of material are the subject for another paper — perhaps by some user of our edition — but I will observe that no other lines in the poem carry a stronger theological and political content than those omitted in these artifacts.

I am confident that the transmissional history of "The Bracelet" reflected on *figure 1* is essentially accurate. It will also be apparent, however, that throughout this presentation and on *figure 1*, I have implicitly called the alteration of "taint" to "fault" in line 11 an authorial revision. This label represents an interpretive judgment on my part, and I should like to explain how I arrived at it:

(1)   While "taint" and "fault" have — or at least can have — the same number of letters and while their second and fifth letters are the same, I have never seen any seventeenth-century hand in which the two words would likely be confused; consequently, I do not think the variant likely to have arisen from a scribal misreading.

(2)   This word appears buried in the middle of the eleventh line of a long poem, a place not particularly likely to have called scribal attention to itself; anyone wanting to alter this word would have had to know it was there and to think it needed changing.

(3)   Though one could elaborate a list of markedly different theological im-
        plications for each of these words, the distinction between angels that
        have "stray'd or gone / From the first State of their Creation" because
        of a "fault" as opposed to a "taint" strikes me as more subtle than any
        scribe, working in the relatively private sphere of manuscript trans-
        mission, would have been likely to make. In context, both words make
        equally good sense, and nothing about either cries out for alteration. I
        cannot imagine an amanuensis copying along from his source text until
        he came to the word "taint" and then thinking, "Oh, my goodness!
        This will never do. I'd better change this to 'fault.'" Whoever changed
        this word, it seems to me, would have had to be someone with a pro-
        prietary interest in the poem — someone who knew "taint" was there,
        who appreciated the fine theological distinction between "taint" and
        "fault," and who felt an owner's freedom to make the switch. I think
        it had to be Donne.

When a text goes public, however, it becomes subject to a different set of
pressures, and this is my final example of the kinds of information that can
emerge from a carefully developed filiation. As noted above, the printed editions — cited at the very bottom of *figure 2*, below the solid line — read
"way" in column five, providing a third alternative to the "taint" and "fault"
found throughout the corpus of manuscripts. "[W]ay" would appear to be a
much less tendentious word than either of the other two, and I think it must
be compositorial. If so, it provides a tantalizing hint as to what the licenser
originally found wrong with the poem and perhaps also to what had previously led Donne to revise "taint" to "fault." From details of the 13 September
1632 entry in the Stationers' Register that records Marriot's effort to license
his book of Donne verses, we can ascertain that he showed the licenser an
exemplum from the traditional "Group I" manuscripts, which include "The
Bracelet" as the first Elegy and which read the line-11 crux as "fault."[3] This
was the form of "The Bracelet" that failed to pass muster for the 1633 edition. As noted above, however, when Marriot illegally printed the poem in
1635 (B on the collation), he did not merely rustle up his former copy and
sneak it into print; he changed copy-texts altogether, using a member of the
λ^3 family, which is an offshoot from the δ^3 branch of the revised-text line of
transmission shown on *figure 1*. A score of distinctive readings corroborate this
point, but I shall cite only two: (1) in line 24, all manuscripts except O21 and

---

[3] See Edward Arber, *A Trainscript of the Registers of the Company of Stationers of London: 1554–1640 A.D.* (London, 1877), vol. 4, p. 249.

Y3 give the normative reading "naturall cuntry rott"; O21 and Y3, however, trivialize this to "Countryes naturall rott," as does B. (2) The second example is that listed on the stemma: in line 104 the λ^3 family reads "Itching," which normatively appears as "Itchy" in the speaker's virulent wish that his rival may experience "Itchy desyre, and no abilitee." "Itching" is also the lection in B.

Since it is clear that a manuscript very like O21 and Y3 was used to set "The Bracelet" into type in 1635, and since there is no manuscript support for the reading "way" in line 11, and since Marriot never subsequently applied for permission to print the excepted elegies, I think we may infer that he came away from his encounter with Sir Henry Herbert and the licensing Wardens in 1632 with a fairly clear notion of what they found objectionable in "The Bracelet" — and Donne's handling of the angels must have been at least one of the controversial topics. Whether Marriot thought the objections too great ever to be answered or too trivial to bother with, he apparently decided to finesse the problem by (a) using a different — and less easily recognizable — copy-text for the poem, (b) altering a significantly offensive word in line 11, and (c) hiding the poem as the twelfth of a newly expanded numbered sequence of elegies, placing it far down the list from the number-one position it had occupied in his Group-I manuscript.

Eclectic Circulation:
The Functional Dynamics of Manuscript and
Electronic Literary Cultures

MARGARET J. M. EZELL

THE TEMPTATION TO SPEAK ABOUT ELECTRONICALLY GENERATED texts in contrast to printed literary creations appears to be almost irresistible. At the 1998 MLA, for example, there were no fewer than eleven sessions under the heading "Electronic Technology in Teaching and Research," as well as individual panels such as this one, "Electronic Editing and Publication," and "Blake and Hypertextuality" which is meeting at the same time. In general, these panels appear to be devoted to explaining how the electronic medium — a phrase which encompasses hypertexts, electronic journals, and scholarly discussion lists as well as the technology which enables their distribution — permits a specific type of written expression which runs counter to our expectations of printed texts.

Since my own interactions with this type of electronic technology are of a recent date and not very impressive — one of my colleagues compared my use of the internet as the electronic equivalent of writing on clay tablets — I can assure you I will offer no startling insights into the nature of the electronic world. What I would like to do instead is take some of the premises on which the models of the electronic text and its author and roles of the editor and reader are constructed and use them to interrogate the ways in which early modern literary culture is characterized, focusing in particular on what I call the circulation of "social" literary manuscripts, especially in the latter part of the seventeenth century.

There are numerous reasons, I think, why the flourishing manuscript literary culture in the first part of the seventeenth century which has been well
studied by Marotti, Woodhuysen, and Mary Hobbs seems to vanish from sight
after 1660.[1] One of them has to do with the interest in the expanded role of
print in the English Civil Wars;[2] another, I think, is connected with early
modern women's participation in the practice and our perceptions of what
they were doing, and finally, with the way the vocabulary of commercial print
literature dominates how we conceptualize the dynamics of literary exchange
and circulation.

There is a strong sense in existing studies that manuscript literary exchange
became the haven of those who dared not print in the period after 1660 —
political subversives and women. The manuscript text in Harold Love's analysis entitled *Scribal Publication* serves largely as a substitute for a printed one,
serving as a means "by which ideologically charged texts could be distributed
through the governing class, or various interest-groups within that class, without their coming to the knowledge of the governed" (177). Women writers
are in Love's model drawn to manuscript culture because "the stigma of print
bore particularly hard on women writers" (the implication here being that
they would be in print if they dared); in his view, women's manuscripts primarily consisted of texts dealing with "the practical conduct of the household," and he notes that such "personal collections on these subjects were regarded with great pride by their compilers" (the implication being but not by
anyone else and certainly not by us) (54, 58). Furthermore, Love's term
"scribal publication" places our attention on those texts which were "the creation of professional scribes, whose work was distributed through organized
markets," and the case studies are of professionally assembled miscellanies,
scribal proceedings from Parliament, and the scribal reproduction of music,
with much less attention to "less organized" manuscript practices (3, 9).

As valuable as Love's study is, it does not represent the range of manuscript
circulation which continued after 1660 well into the eighteenth century, by
both women and men. In addition to the obvious problems of dealing with
gender and genre present in Love's account, there is embedded in it a sense
that what I prefer to call "social" manuscript texts were circulated, edited, and
read in the same fashion as the commercial printed ones. The very term

---

[1] After this paper was given, Peter Beal's important work *In Praise of Scribes:
Manuscripts and Their Makers in Seventeenth-Century England* (Oxford: Clarendon Press,
1998) appeared, offering a sophisticated analysis of the practices involved in creating
scribal books.

[2] See, for example, Harold M. Weber, *Paper Bullets: Print and Kingship under
Charles II* (Louisville: Univ. of Kentucky Press, 1996).

"scribal publication" focuses our attention on the act of transforming a text from a "private" creation to "public" property, without considering alternative modes of circulation available to manuscript texts not found with commercial print.

Through my own experiences in reading later seventeenth-century manuscript literary texts as well as those through the first part of the eighteenth century, I believe that by focusing on the "publication" — that is to say the expanded circulation of a text by making it available to the "public," often through the agency of commercial agents — we are imposing the dynamics of print culture and its circulation of texts among a readership whose obligation to the author ended with the purchase of the text, on the "social" dynamics of manuscript culture, a type of literary community dependent on the active participation of the reader not only with the author, but also with the initial editor of the materials. Such a social literary culture, if examined closely, complicates our notions of a strict division of "public" and "private" and our model of separate, gendered spheres of literary activity.

Clearly, there are many good examples of manuscript volumes which spared no pains to mimic the appearance of the printed page and which participated in the dynamics of a commercial text, and Love's study does an excellent job of representing them. For the other classes of manuscript texts and their authors, early editors, and readers — texts which were not created with any desire or intent for print or commercial distribution, even secret, frustrated desire — I think that the way in which electronic culture describes itself may come to our assistance. The ways in which critics distinguish the nature of electronic editions from printed ones offers an intriguing way to reconceptualize a type of social manuscript practice: in particular, the ways in which the materials circulated between the author and reader, and also between the initial editor (a term I am deliberately using in its widest sense for emphasis) and reader.

For the proponents of electronic texts, one of its innovations is the new relationships created among writer, reader, and text. As early as 1986, Adam Hodgkin was alerting us that electronic publication "is not simply a matter of producing new books by a new method or of reading the classics texts through a computer screen; if we want to gain the benefits of this new technology we have to understand the ways in which it will allow writers to write different kinds of books and also permit readers to construe texts in new ways" ("New Technologies," 151). In a 1997 general introduction to hypertext, Ilana Snyder points to the computer as offering "a medium for writing ... quite different from anything that has preceded it" ("Hypertext," 3), a point I shall contest.

In particular, she observes, the electronic "hypertext differs from printed text by offering readers multiple paths through a body of information: it allows them to make their own connections, to incorporate their own links and to produce their own meanings. Hypertext consequently blurs the boundaries between readers and writers" (ix). One of my colleagues at Texas A&M in geosciences has likewise characterized the electronic medium as consisting of a "parallel world," a "community" based on the exchange of information: Paul Adams situates the interactive nature of the internet as an alternative to "books and television" which "box . . . us up in our houses, [and] had us all separated" ("Another World," C8).

The electronic critic's representation of the history of writing, however, may prove less helpful than the ways in which it configures itself as being different from print. While accounts of current developments politely nod to what Walter Ong called "the chirographic culture" of handwritten manuscripts, the representation of it is brief and pointed: manuscript culture is characterized as a time-consuming, elite activity, restrictive and conservative. The image is of a monk toiling to produce a singularly beautiful art object destined to be chained to the shelf for the pleasure of a select few. This is significant because one of the claims for hypertext over print is that each type of "writing space" supposedly encourages patterns of authorship: "each writing technology permits certain kinds of thinking and discourages others. A blackboard encourages repeated modification, erasure, casual thinking and spontaneity. A pen and paper invite care, attention to grammar, tidiness and controlled thinking. A printed page solicits rewritten drafts, proofing, introspection, editing" (*Orality and Literacy*, 5).

But the icon of manuscript culture being the toiling monk is of course a historically specific one, and one which does not transfer well to early modern Britain. How well would this depiction of manuscript literary culture have captured the nature of the activities of Lady Mary Wroth, whose manuscripts were the object of Josephine Roberts's work? How amused the Restoration poet John Wilmot, the Earl of Rochester, would have been, one suspects, to be informed that his chosen "writing space," his mode of textual production, induced attention to grammar and tidiness.

The electronic critic's depiction of the way in which a hypertext operates in contrast to a print one, however, offers an interesting lever with which to shift our thinking about social manuscripts versus scribal publication. In his book *Writing Space* Jay Bolter distinguishes between three types of textual spatiality. He asserts that for print text, the visual space is fixed, monologic, an object. The visual, physical space of the print text, in turn, engenders a particular view of the relationships among writer, text, and reader: "the visual, physical artifact of the book becomes synonymous with the text itself . . . [where] writing is stable, monumental, and controlled exclusively by the author" (11). The book thus seems like a stand-in for the author, an extension or reproduction of the mind (Johnson-Eilola, "Structure & Text," 101–2). Books, in this formulation, "are essentially repositories for the sequential storage of information" (Snyder, "Hypertext," 17).

Certainly such descriptions might seem to work for those manuscript texts described by Love that were produced by professional scribes to mimic the appearance of print, or, for example, the highly structured manuscript volume Tanner 307 of George Herbert's *The Temple*, probably done by the women of the Collet family at Little Gidding.[3] It is much less true, however, when one looks at other compilation volumes and commonplace books, of which many examples are found in the Rawlinson collection, in which several generations of writers and readers mingle their texts, jostling for space in the margins, reversing the volume and writing from the other end, inserting recipes, poems, and accounts in what to us seems riotous disarray. In this vein, when reading accounts of people's initial encounters with hypertext fiction, I am reminded of problems a modern reader encounters in reading such seventeenth-century social manuscript texts. As Carolyn Handa notes in a review article for *Writing on the Edge*, "the first pass through these [hypertext] stories is likely to be a dizzying experience . . . Something about not being able to read linearly frustrates those of us who have spent so many decades of our lives reading from page one to the end and teaching more or less the same way" (81). As another critic of hypertext points out, part of the novice reader's frustration arises because the hypertext appears "to make a virtue out of lack of organization" (84).

When dealing with what I call social authorship, one encounters, typically, a mess. The problems arise because of the multiple ownership of many manuscript volumes, with dizzying layering of contents, but also because one of the characteristic modes of circulation for most social literature was not as a bound book, but as separate single sheets. The original patterns of circulation of such manuscript materials are almost always lost to us, but traces of them remain behind, in allusions in letters to enclosed texts now lost, in those unsorted bundles of manuscripts labeled "family papers" or "miscellaneous verse" as found in the Portland papers at the University of Nottingham, and also in the efforts of subsequent generations of editors to make books out of this material.

Extensive energy has been devoted by nineteenth- and twentieth-century editors to organize social texts into linear, monologic books with a clearly established authorial presence. Arthur Clifford, the nineteenth-century editor of the Tixall poems — a collection of writings by the Aston family from the

---

[3] See Mario Di Cesare's Introduction to the RETS/MRTS edition of the Tanner manuscript.

mid-seventeenth-century — describes his first encounter with the materials as
being given "a great trunk" filled with papers: "It was a bumper, brimful, and
overflowing, the enormous mass appeared to consist of papers of every sort,
and size: the surface of which was most respectably defended, by a deep and
venerable layer of literary dust" (viii). In order to create his book, a printed
version of the papers, Clifford separated out three bound manuscript volumes
and "a large quantity of loose scraps of paper, sheets, half-sheets, backs of letters, and the like, scribbled over with verses" (*Tixall Poetry*, x). It was Clifford's job as he perceived it to bring order into this seeming chaos and to establish the authorial presence that permits the reader to say that this poem is
by this person on this date.

Because that trunk also preserved the correspondence of the Aston family
members, we also have some idea how the individual manuscript volumes
came into being. One was created by Herbert Aston's wife; he wrote to his
sister Constance Aston Fowler that

> my Mrs. havinge nothinge else to doe this winter, hath made a slight
> collection of all my workes. Wherefore you must make an inquiry into
> all your papers, and if you find any of mine that beginn not as in this
> note, you must send them her by the first opportunity. (xxii)

It is interesting that the author himself had not made a collection of his own
works, and that indeed he was not even sure where his texts could be found,
rather a different situation from the image of the print author in control of his
readers through his or her control of the content — instead, in this eclectic
circulation, it is the reader's contribution of texts back to the initial editor
(Aston's wife) which creates the content of the volume out of the scraps of
verses and loose sheets.

We see the same interesting lack of interest in or control over his texts by
the author in the later example of volume of John Cleveland's verse published
posthumously in 1659. In the preface addressed to "the Discerning Reader,"
E. Williamson, the editorial compiler, lays out the difficulties he had in as-
sembling the volume. "Out of the love he had to pleasure his friends," Williamson announces, Cleveland himself was often "unfurnisht with his own
manuscripts, as I have heard him say often, he was not so happy, as to have
any considerable collection of his own papers, they being despersed among his
friends." Although individual pieces of Cleveland's had been published without his supervision during his lifetime, Williamson desired to "erect ... this
Pyramide of Honour" by gathering Cleveland's works; in the process, however, poems by his friends and readers, Williamson acknowledged, became
"intermixed" in the collection. Unlike a more modern editor, Williamson

apparently lost little sleep over this collage edition, politely asserting that "the world cannot be so far mistaken in [Cleveland's] Genuine Muse, as not to discern his pieces from any of the other Poems." Nor is there any attempt by Williamson to impose a linear chronology or a fixed pathway to follow for reading; it is happily left up to the reader to decide not only who wrote what, but also when, and in what relationship a given piece should be read with other pieces.

For a final example, we see this same intermingling of readers' and named authors' texts in another posthumous edition, Mary Monck's *Marinda. Poems and Translations upon several Occasions*, published in 1716 by her father. Monck did not publish any of her pieces during her lifetime; the content of specific poems makes it clear that she was involved in a literary culture that involved both the exchange and performance of texts among friends. The other contents of the volume are also of interest here; her father announces in the dedication that the materials are "as we found most of them in her Scrittore after her Death, written with her own Hand, little expecting, and as little desiring the Publick shou'd have any Opportunity either of Applauding or Condemning them." The entry on Monck in Janet Todd's *Dictionary of British and American Women Writers* calculates that of the sixty-three poems in the volume, eleven are written to her rather than by her, and several form a series of epistolary exchanges. The posthumous volume thus serves less as a representation of an individual literary career than as mosaic of family and social texts, pieces which are linked through the writers' and readers' social connections like a net or web rather than any specific line of reading imposed by the author or initial editor, where the reader is left to make the connections between the writers and readers whose texts are present.[4]

The oddities and difficulties found in the examples of these three volumes — a nineteenth-century edition of mid-seventeenth-century family papers, and two posthumous editions, one by a male, one by a female — suggest to me not that our forebears were less organized than we are, but that they regarded social literary texts differently from the way we do. Rather than being the simple transmission from a single author to a passive reader, from a book as the linear storage space for texts representing a single voice, what such examples suggest to me is an alternative vision of literary culture. Unlike the commercially produced scribal publications, the book created from social

---

[4] Since presenting this talk, I have further investigated the issue of posthumous publication in "The Posthumous Publication of Women's Manuscripts and the History of Authorship," in *Women's Writing and the Circulation of Ideas: Manuscript Publication in England, 1550–1800*, ed. George L. Justice and Nathan Tinker (Cambridge: Cambridge Univ. Press, 2002), 121–36.

manuscript circulation becomes a receptacle for collaborative labor by the
writer, readers, and compiler and also as the accretion of generations of readers' contributions and annotations, a text which preserves in what we see as
oddities some of the initial dynamics of social literary life.

Social manuscript texts, in their single sheets or manuscript compilations,
represent less the individual writer than the interactive community not too
distant from that envisioned by the electronic critics. The circulation of literary materials was governed not by a separation into public and private spheres
of discourse, nor even of domestic versus commercial production. Instead, to
borrow the terms of the electronic writer, the circulation of literary materials
among a social group serves to create and strengthen bonds between friends,
family, and also generations through actively engaging them in not only the
reading of literary texts but also the compilation and distribution of and contribution to them. What to us may appear textual chaos and disorder may
simply have been the complexity of one aspect of the dynamics of early modern literary culture we have yet to consider.[5]

Works Cited

ADAMS, PAUL. "Another World: A&M Professor says Internet is a True
Community." The Bryan–College Station Eagle. 26 November 1998. C8.

BEAL, PETER. In Praise of Scribes: Manuscripts and Their Makers in Seventeenth-Century England. Oxford: Clarendon Press, 1998.

BOLTER, J. DAVID. Writing Space: The Computer, Hypertext and the History of
Writing. Hillsdale, NJ: L. Erlbaum Associates, 1991.

BROWN, JENNIFER. "Preserving the Past: Monks, nuns get back to scribe
roots with computer-archive Project." AP 21 November 1998 [The
Bryan–College Station Eagle, A13].

CLEVELAND, JOHN J. Cleaveland [sic] Revived. London, 1659.

CLIFFORD, ARTHUR, ed. Tixall Poetry. Edinburgh, 1813.

EZELL, MARGARET J. M. Social Authorship and the Advent of Print. Baltimore:
Johns Hopkins Univ. Press, 1999.

HANDA, CAROLYN. Computers and Community: Teaching Composition in the
Twenty-First Century. Portsmouth, NH: Boynton/Cook, 1990.

---

[5] I pursued these conclusions in more depth in a subsequent monograph, *Social
Authorship and the Advent of Print* (Baltimore: Johns Hopkins Univ. Press, 1999).

HERBERT, GEORGE. *The Temple*, ed. Mario A. Di Cesare. Binghamton, NY: MRTS, for RETS, 1995.

HOBBS, M. *Early Seventeeth-Century Verse Miscellany Manuscripts*. Aldershot: Ashgate, 1992.

HODGKIN, ADAM. "New Technologies in Printing and Publishing: The Present of the Written Word." In *The Written Word: Literacy in Transition*, ed. Gerd Bauman, 151–69. Oxford: Clarendon Press, 1986.

JOHNSON-EILOLA, JOHNDAN. "Review Essay: Structure & Text." *Computers and Composition* 9 (1992): 95–129.

JUSTICE, GEORGE L., and NATHAN TINKER, eds. *Women's Writing and the Circulation of Ideas: Manuscript Publication in England, 1550–1800*. Cambridge: Cambridge Univ. Press, 2002.

LOVE, HAROLD. *Scribal Publication in Seventeenth-Century England*. London: Oxford Univ. Press, 1993.

MAROTTI, ARTHUR F. *Manuscript, Print, and the English Renaissance Lyric*. Ithaca: Cornell Univ. Press, 1995.

MONCK, MARY. *Marinda*. London, 1716.

SNYDER, ILANA. *Hypertext: The Electronic Labyrinth*. New York: New York Univ. Press, 1997.

TODD, JANET, ed. *A Dictionary of British and American Women Writers 1660–1800*. London: Methuen, 1987.

WEBER, HAROLD M. *Paper Bullets: Print and Kingship under Charles II*. Louisville: Univ. of Kentucky Press, 1996.

WOUDHUYSEN, H. R. *Sir Philip Sidney and the Circulation of Manuscripts 1558–1640*. Oxford: Oxford Univ. Press, 1996.

"What Two Crownes Shall They Be?":
"Lower" Criticism, "Higher" Criticism,
and the Impact of the
Electronic Scholarly Edition

R. G. SIEMENS

A N ELECTRONIC MAIL MESSAGE I RECEIVED JUST BEFORE THE 1998 MLA Conference, at which this paper was first presented, told me that an award, of sorts, had been given to the electronic journal I founded at the University of British Columbia in 1994 and have edited until quite recently, *Early Modern Literary Studies: A Journal of Sixteenth and Seventeenth Century English Literature* (*EMLS*). The award, called the "Key Resource Award," was sent to me by a group called *Links2Go*. As I read about this award further, I learned that *Links2Go* uses "Machine Learning and Intelligent Agent technology." Each month, their letter informed me, they

> sample millions of pages from the World Wide Web and analyze those pages to discover relationships between tens of millions of links and thousands of cross-referenced topics. Links2Go provides an interface to these relationships, allowing websurfers to browse links by topic, find links and topics related to an interesting link, and to search for links and topics.

After this news, there followed an apology, issued just in case *EMLS* did not actually fit into the category for which it had received the award. Unfortunately, you see, no one at *Links2Go* had actually looked at the journal before giving the award. The whole process — scanning the internet for materials related to the study of Renaissance literature in English, sorting through those materials, and even writing me (as editor) with news of the award — had been handled automatically!

Happily, I can say that *EMLS* has received other forms of acknowledgment, some even involving human processes of evaluation. An experience such as that given to me by *Links2Go*, though, makes me think that it is, truly (and, in some cases, sadly), a brave new world in which we live and work. And, as in many talks touching on the new technology, while it might be a good rhetorical strategy to echo in my own paper a sense of awe akin to that expressed by Miranda in Shakespeare's *Tempest* (5.1.181), I find myself from time to time more deflated than elated by the promise of the new technologies for our field, the implications of the new technology more muddling than enlightening. In one of these muddled states, I removed part of my talk's title intended to suggest this state; here, I reinstate it. The initial part of my talk's title was intended to be "What two crownes shall they be?" — and, instead of expressing Miranda's awe, it was intended to gesture towards something else, something found in a discussion that takes place between Shakespeare's Lear and Lear's fool, in Act 1, scene 4, of the play. Here, the fool riddles with Lear, "Nuncle, give me an egg, and I'll give thee two crowns." Lear's response, "What two crowns shall they be?," is met with the ironic wisdom of the fool: "Why, after I have cut the egg i'th'middle and eat / up the meat, the two crowns of the egg."

Not in the same spirit of folly or ironic wisdom, but borrowing the same principles of division, in my paper I explore aspects of the impact that the electronic scholarly edition has upon literary criticism; I wish to suggest a way in which we can consider that impact. I do so with two hats on — that of one who studies and explores English Renaissance literature, as an editor and critic, and that of one who practices techniques associated with the growing field of humanities computing.

Models of Critical Interaction: Higher/Lower and "Computer"

I shall begin by cutting the egg, if you will, in the middle, in order to assert a model that suggests the relationship that exists among distinct types of literary critical work; this I adapt from Tim William Machan's introduction to his *Medieval Literature: Texts and Interpretation*. Machan convincingly suggests a division of critical and scholarly work into two chief categories: *Lower Criticism,* which is chiefly textual and bibliographical in nature, and *Higher Criticism*, that which is typified by interpretive studies (3). Lower Criticism, as Machan notes, is most "commonly viewed as the more factual or 'scientific'; it provides numerical, analytical, and categorical information which is used to define . . . realities" (4); Higher Criticism is often seen as "the spirit which gives life to the letters established by the Lower Criticism; it is the intellectual and aesthetic activity which, depending on one's critical viewpoint, reveals, constitutes, or disassembles the meanings of a text" (5). As one who works with either knows, the relationship between the two is mutually influential, for "without the traditional Lower Criticism's constructing of texts, there can be no focus for the theorizing of Higher Criticism, just as without the traditional Higher Criticism's interpretation of texts there can be no contexts within which Lower Criticism can identify facts" (7). In short, each has its own distinct roles and goals, but each also necessarily assists in the definition and development of the other.

Alongside this model of criticism derived from literary studies, I should like to add one from the realm of humanities computing, this one drawn from John Smith's seminal article, "Computer Criticism." Smith there presents a clearly articulated view of the state of literary studies and humanities computing as they existed in the late 1970s. Computer applications for language and literary studies are divided into two groups: the first, "those in which the computer was used to produce through textual manipulation conventional aids for future research (dictionaries, concordances, etc.)," and the second, "those in which the computer was used in the actual analysis of specific works of literature (thematic analyses, stylistic studies, etc.)" (13). I shall return to thoughts about the computer as a critical tool in a moment.

The former of his two groups, the "conventional aids for future research," Smith stated to have had already "been viewed as beneficial or, at least, inevitable" (13). Since the time of Smith's writing, the perception of this group has remained relatively stable, to such an extant that Smith's view of the late 1970s could be shared a decade later by Roseanne Potter, in her preface to *Literary Computing and Literary Criticism*, and by others more recently; as Potter noted, the "practice of computing is widespread and little disputed in these supporting areas of literary study" (xv).

But the past several years *have* seen a shift in views about computing tools for literary studies and for computer-assisted literary criticism. When we speak of undisputedly accepted computing in our literary studies work, we are less often referring to the "conventional aids" that Smith outlined; rather, we speak — as several at the 1998 conference did — of the world wide web, TEI-SGML encoding, database interaction, complex authorship arguments, and cutting-edge editing projects; the last of these are often seen today as the height of computing work as it relates to literary studies. What was little disputed even a decade ago is accepted today; what is little disputed today in this regard will likely be wholly accepted tomorrow.

In large part, I would urge, such acceptance of these "conventional aids" has to do with the societal acceptance of computing practices into nearly all facets of life. But, more specifically, it also has to do with the close identification of this type of work — indexing, concordance-building, collating, etc. — with the accepted projects of Lower Criticism. The computer, in its incarnation of hardware and software even some twenty years ago, was already capable of adding much to these types of critical endeavors. Moreover, while chiefly in a supporting role, such computing tools have quietly assisted in shaping the possibilities for work at higher levels (as is asserted by Machan's model of the interaction between types of criticism).

Smith also outlined computer applications for language and literary studies which bear a closer relationship to the products of Higher Criticism — those "in which the computer was used in the actual analysis of specific works of literature (thematic analyses, stylistic studies, etc.)." Although it attracted the main focus of Smith's attention, this is something about which we do not yet talk in the same manner as we do about those tools more associated with the projects of Lower Criticism. Certainly there have been major studies, a number making significant contributions that have seen acceptance and engagement in the literary studies community (e.g. Foster and Lancashire on Shakespeare); but, on the whole, we cannot today refer to what Smith called "computer criticism" as being "widespread" and "little disputed," nor can we talk in the same way about its being perceived with any real degree of stability.

I suspect, though, that this will ultimately change — and soon; and the key to such change is provided by the scholarly edition in electronic form.

The Electronic Scholarly Edition

A decade ago the scholarly edition in electronic form was something that certainly did not have the prominence that it has today. But it has received excellent consideration of late by our community, notably including such groups as the MLA's Committee for Scholarly Editions (whose guidelines have been positively influential). It has evolved, in real terms, considerably in recent years and promises to evolve much more so in the next few; even so, today there are many excellent examples of which to speak, a few of them in Renaissance studies being the *Arden Shakespeare CD-ROM* (for its implementation) and the three-text *Hamlet* (Q1, Q2, F1) that comes with the MLA publication of *Text Analysis Computing Tools* (Lancashire et al.); in medieval studies, one need only to point to some of the presentations at the 1998 conference, and what has for some time been accorded significant prominence, the electronic edition of *The Wife of Bath's Prologue and Tale.*

More than being editions that differ greatly from what one might find in the print medium, my examples are very different types of *electronic* editions — different beyond, say, the standard distinctions we might draw among editions in print form. As such, I will for a moment focus on them in isolation, before looking at their place in a larger framework.

If we consider these editions with reference to their implementation being favored over theories that drive their production, there are today two basic models for electronic editions of a scholarly nature, each championing one of two relatively distinct approaches to the central matter of electronic editions: the text(s) around which they are built.[1] What each type shares is its promise of an interaction with its text possible only with the assistance of the computer (and impossible, for all practical purposes, in print) — and its promise of a new effect on the critical reader who enjoys that interaction.

The first of these models is referred to as the *dynamic text*; it is an electronic text which, in essence, indexes and concords itself, allowing the reader to interact with it in a dynamic fashion; this model of the electronic edition is made up of the combination of a properly-encoded electronic text with text-retrieval and text-analysis software. What makes this type of edition *dynamic* is the way in which the computer facilitates a non-linear interaction with the text — in essence, structuring and treating it as a database — and allows the reader to draw, seamlessly, on a good deal of text-based information not easily accessible to the reader of the print edition. In addition to linear reading, those using a dynamic edition can also carry out a number of different types of text-based searches, map out the distribution of search results over the course of the text(s) under consideration, and, using the software's statistical analysis capabilities, analyze connotative "clusters" of words associated with the search terms. And more.

The second model is what might best be referred to as the *hypertextual edition*. Seen by some as being the technological manifestation of social theories of editing (especially when presented as "archive"), this type of electronic scholarly edition exploits the ability of hypertextual organisation to facilitate a reader's interaction with the apparatus (textual, critical, and otherwise) that traditionally accompanies scholarly editions, and with relevant external textual and graphical resources, critical materials, and so forth. It also allows one to "jump" from the text to other related documents of this sort.

---

[1] I've discussed this in greater detail elsewhere (see "Disparate Structures" and, more recently, "Shakespearean Apparatus?" and "Unediting and Non-Editions").

One model, the dynamic text, emphasises extant linguistic relationships; its historical roots are in word-based scholarship — concordance-making and indexing, collocation and distribution, attribution and dating, rhyme analysis, content analysis, and so forth — and, by its combination of electronic text and text-analysis software, the dynamic text facilitates an interaction with the text that is unavailable, in practical form, to the reader working with a printed text. The other, the hypertextual edition, is most often embraced for its employment of hypertext to emphasize relationships of textual and extra-textual natures, facilitating the reader's interaction with the text and materials related to it with an ease unknown even in the best of scholarly editions published in print; its historical roots are to be found in the apparatuses of scholarly editions and, in the best of examples, the variorum editions and large scholarly archives.

But what, specifically, of their impact? The dynamic text automates reading-related functions that would likely not be carried out without the assistance of the computer because of the time involved, such that one's *computer-assisted analysis* of the text and one's *linear reading* of it are acts that become so closely affiliated as to be equivalent. The hypertextual edition also facilitates a close affiliation of the acts of reading and analysis, but does so by providing and assisting in the management of a significant amount of related material extra to the text of the edition itself; what is hypothetically available to the reader in a research library, or group of libraries, and beyond is here made immediately available, encouraging use of the resources by the reader in a seamless fashion. As such, the hypertextual edition, like the dynamic text, also makes accessible dimensions of the text not normally or conveniently available to readers, but does so by providing immediate access to a sort of material different from that handled by the dynamic text.

Placing the Electronic Scholarly Edition
in its Critical Context

Ultimately, the new ways in which each type of electronic edition allows the reader to interact with its content(s) suggest that both types of electronic edition have themselves the potential to produce a new type of reader: one more attuned to the specific aspects of the text favored by its electronic edition-type, a reader who has the potential to be better informed about the text and its content. For this reason, electronic scholarly editions occupy an important place in our thinking today.

But electronic scholarly editions also occupy an important place when we think about what both Machan and Smith address: the influence of Lower

Criticism on Higher Criticism and the influence of humanities computing on literary studies in the form of "computer criticism." Here the electronic edition plays a pivotal role. In addition to being a flagship today for the work of humanities computing in the field of literary studies, electronic editions of both sorts — *dynamic* and *hypertextual* — represent the culmination of decades of humanities computing work that has both supported and directly participated in interpretive studies.

Recalling, for example, Smith's division of computing applications for language and literary studies between "those in which the computer was used to produce through textual manipulation conventional aids for future research ... and those in which the computer was used in the actual analysis of specific works of literature," one recognizes a number of pertinent points. One is that the idea of an electronic text is central to each type of computing application; it is the basis for the dictionaries and concordances generated as "aids" for other research, much as it is the basis for the sorts of textual manipulation necessary for thematic analyses and stylistic and authorship studies. Another is that electronic editions today — especially those which follow the model of the *dynamic edition* and appear as a combination of electronic text and text-analysis software — act as their own conventional aids.

Recalling also the model of critical interaction outlined by Machan, we see that such a model suggests the affinity of those accepted computing-derived research aids and the work of Lower Criticism into which computing practices have been accepted. It also brings into focus, from a literary-critical perspective, the areas of literary criticism beyond "aids for future research" upon which computing tools have thus far had their greatest impact: again, this is the Lower Criticism, what is "factual" and "enumerative," the area of textual studies and bibliography, and, ultimately, that of the electronic scholarly edition.

The models of Machan and Smith also help us consider the ways that traditional humanities computing concerns necessarily project themselves into concerns of literary interpretation through the electronic edition. Dynamic interaction with a text — a process which enacts accepted lower critical practices upon a text — is a critical process that duplicates the sorts of tasks that Smith outlines as making up much of computer criticism; restated, such interaction is itself an interpretative process, the software enabling the lower-critical tasks to be carried out swiftly and seamlessly. This is true of the hypertextual edition as well; here, the tools that allow hypertextual interaction also facilitate a unique level of critical interaction with the text (though this type of computer-critical act is outside the realm of Smith's concern).

In short, it is through the electronic edition that, today, one can most easily witness the influence of what is chiefly textual and bibliographical in nature upon what is more interpretive by nature — as well as the concomitant influence that schools of interpretation exert upon what is most "commonly viewed as the more factual or 'scientific,'" what "provides numerical, analytical, and categorical information which is used to define ... realities" (Machan, "Higher and Lower Criticism," 4).

Conclusion

Returning to the exchange between Lear and his fool, we might well ask, as Lear does, with a more obvious frame of reference: "What two crowns shall they be?" Regarding the electronic scholarly edition — and within the framework of the binary models suggested by both Machan and Smith — are we dealing with Higher Criticism? Lower Criticism? Are we dealing with Computer Criticism? Or supporting aids to analysis? Are we dealing with none? or, alternatively, all, of the above?

My best answer is that when we consider the critical impact of the electronic scholarly edition as it is developing today — and if we accept ways of looking at what we do as scholars and critics in terms such as those used by Smith and Machan — we less consider two crowns, separate though related, and more explore the meat that lies between them. Potentially, we are participating in a process that may ultimately lead to a re-conception of the thing itself.[2]

Works Consulted and Cited

CHAUCER, GEOFFREY. *Chaucer: The Wife of Bath's Prologue on CD-ROM*. Peter Robinson, gen. ed. Cambridge: Cambridge Univ. Press, 1996.

Early Modern Literary Studies: A Journal of Sixteenth and Seventeenth Century English Literature (EMLS). <URL: http://purl.oclc.org/emls/emlshome.htm>.

FAULHABER, CHARLES B. "Textual Criticism in the 21st Century." *Romance Philology* 45 (1991): 123–48.

FINNERAN, RICHARD J., ed. *The Literary Text in the Digital Age*. Ann Arbor: Univ. of Michigan Press, 1996.

FOSTER, DONALD W. *Elegy by W. S.: A Study in Attribution*. Newark, DE: Univ. of Delaware Press, 1989.

---

[2] I wish to thank the Killam Trust, and the University of Alberta, for its generous support during the time in which this paper was written.

————. "*A Funeral Elegy*: W[illiam] S[hakespeare]'s 'Best-Speaking Witnesses'." *Publications of the Modern Language Association* 111 (1996): 1080–1105.

————. "A Romance of Electronic Scholarship; with the True and Lamentable Tragedies of *Hamlet, Prince of Denmark*. Part 1: The Words." *Early Modern Literary Studies* 3.3 / Special Issue 2 (1998): 1–42 <URL: http://purl.oclc.org/emls/03-3/fostshak.html>.

————. "*SHAXICON* 1995." *The Shakespeare Newsletter* 45 (1995): 25–32.

HARNAD, STEVAN. "The PostGutenberg Galaxy." *Times Higher Education Supplement.* May 12, 1995.

HILL, W. SPEED. "Editorial Theory and Literary Criticism: Lamb and Wolf?" *Review* 19 (1997): 37–64.

LANCASHIRE, IAN. "Computer Tools for Cognitive Stylistics." In Ephraim Nissan and Klaus M. Schmidt, eds., *From Information to Knowledge: Conceptual and Content Analysis by Computer*, 28–47. Oxford: Intellect, 1995.

————. "Phrasal Repetends in Literary Stylistics: *Hamlet* III.1." In Susan Hockey and Nancy Ide, eds., *Research in Humanities Computing 4: Selected Papers from the 1992 ACH/ALLC Conference*. Oxford: Oxford Univ. Press, 1996.

————. "Uttering and Editing: Computational Text Analysis and Cognitive Studies in Authorship." *Texte: Revue de Critique et de Théorie Littéraire* 13/14 (1993): 173–218.

————, et al. *Using TACT with Electronic Texts: A Guide to Text-Analysis Computing Tools*. New York: Modern Language Association, 1996.

LINKS2GO. <URL: http://www.links2go.com/>.

MACHAN, TIM WILLIAM. "Late Middle English Texts and the Higher and Lower Criticisms." In Machan, ed., *Medieval Literature: Texts and Interpretation*, 3–16. MRTS 79. Binghamton, NY: Medieval and Renaissance Texts and Studies, 1991.

MARDER, LOUIS. "Thoughts on a 'Definitive' Edition of Shakespeare: Is it Possible?" *The Shakespeare Newsletter* 32 (1982): 27–29.

MLA OF AMERICA, COMMITTEE ON SCHOLARLY EDITIONS. "Guidelines for Electronic Scholarly Editions." <URL: http://sunsite.berkeley.edu/MLA/guidelines.html>.

O'DONNELL, JAMES J., and ANN OKERSON, eds. *Scholarly Journals at the Crossroads: A Subversive Proposal for Electronic Publishing*. Washington, DC: Association of Research Libraries, 1995.

POTTER, ROSEANNE, ed. *Literary Computing and Literary Criticism: Theoretical and Practical Essays on Theme and Rhetoric.* Philadelphia: Univ. of Pennsylvania Press, 1989.

SHAKESPEARE, WILLIAM. *The Arden Shakespeare CD-ROM: Texts and Sources for Shakespeare Study.* Walton-on-Thames: Arden Shakespeare, 1997.

SIEMENS, R. G. "A New Humanism? Toward a Reconsideration of the Ideals and Pragmatics Shaping Electronic Scholarly Publication in the Arts Today." In Siemens and W. Winder, eds., *Scholarly Discourse and Computing Technology: Perspectives on Pedagogy, Research, and Dissemination in the Humanities*, 167–81. [A special issue of *Text Technology* 6.3 (1996) and *Computing in the Humanities Working Papers* B.33 (1997).]

————. "Disparate Structures, Electronic and Otherwise: Conceptions of Textual Organisation in the Electronic Medium, with Reference to Editions of Shakespeare and the Internet." In Michael Best, ed., *The Internet Shakespeare: Opportunities in a New Medium*, 1–29. *Early Modern Literary Studies* 3.3 / Special Issue 2 (1998) <URL: http://purl.oclc.org/emls/03-3/siemshak.html>.

————. "Shakespearean Apparatus? Explicit Textual Structures and the Implicit Navigation of Accumulated Knowledge." *TEXT: An Interdisciplinary Annual of Textual Studies.* Electronic preprint published in *Surfaces* 8 (1999): 1–34 <URL: http://www.pum.umontreal.ca/revues/surfaces/vol8/siemens.pdf>.

————. "Unediting and Non-Editions." *The Theory (and Politics) of Editing.* [A special issue of *Anglia* (2002); forthcoming.]

SMITH, JOHN B. "Computer Criticism." In Potter, ed., *Literary Computing and Literary Criticism*, 13–44.

SUTHERLAND, KATHRYN, ed. *Electronic Text: Investigations in Method and Theory.* Oxford: Clarendon Press, 1997.

Julie Palmer's "Centuries":
The Politics of Editing
and Anthologizing Early
Modern Women's Manuscript Compilations

VICTORIA E. BURKE &

ELIZABETH CLARKE

PERHAPS THE MOST PRESSING ISSUE FOR ANY EDITOR OF AN EARLY modern woman's manuscript compilation is academic politics at the start of the millennium. Texts by women are still not as freely and cheaply available as feminist pioneers in the 1970s and 1980s would perhaps have dreamed: the mainstream anthologies from which so much Renaissance literature is taught make very few gestures towards early modern women's writing of any sort, leaving undergraduate courses in women's writing the sport of the few. A welcome exception is the recent anthology edited by David Damrosch (*The Longman Anthology of British Literature*, published in New York by Longman in 1999) that includes fourteen women writers from the mid-sixteenth to the late seventeenth century. A survey during the academic year 1992/1993 conducted of British institutions of higher education by Elaine Hobby and Bill Overton about teaching provision for the period 1640–1700 revealed a variety of factors for a reluctance to integrate women writers. These included the availability of texts, the impact of modularization, and the sentiment voiced by one respondent: "There is not space for Margaret

Cavendish and Dryden."[1] This attitude is partly of course a function of the infrequency of women's ventures into print in the early modern period. The imperative driving the Perdita Project,[2] to make scholars and students aware of women's manuscript material that survives from the period, is an overtly feminist one: to heighten awareness of the amount of women's writing that took place in the sixteenth and seventeenth centuries. This is clearly not a universally accepted priority: Sara Jayne Steen in 1990 cited the case of a grant proposal being refused for an edition of early modern women's writing because "anything worth reading by Renaissance women was already in print."[3] However, in order to change the face of women's-writing courses, or perhaps more importantly of survey courses in Renaissance literature, our kind of archival research must be linked with a publishing project which makes available at least some of this material. The RETS edition of *The Southwell-Sibthorpe Commonplace Book* by Jean Klene was a pioneering and very welcome venture in manuscript publication.[4] The Perdita team is producing an anthology of early modern women's manuscript verse to be published by Manchester University Press in 2004.

Paradoxically, however, the editing of women's manuscript writing could be seen to be undermining the feminist project. The complexity of the medium within which any such writing is enscripted is an immediate barrier to non-specialist readers. Manuscript material tends to be, literally, difficult to read: moreover, it is sometimes unfinished, sometimes collaborative, often unattributed. Manuscripts tend to fall apart and be put back together incorrectly: Jonathan Gibson, Research Fellow on the Perdita Project, has noticed that one of Anne Southwell's poems most interesting to a feminist reader, a Defence of Eve, is back to front in the printed edition as the folio (fol. 26) has obviously been inserted the wrong way round. The poem, then, actually begins with the lines,

---

[1] Elaine Hobby and Bill Overton, " 'There is not space for Margaret Cavendish and Dryden': Higher Education Teaching 1640–1700," *Women's Writing* 1 (1994): 257–75.

[2] <http://human.ntu.ac.uk/perdita>

[3] Sara Jayne Steen, "Behind the Arras: Editing Renaissance Women's Letters," in *New Ways of Looking at Old Texts: Papers of the Renaissance English Text Society, 1985–1991*, ed. W. Speed Hill (Binghamton, NY: RETS, 1993), 229–38, here 238.

[4] Jean Klene, ed., *The Southwell–Sibthorpe Commonplace Book: Folger MS V.b.198*, MRTS 147 (Tempe, AZ: Medieval & Renaissance Texts & Studies, for RETS, 1997). See also the essay by Klene in this volume.

> Sir give mee leave to plead my Grandams cause.
> and proove her Charter from Jehovas lawes.
> Wherby I hope to drawe you ere you dye
> from a resolv'd and wilfull herresye
> In thinkinge ffemales have so little witt
> as but to serve men they are only fitt; . . .[5]

The misordering of this poem raises important issues for an anthologist, because it is not simply a matter of printing fol. 26v before fol. 26r. The poem exists in another version earlier in the manuscript (an allegorical account of the fall and redemption of Adam which lacks the 46-line feminist digression, fols. 18r–19r), and this alternative version hints at what the original ending of this incomplete poem may have been. Perhaps this possible ending should be tacked onto the Defence of Eve poem; perhaps it should be included as an appendix. This example demonstrates that anthologizing women's manuscript writing throws up issues different from editing an anthology from printed works. By taking the collation of a manuscript into account, we can see that the currently accepted order of a poem is incorrect. By examining alternate versions of the same poem in a manuscript, we address issues of authorial intention.

The authorship conditions within which manuscript verse was composed and circulated problematize the stable versions of authorship and text which are offered by the layout of our modern anthologies. The poetry anthology which is being prepared by six of us who work on the Perdita Project is arranged differently from conventional author-centered anthologies. *Early Modern Women's Manuscript Poetry* centers on fifteen individual manuscripts. Our attention to the physical characteristics of the manuscripts from which we are constructing our anthology should alert us to textual problems and prevent us from reproducing a nineteenth-century binder's mistake, as occurred in the Southwell case. Many anthologies of women's writing from our period favor print sources over manuscript, giving a skewed picture of women's literary production of the period; our poetry anthology will help correct that erroneous perception, by including more celebrated writers such as Mary Sidney and Mary Wroth, alongside less well-known writers like Octavia Walsh, Anne Ley, and Hester Pulter. We face issues of manuscript transcription, such as the extent to which we should reproduce every correction, erasure, abbreviation,

---

[5] Folger Shakespeare Library MS V.b.198, fol. 26v. We are following Michael Hunter's suggestions for transcription (see discussion below). In line 4, *resolv'd* replaces *perverse* deleted.

blank space, and change of hand. Perhaps more crucial is the choice of texts. In a recent review of Kate Aughterson's *Renaissance Women: A Sourcebook*, Jeffrey Kahan points out that all editors of anthologies choose particular texts over others and certain extracts over others, but he criticizes Aughterson for allowing her own interpretive strategy, one that places a transgressive or subversive reading of the extracts in the foreground, to dominate the volume.[6] In their anthology (which includes a poem by Julia Palmer), Jane Stevenson and Peter Davidson have selected poems which demonstrate the range of women's writing across lines of class, religion, location, and language. In the case of poems of uncertain authorship, the editors consider those poems that contain non-stereotypical versions of femininity as likely to have been female-authored.[7] Another issue, that of contextualizing women writers, is raised in a review in *The Times Literary Supplement* by Katherine Duncan–Jones of Marion Wynne–Davies' 1998 anthology of early modern women's poetry. Duncan–Jones criticized the editing of Mary Wroth who she felt was unintelligible without detailed reference to Sir Philip Sidney.[8]

We were offered by the late Jeremy Maule the chance to publish the "Centuries" of Julia Palmer, dated 1671–73 (William Andrews Clark Memorial Library, UCLA, MS. P1745 M1 P744 (1671–73 Bound) in his Renaissance Texts from Manuscript series. The first two volumes of the series have been published,[9] but his death has put the future of the series in doubt, and we were advised to find another publisher. We have in fact chosen to go with the imprint of our former employer, Nottingham Trent University, called "Trent Editions," which is dedicated to the recovery in affordable editions of unknown texts. The Palmer edition is the first volume to be published in the "Early Modern Women's Writing" series of "Trent Editions"; forthcoming

---

[6] J. Kahan, review of K. Aughterson, ed., *Renaissance Women: A Sourcebook* (London and New York: Routledge, 1995), *Renaissance Quarterly* 51 (1998): 693–94.

[7] Jane Stevenson and Peter Davidson, eds., *Early Modern Women Poets (1520–1700): An Anthology* (Oxford: Oxford University Press, 2001), xxix–xxxvii.

[8] K. Duncan-Jones, review of M. Wynne-Davies, ed., *Women Poets of the Renaissance* (London and New York: Routledge, 1998), *Times Literary Supplement*, 8 January 1999, 22.

[9] *A Reformation Rhetoric: Thomas Swynnerton's The Tropes and Figures of Scripture*, ed. Richard Rex, Renaissance Texts from Manuscript 1 (Cambridge: RTM Publications, 1999); Meric Casaubon, *Generall Learning: A Seventeenth-Century Treatise on the Formation of the General Scholar*, ed. Richard Serjeantson, Renaissance Texts from Manuscript 2 (Cambridge: RTM Publications, 1999). This series is now copublished by Medieval & Renaissance Texts & Studies. <http://www.asu.edu/clas/acmrs/publications/mrts/rtfm.htm>

editions include Alice Thornton's autobiography and the letters of Katherine, Lady Ranelagh.[10] This allows us to fulfil one part of our political agenda: Julia Palmer's "Centuries" is now available in a cheap edition.

Palmer's manuscript is more like a verse miscellany than a traditional woman's commonplace book. It is not typical of the majority of items we are describing and cataloguing for Perdita; about one-quarter contain poetical material, but much of that is transcribed from other sources and can give valuable insight into women's interjections into manuscript culture. Something like Constance Fowler's miscellany, published by RETS in 2000,[11] presents different editing choices from those found in an authorial fair copy of original poetry. But there are still many choices to be made in producing such an edition.

In the textual introduction to our edition we highlight the material characteristics of the Palmer manuscript. This collection of two hundred poems exists in an autograph fair copy in octavo format, bound in contemporary brown calf, with only blind ruling for ornamentation. It is not ostensibly a presentation copy, instead containing authorial revisions at various points, but it is neatly produced. Palmer copied her poems from another source, probably her rough papers, and possibly much later after she composed them.[12] The first flyleaf consists of the author's signature, the date 1671, and a note indicating that she wished the manuscript to be read by two apparently like-minded people who held powerful positions in the Society of Apothecaries: "I Leave this Book to Mr Joseph Bisco senior. if he out Live me otherwiss. I Leave itt to Mr James pitson Apothicary." This note and the signature on the flyleaf are in the same hand as the rest of the manuscript, leading us to describe the manuscript confidently as autograph.

We have traced these two men in the Court Minutes of the Society of Apothecaries. Joseph Biscoe (1637–4718) was an officer in the Society in the early eighteenth century becoming Master in 1711–12, and he took James

---

[10] <http://human.ntu.ac.uk/trenteditions/>

[11] *The Verse Miscellany of Constance Aston Fowler: A Diplomatic Edition,* ed. Deborah Aldrich–Watson, MRTS 210 (Tempe, AZ: MRTS, 2000). See also the essay by Aldrich–Watson in this volume.

[12] There are several indications of this: three times Palmer skips ahead in her transcription, needing to cross out a line. See pp. 5 (line deleted between ll. 1 and 2), 128 (between ll. 46 and 47), and 134 (between ll. 18 and 19). Also, a poem has been copied out of sequence given the dates of transcription — a poem composed on 26 September (p. 214) has been transcribed before two written on 22 and 25 September (pp. 218 and 219). It is not easy to date the paper since its horn watermark is very common, and the tight binding and octavo format make it difficult to see defining characteristics.

Pitson (b. c. 1658) as his apprentice on 7 May 1672. Pitson was freed in 1680 and was active in the Society, holding several positions including Master, in 1723–24.[13] The Biscoe family appears in the records of St. Margaret's, Westminster. In those parish registers is listed the baptism of a Samuel Palmer on 17 June 1667, son of Nicholas and Julia Palmer.[14] She was probably the Julia Hungerford who married Nicholas Palmer on 12 May 1664 at All Hallows London Wall.[15] This may be our poet, since Julia is an unusual name at this point in history. *The Oxford Dictionary of English Christian Names* claims that it was not used in England as a first name until the eighteenth century.[16] Julia Palmer's absence from later Anglican records suggests that she became a Nonconformist; while she lived in Westminster she may have belonged to the large Presbyterian congregation led by Thomas Cawton and later Vincent Alsop.

Her manuscript and extant records indicate that Julia Palmer knew the Biscoes, a powerful family with Presbyterian affiliations. Julia Palmer was linked with Joseph Biscoe through Nonconformity: her manuscript indicates that she wishes her manuscript to be used for the spiritual good of others, so it is likely that both Biscoe and Pitson were sympathetic to her views. In fact Biscoe has impeccable Nonconformist credentials. His nephew married Vincent Alsop's granddaughter at All Hallows London Wall, and Biscoe himself later became a parishioner of John Nesbitt, pastor of an Independent congre-

---

[13] John Challenor Covington Smith, *Pedigree of the Family of Biscoe* (London: Mitchell and Hughes, 1887), 4–7; Arthur Meredyth Burke, ed., *Memorials of St. Margaret's Church Westminster Comprising the Parish Registers, 1539–1660 and the Churchwarden's Accounts, 1460–1603* (London: Eyre and Spottiswode, 1914), 134; Guildhall Library, Court Minutes of the Society of Apothecaries 1651–80, MS. 8200/2, fol. 160; Court Minutes 1680–94, MS. 8200/3, fol. 6; Penelope Hunting, *A History of the Society of Apothecaries* (London: The Society of Apothecaries, 1998), 302; C. R. B. Barrett, *The History of the Society of Apothecaries of London* (London: Elliott Stone, 1905), 122–31. See Court Minutes 1694–1716, MS. 8200/4; Court Minutes 1716–26, MS. 8200/5; and Court Minutes 1726–1745, MS. 8200/6 for Biscoe's and Pitson's activities as officers of the Society. Since apprentices were usually bound to a master when they were fourteen (Hunting, *History*, 45), Pitson was probably born in 1658. The last mention of Pitson in the Court Minutes is 16 March 1732/3, so he may have died shortly afterwards.

[14] Herbert F. Westlake and Lawrence E. Tanner, eds., *The Registers of St. Margaret's Westminster London 1660–1675*, Harleian Society vol. 64, Register Section (London: Harleian Society, 1935), 64.

[15] International Genealogical Index <http://www.familysearch.org>; Guildhall Library, All Hallows London Wall parish registers, MS. 5085, fol. 55v.

[16] E. G. Withycombe, *The Oxford Dictionary of English Christian Names*, 3rd ed. (Oxford: Clarendon Press, 1977), 183. Withycombe points out that the name Julia was used by Shakespeare, in *Two Gentlemen of Verona*, and of course by Herrick.

gation at Hare-court, Aldersgate Street, and also a lecturer at Pinners' Hall.[17] (Pinners' Hall was the site of a weekly lecture by Presbyterian and Independent ministers.) Julia was probably also interested in the connections of both dedicatees with the Society of Apothecaries. In the Court Minutes of the Society of Apothecaries on 7 July 1682, Samuel Palmer, bound as an apprentice to the apothecary Edward Baker for eight years, is listed as the son of the deceased Nicholas Palmer of New Windsor in Berkshire.[18] That this Samuel is Julia and Nicholas's son is made more likely by the fact that the Nicholas Palmer buried at New Windsor on 28 February 1681[19] was a Presbyterian preacher, a very plausible occupation for the husband of the Julia Palmer whose Presbyterian sympathies are displayed so clearly in the manuscript. "Mr Palmer of London" preached at New Windsor in 1669; on 24 May 1672 a licence was requested for "Nicholas Palmer, Presbyterian, at Mrs. Jane Price's new house, Frogmore, New Windsor, Berkshire," which was granted on 10 June.[20] The move to New Windsor was probably part of a Presbyterian outreach made possible by the Declaration of Indulgence. Julia's dedication of the manuscript may have been an attempt to gain favor for her son whose career as an apothecary seems to have been unsuccessful; he never completed his apprenticeship. The date of the inscription to Joseph Biscoe is clearly later than the date of composition of the poems as it refers to "Joseph Biscoe, senior." The younger Joseph was baptized on 7 August 1676;[21] Palmer's transcription, then, must postdate 1676, and probably dates from a time in the 1680s when the patronage of Biscoe and Pitson could have been useful to young Samuel.

Biscoe was probably also a neighbor of the Palmers while they were in Westminster. According to the Westminster tax assessment for 1694, Joseph

---

[17] Walter Wilson, *The History and Antiquities of Dissenting Churches and Meeting Houses in London, Westminster, and Southwark* (London: Maxwell & Wilson, 1810), 3: 282–87; Smith, *Family of Biscoe*, 6. Biscoe bequeathed two guineas to "my Reverend Pastor Mr John Nesbit" in his will dated 1 February 1713/14 and proved 11 December 1723 (City of Westminster Archives Centre, Will Accession 120/1853, fol. 128).

[18] Guildhall Library, Court Minutes of the Society of Apothecaries 1680–1694, MS. 8200/3, fol. 64. Presumably Samuel Palmer never completed his eight-year apprenticeship because he is not listed as having been freed.

[19] Berkshire Record Office, New Windsor parish registers, MS. D/P149/1/1 (no foliation).

[20] A. G. Matthews, *Calamy Revised: Being a Revision of Edmund Calamy's Account of the Ministers and Others Ejected and Silenced 1660–1662* (Oxford: Clarendon Press, 1934), 380; F. H. Blackburne Daniell, ed., *Calendar of State Papers, Domestic Series, May 18th to September 39th, 1672* (London: HMSO, 1899), 55, 196, and 216.

[21] Winifred Ward, ed., *The Registers of St. Margaret's Westminster*, part 2, Harleian Society vol. 88, Register Section (London: Harleian Society, 1968), 8.

Biscoe lived in a grand house in the Sanctuary and Deanery. He owned a great deal of property in Westminster, including the houses next door to "Mr. Alsop's meeting house" in New Way. It is possible that he donated or sold the land for the meeting house to the Presbyterian congregation. Tantalizingly, a Samuel Palmer lived close by in Orchard Street: we do not know whether this is Julia's son.[22] There is no record of Julia Palmer moving to New Windsor, but if she did go there with her husband it is likely that she returned to Westminster with her son after her husband's death.

The choices anthologists make, whether it is in trying to claim a "tradition" of women's writing by isolating it from male contemporaries' work, or in placing works in print in a privileged position over those in manuscript, affect how students and the academy alike see women's writing in this period. Editors of women's complete works face similar challenges. Besides textual and biographical information, our introduction also contains vital information on the appropriate context for the verse, arguing that Palmer should be read through the lens of Nonconformist beliefs rather than as part of a distinct female tradition. Feminist scholars have been at pains to discern a tradition of women's writing in the early modern period, a project that is undermined by the fact that many women who wrote would probably never have read any printed book written by another woman, at least until the dissemination in the late seventeenth century of Katherine Philips's poetry.[23] We would suggest that there is a kind of poetry thought of as ideal women's poetry, which is often explicitly "authorized" by men in this period. In the earlier seventeenth century there are several prose works by women, each of which also contains a poem by the author of the treatise herself: Anne Lock's translation of Jean Taffin's treatise *Of the Markes of the Children of God* (1592, 1609); Dorothy Leigh's *The Mother's Blessing* (1616); Elizabeth Richardson's *A Ladies Legacie* (1645); Frances Cooke's *Meditations* (1650). These poems are similar in that they are all devotional, and simple in meter and rhetoric: they resemble most closely

---

[22] Corporation of London Record Office, Assess. Box 40.22.

[23] The "matchless Orinda" inspired "Ephelia," Anne Killigrew, and Jane Barker, among others (Patrick Thomas, "Introduction," in *The Collected Works of Katherine Philips "The Matchless Orinda,"* ed. Thomas [Essex: Stump Cross, 1990],1:25–28). For example, Jane Barker wishes to "reach fair Orindas height" in "The contract with the muses writ on the bark of a shady ash-tree" (*The Poems of Jane Barker: The Magdalen Manuscript*, ed. Kathryn R. King [Oxford: Magdalen College, 1998], 40). An earlier exception is the mother's-advice writer Elizabeth Richardson who read and responded in the form of a meditation and *précis* to Mary Sidney's translation of De Mornay's *The Triumph of Death*, as Margaret Hannay has discovered ("Elizabeth Ashburnham Richardson's Meditation on the Countess of Pembroke's *Discourse*," *English Manuscript Studies 1100–1700* 9 [2000]: 114–28).

the psalm paraphrases that are seen to be holy because they are unrhetorical, transparent, and follow biblical language closely. Since several of these works appear under male patronage, we think this must constitute the type of poetry considered suitable for a woman in the first half of the seventeenth century.

Julia Palmer's poetry fits very well into this category. Her poetry is simple in meter, very biblical, and supremely devotional. However, Palmer may not have been aware of any "women's tradition" of devotional writing; she probably wrote "Centuries,"[24] i.e. two groups of one hundred poems, because of the popularity of William Barton's *Centuries* of biblical verse. In the end he wrote six *Centuries*, but the first *Century of select hymns* was published in 1659 and three more *Centuries* were published in 1668. Many Nonconformists, particularly Presbyterians, appreciated Barton's poetry, Richard Baxter and Matthew Henry among them. Julia Palmer's Nonconformism is indicated not only by her biography (the fact that her husband became a Presbyterian preacher) but also by the strong Calvinism and distinctive phraseology in her poetry. She frequently celebrates "free grace" (God's mercy in saving people and sustaining them with blessings, expecting nothing in return), and uses the verb "give in" instead of "give" to describe the direct blessings of God. Poem 40 in the "First Century," entitled "Desires," describes the ideal Nonconformist deathbed scene as rendered sacred by Samuel Clarke's 1662 volume *A collection of the lives of ten eminent divines*. The poem includes some distinctively Nonconformist if rather unpoetic jargon such as "Let an abundant entrance be / Administred then unto me" (p. 66, ll. 31–32). Throughout her poetry Palmer emphasizes the importance of "ordinances" and "duties" (set services ordained by authority such as holy communion), suggesting that she was Presbyterian rather than a member of a more radical sect. She was certainly not Baptist, where the use of poetry in spiritual matters was controversial throughout the second half of the seventeenth century: the issue caused a split in the movement in the early 1690s. The very action of writing poetry excludes her from more radical sects such as the Quakers, for whom all rhetorical play was suspect.[25] Before the publication of Mary Mollineux's *Fruits of Retirement* in 1702

---

[24] Palmer did not title her own poems "Centuries": an extract of a sale catalogue preserved with the manuscript at the Clark Library has done so, evidently noting that her poems fit this format.

[25] The Quaker Mary Pennington and her husband "scrupled" the use of psalm paraphrase because it was too indebted to human invention. Peter Collins, Lecturer in Sociology at the University of Durham, gave a paper on Quaker discipline in the late seventeenth century at "Heterodoxy and Orthodoxy," the Seventeenth Century Conference at Durham, July 1999. In answer to a question he said that he believed the writing of poetry would be absolutely taboo for a Quaker.

only one other verse publication had been approved by the Second Morning Meeting, and that was also issued posthumously: William Sixsmith's *Some Fruits brought forth through a Tender Branch in the Heavenly Vine* in 1679.[26] Abigail Fisher was told to rewrite her verse in prose.[27]

Julia Palmer's poems are not only extremely biblical but also profoundly intimate: they deal almost exclusively with her spiritual union with Christ. The intensive period of composition — two hundred poems in two years — means that in some ways the poetry functions as a spiritual journal, many of the poems being located in a particular occasion, or attached to a particular date. Like the spiritual journal, there is no real sense of progress throughout the time period involved: a typically Calvinist spirituality of depths and heights is charted, God being responsible for both. Palmer has given the title "Experience" to four of her poems, the technical term for the subject matter of the spiritual journal.[28] As with other Nonconformist women, the romance with Christ held out to her as life's greatest blessing, and consummated fully at death, leads her to long for death with a passion that was clearly thought rather dangerous by one man in authority. She writes a rather indignant poem to a Mr H who dared to suggest there was nothing wrong in desiring a long and happy life (pp. 222–24), stating,

> But as for those, that have a sight
> And tast, of Christ, there harts delight
> All your perswasions ar in vain
> To make them wilingly, remain
> In this sad, distant, absent, state
> Your arguments ar come to late   [70]
> Ther harts they ar already gone
> To'th object, they would live upon
> And tis beyound your skill, to tole
> Ther harts back, to this durty hole
>
> (p. 223)

---

[26] London, Friends House Library, Morning Meeting Book, vol. 1 (1673–92), 23, and vol. 3 (1700–1711).

[27] Margaret J. M. Ezell, *Writing Women's Literary History* (Baltimore: Johns Hopkins University Press, 1993), 158.

[28] See the headings in the ideal spiritual diary laid out in Isaac Ambrose, *Media* (London, 1657), 87–88, 163–68, and Elizabeth Clarke, "Diaries and Journals," in *A Companion to English Renaissance Literature and Culture*, ed. Michael Hattaway (London: Blackwell, 2000), 609–14.

Her siting of the poems within a model of spiritual marriage locates her firmly on one side of a religious debate with political overtones that took place in the 1670s. In a tract of 1674 William Sherlock, Master of The Temple, attacked Nonconformist spirituality, particularly the Independent John Owen, who had characterized the believer's relationship with Christ in terms of the erotic poetry of the Song of Songs, and the Presbyterian Thomas Watson, whose 1657 treatise *Christs Loveliness* epitomized the spirituality of poetic desire at the heart of Nonconformist religion. Sherlock was particularly scathing about the preacher Thomas Vincent, who had suggested to unmarried young women that they consider Christ as their husband.[29] The debate turned on the status of metaphor, Nonconformists arguing that the very metaphors in which Scripture is couched were inspired, whilst Anglicans preferred to locate inspiration in the rational interpretation of such tropes.[30] Tory Anglicans were most worried by the image of the believer as the spouse of Christ, which posed a political problem: such an intimate relationship of Christ and the believer bypassed authority and all external constraint. Many Nonconformists answered Sherlock, including Vincent Alsop: he was appointed successor to Thomas Cawton in 1677 on the basis of the volume *Antisozzo*.[31] The fact that the best Nonconformist answer to Sherlock was written by Robert Ferguson rather proved the Tory Anglican point: he was the Earl of Shaftesbury's chief pamphleteer during the Exclusion Crisis, the main organizer of the Rye House Plot in 1683 to assassinate the King and the Duke of York, and the composer of Monmouth's *Declaration* at his landing in the West Country in 1685. Dryden considered him the archetypal traitor:

> *Judas* that keeps the Rebells Pension-Purse;
> *Judas* that pays the Treason-writers Fee,
> *Judas* that well deserves his Namesake's Tree [.][32]

---

[29] William Sherlock, *A Discourse Concerning the Knowledge of Jesus Christ, and our Union and Communion with Him* (London, 1674), 383.

[30] The Anglican Sherlock argues in *A Discourse* that only the meaning of the metaphor is inspired. In contrast, Robert Ferguson, in *The Interest of Reason in Religion, with the Import and use of Scripture Metaphors; and the nature of the Union betwixt Christ and Believers* (London, 1675), argues that the metaphor itself is inspired. Better known works which treat this issue are John Owen's *Truth and Innocence Vindicated* (London, 1669), a Nonconformist reply to Samuel Parker (the Bishop of Oxford)'s *Discourse of Ecclesiastical Politie* (London, 1670), despite the dates.

[31] Wilson, *The History and Antiquities of Dissenting Churches*, vol. 2 (London: Maxwell & Wilson, 1808), 61.

[32] *The Second Part of Absalom and Achitophel. A Poem* (1682), ll. 321–23, in *The Poems of John Dryden*, ed. James Kinsley (Oxford: Clarendon Press, 1958), 1:280.

This particular aspect of Nonconformist spirituality, the believer as bride of Christ, gives Julia Palmer both spiritual and poetic confidence. Her sense of closeness to Christ enables her to resist authority as represented in Mr H, while the discourse of the Song of Songs offers her a biblically-sanctioned female poetic voice to imitate in an age when poetry was suspect as a vehicle of true devotion. She is convinced of the worth of her manuscript because it is in many ways the precisely correct response to the teaching of John Owen, Thomas Watson, and many other respected London Nonconformist ministers. There is no humility topos at the start of the manuscript, simply an assumption that God will use her as an amanuensis.

> Blessed spirit, doe thou endite
> Help me to speak thy praise
> That soe I may others envite
> To love thee, all there days
>
> A blessed sun, oh Lord thou art   [5]
> Let still thy beames of glory dart
> To warm, and quiken, my dull hart

The first poem of "The Second Century," in a similar vein, finishes with an even stronger statement of an expected readership: "That I to others, still may be / A light, to lead them unto thee" (p. 162, ll. 7–8). Later in "The Second Century" Palmer reiterates this desire. In poems 14 and 32 she yearns, "Oh that, I might, make others fall / in love with thee, and take / Thee, for their only all, in all" (p. 178, ll. 45–47) and "In this my day, or rather night / let holy nese in me, / Bee still a constant growing light / to lead many, to thee" (p. 203, ll. 33–36). Palmer must have considered her poetry worthy to leave to such a rich person as Biscoe; comparing their rents in 1694, Samuel Palmer paid £7 while Biscoe, at a house in The Sanctuary and Deanery, paid £30.[33] Palmer's poetry may have circulated among sympathetic apothecaries and Nonconformists, perhaps among members of her husband's congregation in New Windsor, among the Hare-court congregation that Biscoe attended, or even among those who attended the lectures at Pinners' Hall. These congregations may have sung Palmer's poems: the meter of many of them is iambic dimeter in combinations of four, three, and two feet, the standard components of the hymnbook. Palmer also used many of the meters in William Barton's *Centuries*. Isaac Watts's early hymns were "lined out" to a congre-

---

[33] Corporation of London Record Office, Assess. Box 40.22.

gation singing them as hymns from a manuscript copy; perhaps Palmer's were as well.

§

For a combination of reasons we have produced a near-diplomatic transcription of the manuscript for our edition. We have generally preserved punctuation, since it is not usually a barrier to comprehension in Palmer's text, but we regularized certain aspects: we expanded abbreviations, and switched her peculiar usage of commas instead of apostrophes to normal usage.[34] We emended Palmer's words when they seem obviously incorrect, since, as Speed Hill puts it, "an error is an error, even if it has the authority of the author itself."[35] We tried to replicate the experience of reading the manuscript as closely as possible, without making choices which fetishize the physical object above the sense of the words (or, in Jerome McGann's terms, the bibliographical codes above the linguistic codes).[36]

As the edition we have produced is "non-critical" rather than "critical," we did not need to be concerned with the controversies among the Greg–Bowers–Tanselle school of eclectic editing based on a copy-text, since we have just one autograph text. Nor do the critics more interested in production and reception of texts above authorial intention, such as D. F. McKenzie, Jerome McGann, and Donald Pizer, have direct relevance for us, again because the only agent of production seems to have been Palmer herself, and because nothing concrete is known of her readership.

Using D. C. Greetham's definition of the span of non-critical editions, we considered photographic reproduction, type facsimile, and diplomatic tran-

---

[34] On punctuation as a substantive rather than accidental variant see W. W. Greg, "The Rationale of Copy-Text," in *Collected Papers*, ed. J. C. Maxwell (Oxford: Clarendon Press, 1966), 374–91. See also Malcolm Parkes, *Pause and Effect: An Introduction to the History of Punctuation in the West* (Aldershot: Scolar, 1992); and Anthony Hammond, "The Noisy Comma: Searching for the Signal in Renaissance Dramatic Texts," in *Crisis in Editing: Texts of the English Renaissance*, ed. Randall M. McLeod (New York: AMS, 1994), 203–49.

[35] W. Speed Hill, "The Theory and Practice of Transcription," in *New Ways*, ed. Hill, 25–32, here 27–28. T. H. Howard-Hill makes a similar point, and argues that editors must establish which textual features are "intention carriers" for a particular author ("Modern Textual Theories and the Editing of Plays," *The Library*, 6th ser. 11 [1989]: 109, 96).

[36] Jerome J. McGann, "What Is Critical Editing?" *Text* 5 (1991): 15–29.

script.[37] We decided ultimately to produce a diplomatic transcript, but wondered how diplomatic we should be. One end of the spectrum is found in Mary Hobbs's edition of the Stoughton manuscript, an important source for Henry King's poetry.[38] In the transcription to accompany her facsimile reproduction, Hobbes has preserved not only original spelling and punctuation but also abbreviations, superscriptions, tildes, and u and v (with occasional slips). But Michael Hunter, in an extremely valuable article entitled "How to Edit a Seventeenth-Century Manuscript: Principles and Practices," has asked for scholarly agreement about conventions of transcription, pointing out how each editor tends to re-invent the wheel, and insufficiently to theorize his or her choices.[39] Though his sources, mainly late seventeenth-century letters and autobiographies concerning the history of science, exist typically in one autograph copy, as is the case with Julia Palmer, he points out that significant issues are at stake. He advocates retaining original spelling and capitalization, and punctuation as well, though with some latitude. He argues for normalizing i/j and u/v on the basis that it would be inappropriate to replicate a purely manuscript usage which would have been regularized by a contemporary printer, as would be the case with abbreviations, and so he advocates silent expansion. Hunter proposes several alternatives for noting additions and deletions to the text; we have chosen the "clear-text" method (rather than the "inclusive text," which uses brackets, italics, and diacritics), so that readers can see what the author intended as the final form of the poem, and can decide whether to consult notes or not.

Hunter neglects to mention that a seventeenth-century printer would also, of course, have normalized the spelling of a manuscript text. By the logic of his earlier examples (normalizing u/v and expanding abbreviations) we should then modernize spelling (though of course the exact variant a seventeenth-century printer would have used could only be guessed). He argues, however, that "modernization is by its very nature an unacceptably arbitrary procedure, and it is best avoided."[40] This is a view shared by many editors. But there

---

[37] D. C. Greetham, *Textual Scholarship: An Introduction* (New York: Garland, 1994), 347–51. For a similar definition of a documentary edition see W. Speed Hill, "Editing Nondramatic Texts of the English Renaissance: A Field Guide with Illustrations," in *New Ways*, ed. Hill, 1–24, here 5; and G. Thomas Tanselle, "Editing Without a Copy-Text," *Studies in Bibliography* 47 (1994): 1–22, here 3.

[38] Mary Hobbs, ed., *The Stoughton Manuscript. A Manuscript Miscellany of Poems by Henry King and his Circle, circa 1636* (Aldershot: Scolar Press, 1990).

[39] Michael Hunter, "How to Edit a Seventeenth-Century Manuscript: Principles and Practice," *The Seventeenth Century* 10 (1995): 277–310.

[40] Hunter, "How to Edit," 290.

are some powerful political arguments to be made in favor of modernization. Many aristocratic households employed secretaries who produced scribal copies of the family's literary texts. John Rolleston was the Cavendish family's secretary, transcribing some of the Duke of Newcastle's works, but also of those of his daughter, Jane Cavendish.[41] No doubt Rolleston altered her spelling and any grammatical infelicities, probably with Cavendish's approval. Seventeenth-century women often solicited correction of their work by male contemporaries. Anne, Lady Southwell, asked a friend, the curate Roger Cox, to "Condemne, amend, or rattifye this scrole," but if he felt unequal to the task to "Pass it to oure beloved Docter Featlye / his tongue dropps honnye, and can doe it neatlye."[42] Julia Palmer was probably not sufficiently wealthy to employ a scribe, even if such an extravagance were acceptable within Nonconformist culture. It seems to do her poetry a disservice to present it in a less regularized form than she would have enjoyed had a professional transcribed her verse. This is of course a class rather than a gender issue. Many anthologies modernize the spelling of their authors: in our experience students have found it a barrier to women's poetry when Donne and Milton are presented in modern spelling, but Anne Lock and An Collins are presented in the original. It surrounds women's poetry with an aura of quaintness, and gives the impression that women were more ignorant than their male contemporaries. In spite of these views in favor of modernization, we have chosen to prefer a scholarly audience and have retained her individualistic spelling, not least because the manuscript cannot be microfilmed, and the Clark Library is too far away for many scholars to travel to. We are lucky, however, that Palmer's practices are not impenetrable to a student reader. We have also chosen to follow Hunter's prescriptions for our Perdita anthology, for similar reasons.

§

However much annotation we offer to explain religious difference or to contextualize the poetry, the problem with Julia Palmer's verse is that it is so different from other works of the 1670s that tend to be studied. In 1672, another edition of Cowley came out,[43] Milton was still alive, and Dryden had

---

[41] Two copies of Jane Cavendish's poetry and drama transcribed by Rolleston are now Bodleian Library, MS. Rawl. poet. 16, and Beinecke Library, Yale University, Osborn MS. b. 233.

[42] Folger Shakespeare Library MS. V.b.198, fol. 26r.

[43] *The works of Mr. Abraham Cowley: consisting of those which were formerly printed: and those which he design'd for the press, now published out of the authors original copies*, 3rd ed. (London, 1672).

started his poetic career. This poetry needs a completely different kind of reading. Even if it is treated in a separate category of "woman's poetry," Katherine Philips, whose poems were issued in the 1660s, is the inevitable comparison. Yet Julia Palmer was completely excluded from the kind of community in which our idea of seventeenth-century poetry is fostered: in turn, her verse deliberately excludes aristocratic modes of rhetoric, with their associations of royalism and conformity. It is worth noting that Philips was brought up in a middle-class London Puritan family, and attended a boarding school run by a Presbyterian schoolmistress,[44] which suggests a parallel with Palmer's probable upbringing, but Philips's writing does not explore one's spiritual marriage with Christ — something a royalist would not do. In obviously striving to enter an elite community on the basis of her rhetorical skill, Philips is doing something profoundly different from Julia Palmer, who is also interested in an elite community (as the inscription to Joseph Biscoe points out) but a holy one. Palmer's priorities are entirely different, but they are not unique among other Nonconformist women's writings, mostly spiritual journals, which have survived from this period. Elizabeth Turner goes through a kind of marriage service with Christ (Maidstone, Centre for Kentish Studies, U1015 F 27, pp. 58 and 60) and Mary Rich's journal traces her romance with Him (British Library Add. MSS. 27351–27358). That this is a gendered model of ideal Nonconformist piety is suggested by the Thomas Vincent sermon entitled *Christ the Best Husband, or an invitation of Young Women unto Christ* (London, 1672).

Self-consciously holy poetry does not have to be good, and in fact it rather adds to the author's sanctity if it is not (even George Herbert makes noises in this direction in "The Forerunners," "A true Hymne," "Jordan (i)" and "Jordan (ii)"). The Presbyterian minister Oliver Heywood wrote in an autograph manuscript:

> these verses I compile
> in heat of my devotion,
> not caring for the stile
> nor yet intending notion
> rouzing my heart the while
> to some diviner motion
>
> Written in my study at Coley-Hall may the 18 1667[45]

---

[44] *Collected Works*, ed. Thomas, 1:2.

[45] Oliver Heywood, *His Autobiography Diaries, Anecdote and Event Books*, ed. J. Horsfall Turner, vol. 1 (Brighouse, Eng.: A. B. Boyes, 1882), 131.

John Bunyan worried that poetry might be seen to distort truth, stating defensively in the opening poem to his *Profitable Meditations* (1661),

> 'Tis not the Method, but the truth alone
> Should please a Saint, and mollifie his heart:
> Truth in or out of Meeter is but one;
> And this thou knowst, if thou a Christian art.[46]

A generation later, Isaac Watts went so far as to ignore aesthetic considerations; he wrote of his popular hymnbook: "Some of the Beauties of Poesy are neglected, and some wilfully defac'd."[47] Many of Palmer's poems are long. Moreover, although she has a kind of facility in simple rhyme schemes, she is not that scrupulous about a bad choice of rhyme or a lapse in meter. However much contextualization is offered, the non-specialist reader is not going to forgive her these faults. Her reputation would, in fact, benefit hugely from selection: some of her shorter lyrics reach a kind of simple sublimity, such as "The Child in a strangers arms," (pp. 129–30), which begins,

> Oh world, what means thy tempting charms
> I'me like a litle Child
> Infolded in, a strangers arms
> whilst in thee, I am held
>
> If the Child doe, its father spy   [5]
> it then can take no rest
> But will strecth out, its arms, and cry
> in'ts fathers arms to nest
>
> Whatever you. to it can give
> it will not satisfie   [10]
> Nothing can to it give releife
> But still twill moane, and cry
>
> Untill its father, do it take
> and then its crys, doe cease

---

[46] Cited in Graham Midgley, "Introduction," in *The Poems, The Miscellaneous Works of John Bunyan* 6 (Oxford: Clarendon Press, 1980), xv–lxii, here xviii.

[47] Isaac Watts, *Hymns and Spiritual Songs in Three Books*, 10th ed. (London, 1728), vii.

Its fathers arms can only make   [15]
it still, & be at peace

Oh pity Lord, my weary soull
still reaching after thee
And cannot rest, till thou condole
and strecth thine arms, to me   [20]

The poem ends with Palmer begging Christ to fetch her to his throne. Lyrics such as these could not unfavorably be compared with those of Isaac Watts, and also with Bunyan's. Bunyan's editor addresses the problem of critics who have weighed Bunyan against "highly self-conscious and cultivated poets" like Herbert, Crashaw, Baxter, and Quarles and have found his verse wanting; he suggests that the context in which Bunyan's verse should be read is that of popular folk literature: religious broadside ballads, metrical versions of the psalms, emblems, and fables.[48]

Scholars of women's writing in the period need to know about Julia Palmer's poetry: it is, in many senses, extraordinary, and if a proper literary history for women is to be compiled, her work should figure in it. Her poetry is remarkable, considering her gender, her lack of an elite education, and the prohibitions against rhetoric within her particular culture. Our presentation of Julia Palmer's manuscript should ideally fulfil the needs of teachers and researchers of women's writing at the same time, an extremely difficult task. The political decision to approach the scholarly readership first may not be the correct one, in view of the need for cheap student editions that could form part of an academic syllabus. However, there is the wider context of academic politics, in which researchers of women's writing still have a great deal to prove. A recent reviewer of a biography of the writer Bathsua Makin called its subject a "minor schoolmistress" and accused "the early modern women's studies industry" of "displaying the classic symptoms of over-rapid expansion, where the quantity of production has outstripped the underlying rate of research."[49] It is probably impossible to combat this kind of prejudice: what we have done is to edit this manuscript according to the highest editorial standards and hope that the academic community will be receptive to Julia Palmer. No doubt she would have been equally unreceptive to its criticism or praise.

[48] Midgley, "Introduction," in Bunyan, *Poems, Miscellaneous Works*, 6:xxv–xlvii.

[49] Noel Malcolm, review of Frances Teague, *Bathsua Makin, Woman of Learning* (London: Associated Univ. Press, 1998), *Times Literary Supplement*, 5 Nov. 1999, 28.

Editing a Renaissance Commonplace Book: The Holgate Miscellany

MICHAEL ROY DENBO

T HE HOLGATE MISCELLANY IS AN EARLY SEVENTEENTH-CENTURY
verse commonplace book housed at the Pierpont Morgan Library,
New York City.[1] It is a quarto gathered in fours comprising 164
leaves. Among the poets represented are John Donne, William Shakespeare,
Ben Jonson, Francis Beaumont, William Herbert, Henry King, Thomas Carew, William Strode, Richard Corbet, and Sir Henry Wotton. There are also
seven poems by the compiler, William Holgate, and many anonymous poems,
several of which are first published in this collection. Some of the poems
chronicle political events of the period, including the proposed marriage of
Charles, Prince of Wales, to the Spanish Infanta. In addition to the poetry,
there are a few prose entries, most recording speeches by well-known
dignitaries who visited Saffron Walden, the home of William Holgate. Virtually all the poems were transcribed from other manuscripts, but a few were
transcribed from printed materials. It is written in a generally readable Italic
hand, but Holgate occasionally wrote individual letters in secretary. As to be
expected, his orthography is inconsistent, at times spelling the same word

---

[1] Michael Denbo, "The Holgate Miscellany (Pierpont Morgan Library MS 1057):
A Diplomatic Edition" (Ph.D. diss., Graduate Center, CUNY, 1997), and Denbo,
"Print as Copy-text in the English Renaissance Manuscript Tradition," *Renaissance
News & Notes* 10 (1998): <http: www.r-s-a.org/rnn10-1_d_g.htm#Denbo>.

differently from one line to the next. The manuscript also includes a section of eighteenth-century entries, transcribed by John Wale, a descendant of the Holgate family.

My first impression upon seeing the Holgate was that it is a book of uncommon natural beauty. The handwriting is neat, the pages nicely organized and compact, giving the impression of an intelligently collected book of poems. It is not overly ornate as some miscellanies are. I recognized only a few of the poems. I was not sure who William Holgate actually was. I could not even read all the poetry. How was I to find an organizing principle that would intelligently explain how the book was brought together, under what circumstances and when, and how it added to our general knowledge of Renaissance poetry? Of course, I knew it was the cultural significance of texts that brought me to this manuscript, but just knowing that did not explain what I had to do to make this text meaningful to the scholarly community.

What spoke to me most clearly was a sense I immediately had of the man who first created it. Surely he, despite the fact that I knew so little about him, was the key to understanding the text as a social document. To discover as much as possible about him was my primary concern. I hoped to find copies of the poems that were exactly like the texts I saw in the Holgate, with the belief that if I could trace the source of a particular text, I might be able to place Holgate himself at a specific time and place. I also wanted to learn as much as possible about the individual texts, who they were about, and who, if possible, wrote many of the anonymous poems transcribed into the miscellany. Indeed, the anonymous and unusual poems became the most valuable because they might bring me closer to Holgate. In other words, I wanted to make my information as personal as my own sense of the document. It would be a gigantic task, but one well worth doing if I could recreate some of my own immediate sense of the document.

A second issue presented itself from the outset. Despite the fact that Holgate included seven of his own poems, the manuscript itself is the work of a reader and not a writer. This implied that I had to address the reception of poetry more than its production. Why did he keep these particular poems? It is easy to assume that they were the poems he liked, but on what basis do I make that assertion? Maybe some were collected because he wanted exemplars of what he considered bad poetry. In what way did they become his property once he recorded them? Did he feel free to change the poems to suit his own taste?

Perhaps some were included only as a testament for people who were dead. Others may have been transcribed for reasons of patronage, as some commentators on the miscellany have suggested. Ultimately, these are questions of interpretation, but not interpretation as it is usually applied to literary studies.

This would be interpretation that accounts for the reading habits of one particular individual, but the explanation for those habits could not be shown based only on my own assumptions.

Indeed, it is the contemporary use and understanding of "manuscript" that underlie the guiding principles of my edition. Unlike an edition that focuses on a particular text as something to read, this edition seeks to understand the activities and practices that were required so that the document *could* be read. No other poetry that I know affords us the opportunity to examine literature in this manner, because, to my knowledge, no period in literary history has left such a material record as to who read its poetry and why. Who was this William Holgate whose name is attached to this manuscript? Who were his friends? What role did manuscript poetry play in his friendships? How and why were the poems actually transcribed? What values can we infer from the poems found in the miscellany? In what ways were the poems either socially acceptable or unacceptable? What materials were used to create this and other miscellanies, and how were they maintained? The simplicity of these questions only disguises how difficult they proved to answer. In a sense, they are the questions we align with prose, which is how I describe the miscellany tradition: it is the prosaics of Renaissance poetry, the common practices that create identity and produce coherent meaning in an interactive social community; indeed, the very community that allowed the miscellany to exist in the first place. What meaningful actions did Holgate have to perform in order to create his miscellany?

From this perspective, it is not hard to justify what editorial choices had to be made to edit this text: anything and everything that could be reduced to an *activity* required to produce the manuscript needed to be analyzed. Poems and poets had to be identified; topical information had to be confirmed or accounted for. As many miscellanies as possible had to be consulted, and when appropriate, collations supplied to substantiate common copy-texts. Collation alone is what brings texts together. The edition is therefore diplomatic. I tried to reproduce each manuscript page in a readable fashion. The original manuscript page measures 19 x 14½ centimeters. The poems are neatly copied; the space is carefully used. Stanzas and marginalia are clearly defined. First letters of stanzas and, in general, proper nouns, are written with a visual flourish that adds to the aesthetics of the page. Special notations, such as the majuscule ligature Æ in "Æolus" in the first lines of the stanzas noted 10 and 11 May, are clearly set off (*figure 1*). Indeed, all stanza forms are consistent throughout the poem. As with many poems in the Holgate, Latin notations, in this case "Maris ostium," are included. Note, too, the secretarial minuscule 'd', penultimate stanza, line 3, is altered (or corrected) to a majuscule italic '*D*' in "Bedith Downes."

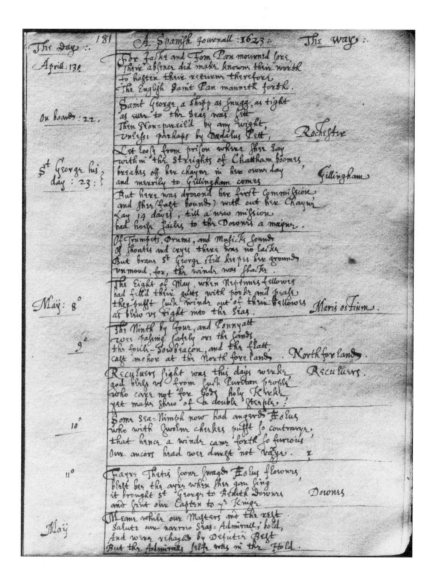

Individual poems also suggest important clues about Holgate and his reading. *Figure 1* is the front page of a poem entitled "A Spanish Iournall: 1623: The Way." It is 408 lines long, the second longest poem found in the Holgate. To my knowledge, this is the only surviving copy of this poem. Although it is anonymous, it was clearly written by someone on board the ship *Saint George*, one of the follow-up ships sent by James I to bring Prince Charles and the Spanish Infanta back to England had the negotiations for their proposed marriage been successful. Charles and the Duke of Buckingham traveled incognito to Spain, calling themselves Jacke and Tom Pan. James himself wrote of their exploits, "Off Jacke and Tom," reprinted in *The Poems of James VI of Scotland*, Ed. James Craigie, 2 vols. (Edinburgh: Scottish Text Society, 1955–58). Many of the events described in the poem are confirmed by the *Calendar of State Papers Domestic*. For example, the failure of the *Saint George* to sail out of English waters described in stanza 3 is recorded in a letter dated 22 April from Sir Francis Steward, Captain of the *Saint George*, to Secretary of State Conway. A second letter, dated 24 April, from Lord Brooke to Secretary Conway also confirms information about the chain (line 14) and Gillingham (line 12, margin).

The first question, of course, is who wrote the poem. Unfortunately, I do not know, but I certainly hope that this is indeed not the only copy of this poem and that someday the poet will be identified. Needless to say, it is a unique historical and cultural document. It adds to our general sense of the excitement and concern the public held over the proposed Spanish match. The Holgate itself contains two other poems about the match he was against. Because this is the only known copy of the poem, it is also possible that Holgate himself was part of the diplomatic mission or a member of the crew. The possibility that Holgate was in some way attached to the mission makes other seagoing poems found in the Holgate potentially important because they may help trace lines of lineage between manuscripts. These include John Donne's "Hymn to Christ," Donne's verse epistle to Christopher Brooke, "The Storme," and Brooke's probable reply to Donne, "Of Teares," all found in the Holgate.

But the most interesting connection for this poem comes not from the poem itself, but from Edward, Viscount Conway, Secretary of State, addressed in the two letters noted in the *Calendar of State Papers Domestic*, because the Holgate shares a remarkable resemblance to a miscellany found among the Conway Papers, British Library Add. MS. 23229. This manuscript is important to Donne scholars because one of its sections was transcribed by Sir Henry Goodyer, Donne's close friend. However, another section is most important because in one sequence the Holgate and the British Library manuscripts are remarkably similar. Between pages 69 and 72, the Holgate has four

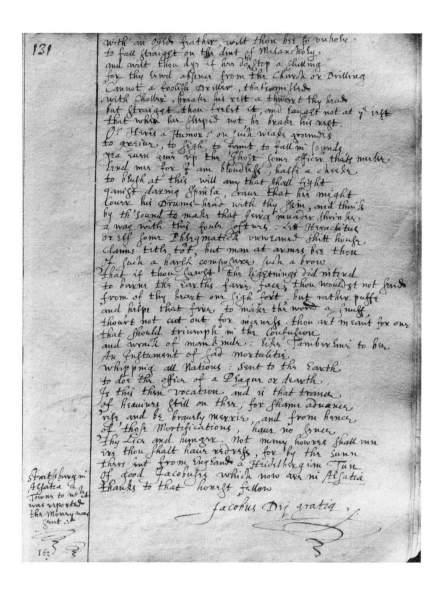

Figure 2. By permission of the Pierpont Morgan Library, New York, MA 1057, p. 131. The final page of "On the Money Newes so Current in Frankendale about Iune 1621," anonymous. Note the similarity of the signatures in this and *Figure 3*, British Library 23229.

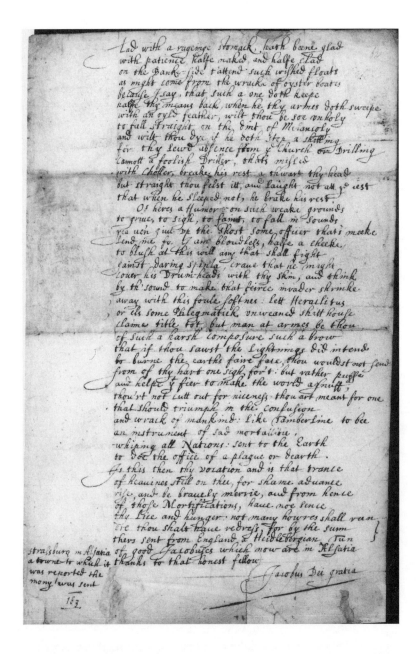

Figure 3. By permission of the British Library 23229, f. 62. The similarity of
several poems in both manuscripts suggest identical copy-texts, or that one
served as the copy-text of the other.

poems, two of which are found in only two other manuscripts. The four poems appear in an identical grouping in Add. MS. 23229, and the texts of all the poems are virtually identical. The same handwriting is also found in two poems preserved in the *State Papers Domestic*, "Upon Prince Charles, His Coming out of Spaine," and "An Answer to Dr. Corbet's Verses to the Duke of Buckingham," again, both of which share virtually identical texts with the Holgate.

Most significant of all, however, is "On the Money Newes so generally Current in Frankendale about Iune 1621," subscribed satirically "Iacobus Dei gratia," pages 128–31 in the Holgate. The last page of the same poem is found in Add. MS. 23229, again with virtually an identical text. So identical are the two texts that the mock signature "Iacobus Dei gratia" appears to be written by the same person (*figures 2, 3*). In addition, these are the only two copies of the poem I have been able to locate. It is a biting satire describing the mistreatment of English troops at the siege of Frankendale, June 1621. Had the poem been written today, we would consider it an antiwar poem. It is a political tract that ridicules English involvement in the war and is replete with local idioms that I am sure would be understood only by members of the regiment actually engaged in the siege.

Several comments can be made about the similarity of these two texts. Since a miscellany is essentially a copy book, how and under what circumstances a copy was made is the essence of understanding this text as a social document. More than likely, Holgate knew the creator of Add. MS. 23229. Although the hand of that manuscript has never been identified, its writer was certainly close to Edward Conway and the inner workings of the government. History tells us what the government did; personal commentary and activity tell us how people understood and adapted to the current circumstances as an organizing social principle. We can also examine the value system involved in the simple act of transcribing a text. Is the text itself sacrosanct or can it be adapted to fit the needs and/or tastes of a particular reader? My overwhelming impression is that Holgate was a very careful transcriber, even to the point of spelling words exactly as he saw them in his textual models. This is especially clear in sections that Holgate used printed materials as his copy-texts. In one poem, "Muld-Sacke," a satire about confused gender roles, he actually describes the physical characteristics of the book from which he transcribed the poem.

But I still have not answered the question, who was William Holgate? I have deferred answering this question because I feel his identity typifies so much of the editorial work required for this type of edition. William Holgate shares the same initials as the enigmatic "W. H." of Shakespeare's Sonnets, and because the miscellany contains one of only two extant manuscript copies of Sonnet 106, there has always been at least the possibility that Holgate was indeed "W. H." I am positive, however, that he was not. Edward Dring, a London bookseller who eventually sold the manuscript to the Morgan Library, went to great efforts to find out if there was a connection between the two. Fortunately, all his efforts are recorded in an unpublished bound volume maintained by the library, "The History of the Holgate family as collected by E. H. Dring." What was interesting to me is that Dring set out to find a specific piece of information — was William Holgate W. H.? — and proceeded logically to investigate Holgate's identity within that narrow perspective. But identity, in terms of social criticism, is not that narrow. As commentators such as Lacan tell us, identity is created by conventional symbols that allow us to identify ourselves within a particular social circumstance; who or what we mean by the universal pronoun "I" is thoroughly bound in the symbolic system that allows meaning to exist in the first place. Thus, I confess, I never fully discovered who William Holgate was, i.e., his profession, his position in society, etc. There are no autograph documents or texts to help me with that. I do know that he was born in Saffron Walden, Essex, and that his father was a landowner. He had one son, also William, who was killed in the Civil War. He himself died sometime after 1649. There is strong evidence that his marriage was not successful. He was clearly educated, but there is no extant record of his being enrolled in any school. But I also learned about many of the things that made him the person that he believed himself to be, how he saw the world, and how he existed in it. He was actively concerned with public affairs, including the Spanish Match, the murder of Sir Thomas Overbury, and the death of Prince Henry. More than likely he was a royalist, but one often critical of James. Although some of the poems reflect Catholic sentiment, I doubt that he was a recusant. He certainly was serious about his religious beliefs. But because the miscellany itself has such a personal feel, he looms over it as a character living out the story of his own life, recorded in a polyphonic text, brought to life by the actions he and everyone else around him understood. What actually happened to make the miscellany possible? Nothing was too insignificant, and nothing is more important than anything else. It is the ultimate act of realism: what can we say for sure that allowed *and allows* this text to exist?

Finally, there is nothing exclusive about the Holgate: it is one of many texts that need to be edited. Much of the information that I left out will be discovered when all the surviving miscellanies are examined carefully. None of them exists alone, and none can be understood without important information found in all the others. Someday, all of that will be completed, and we will all know much more about this very important period of English literature.

Richard Hooker and the
Rhetoric of History

W. SPEED HILL

ICHARD HOOKER'S PERVASIVE HISTORICISM IS, ODDLY ENOUGH, often overlooked. Restricting himself in the *Lawes* to issues of polity, ministry, and worship, his focus on church discipline means that he is constantly citing, interpreting, and weighing historical materials, what he calls the "helps and furtherances of direction which Scriptures, councels, Fathers, Histories, the lawes and practises of all Churches, the mutual conference all mens collections and observations may afford" (*Folger Library Edition of the Works of Richard Hooker* [hereafter FLE]: FLE 2:6; V.Ded.9). By "histories" Hooker means "all those old Historiographers, out of which *Eusebius* gathereth his story," referring to the *Historia Ecclesiastica* initiated by Eusebius, the fourth-century Bishop of Caesarea. Hooker cites this compilation some fifty-nine times. Unlike the Sir Philip Sidney's hapless historian, "loaden with old mouse-eaten records, authorising himself (for the most part) upon other histories, whose greatest authorities are built upon the notable foundation of hearsay, ..."[1] Hooker's sources were authoritative. They include the historical texts preserved in Scripture, praised as "looking glasses to behold the mercie, the truth, the righteousnes of God towards all that faithfullie serve, obey and honor him" (FLE 1:124; I.13.3), and they include the letters and tracts of the

---

[1] *An Apology for Poetry*, ed. Geoffrey Shepherd (London: Thomas Nelson, 1965), 105.

early Church Fathers,[2] collections of canons adopted by general councils, and legal citations from standard compilations like the *Corpus Juris Civilis* and the *Corpus Juris Canonici*. Individual historians range literally from *A* (Aelius Lampridius, a fourth-century Roman historian) to *Z* (Joannes Zonaras, a twelfth-century canonist); I count sixty-four named individuals. But virtually every citation of every author or compilation, legal or conciliar, has a historical point to make, and all the texts Hooker cites, whether formally denominated as "histories," sacred or secular, are treated as historical texts.

Above all, the basic historical document is the Bible,[3] citations of which overwhelm those from non-scriptural sources. The historical character of his citations[4] only states the obvious, as the point at issue was fundamentally a historical one: what exactly was the polity of the early Church? Did God through Christ outline a model of what that early church polity should be? Was it documented? If so, was that model normative, in the late sixteenth century, for a reformed Church of England? In rebutting the disciplinarian challenge to the Elizabethan Settlement (see FLE 1:338; 2:352), Hooker, trained as a theologian, was obliged to refashion himself into a historian of that early Church.[5]

§

In surveys of Tudor historians,[6] church history itself enjoys a distinct histori-

---

[2] Augustine, Cyprian, and Tertullian principally, but others as well, many newly edited by Erasmus and his fellow humanists. See William P. Haugaard, "Renaissance Patristic Scholarship," *Sixteenth Century Journal* 10 (1979): 37–60; for a detailed enumeration see FLE 7 (*Index*).

[3] See Indexes of Scriptural References, FLE 5:851–909 and 6:1101–1156.

[4] His collaborators, Edwin Sandys and George Cranmer, were at pains to insist that Hooker supply accurate references in each of them. For a discussion of Hooker's citations, see W. Speed Hill, "Commentary on Commentary on Commentary: Three Historicisms Annotating Richard Hooker," in *Margins of the Text*, ed. D. C. Greetham (Ann Arbor: Univ. of Michigan Press, 1997), 323–52.

[5] Richard Schoeck rightly observes that Hooker's initial training at Corpus Christi was primarily humanistic: "in point of fact, he read the classics in a program that was a forerunner of the nineteenth-century greats" (private communication). So prepared, he would then have gone on to read in theology, the queen of the sciences at sixteenth-century Oxford, a course of study he did not complete, as Secor observes: Philip B. Secor, *Richard Hooker, Prophet of Anglicanism* (Turnbridge Wells: Burns & Oates, 1999), 88 ff.

[6] F. J. Levy, *Tudor Historical Thought* (San Marino, CA: The Huntington Library, 1967); W. K. Ferguson, *The Renaissance in Historical Thought* (Boston: Houghton Mifflin, 1948; repr. New York: AMS Press, 1981); Herschel Baker, *The Race of Time*

ography.[7] Augustine in *The City of God* is generally credited with its initial formulation in the West, which he envisioned as a counter to the meaningless flux or, alternatively, the endless cyclicality of pagan historiography; what he termed "this fantastic vicissitude ... a ceaseless transmigration between delusive blessedness and real misery."[8] For Augustine, human history has a shape that is theologically meaningful. It begins with the Creation, is punctuated by the Flood and the Incarnation, and ends with Christ's second coming, at which time temporality as we experience it simply ceases. Later chronologists supplied a precision and a tripartite symmetry that Augustine himself declined to impose.[9] Familiar to most of us is James Ussher's deduction that Creation itself took place in 4004 B.C.: "Which beginning of time, according to our chronologers, fell upon the entrance of the night preceding the 23rd day of October in the year of the Julian Calendar, 710. ..."[10] The Flood occurred two thousand years after Creation,[11] the Incarnation was another 2000 years in coming, and the Last Judgment would close out the third bimillenium. The first two thousand years were the realm of Nature, the next of the Law, and the final one of Grace.[12] Using the prophecies enunciated in the Book of

---

(Toronto: Univ. of Toronto Press, 1967), and F. Smith Fussner, *Tudor History and the Historians* (New York and London: Basic Books, 1970). A more recent survey, D. R. Woolf, *The Idea of History in Early Stuart England* (Toronto: Univ. of Toronto Press, 1990), treats post-Tudor historians.

[7] See Donald R. Kelley, *Faces of History* (New Haven and London: Yale Univ. Press, 1998), chap. 7; Levy chap. 3, and Ferguson chaps. 5, 6. Sir Francis Bacon subdivides History into Natural, Civil and Ecclesiastical, the latter being further subdivided into History of the Church, of Prophecy, and of Providence: see *The Advancement of Learning*, ed. William Aldis Wright, 4th ed. (Oxford: Clarendon Press, 1891), chart facing p. 75, and 98–100.

[8] *The City of God*, trans. Marcus Dods (New York: Random House, 1950), 393; see esp. Book 11, chaps. 5, 6; Book 12, chaps. 11–13.

[9] On the complex problem of periodization in the history of the Church, see John M. Headley, *Luther's View of Church History* (New Haven and London: Yale Univ. Press, 1963), chap. 3, esp. 109, 145–51.

[10] *Annals of the Old and New Testament* (1650); from the 1658 trans., p. 1; cited by Peter Burke, *The Renaissance Sense of the Past* (New York: St. Martin's Press, 1969), 48.

[11] Hooker is uncertain as to just when Adam and the angels fell: "concerning some thinges we may lawfully doubt and suspend our judgement ... as namely touching the time of the fall both of man and Angels ..." (FLE 1:179; II.7.5).

[12] As Hooker puts it, "There have been in the world from the verie first foundation thereof but three religions, *Paganisme* which lived in the blindnes of corrupt and depraved nature, *Judaisme* embracinge the law which reformed heathnish impietie, and taught salvation to be looked for through one whome God in the last daies would send and exalt to be lord of all, finallie *Christian beliefe* which yeeldeth obedience to

Revelation, Protestant historians further subdivided the final two thousand years with the coming of the Anti-Christ, identified by many as the Pope (see FLE 6:348 n.18), and of the apocalyptic days preceding the Last Judgment.

For Hooker, as for Augustine, human history is above all purposive: its *telos* is nothing less than the restoration of eternal life to deserving human believers. Humans experience that intervention as Divine Providence, which may work in ways mysterious to men but which is nonetheless omnipresent, whether visibly active or not.[13] Hooker reiterates his personal belief in Providence (I count over twenty references), and, while he does not elaborate on "the worldes end," he does limit human temporality to "as long as the present world doth last" (FLE 3:396; VIII.6.9), anticipating that God "in that day shall condemne the wicked" (FLE 3:397).[14]

Corresponding to the dual worlds of eternity vis-à-vis history, reformed ecclesiology divided the Church into a "mystical" or spiritual body, whose members are known only to God, and a "visible" or worldly body, whose membership required (for Hooker) only baptism and a formal profession of faith.[15] Only the latter aspect of the church can be properly historicized.

Hooker thus participates in that distinguishing characteristic of Judaeo-Christian religious tradition, which holds not only that God is an active participant in human affairs (Homer does as much) but also that his participation, recorded by generations of scribes, constitutes an ongoing, continuously updated and retransmitted textual witness to that divine activity. A divinely hypostasized history, then, becomes textualized in the narrative we know as Holy Scripture, a narrative first of Jews, then of Christians. This participation sustains Hooker's reading of Scripture and, by extension, that of the early Church Fathers, whose letters, tracts, and homilies continue the sacred

---

the gospell of Jesus Christ, and acknowledgeth him the Savior whome God did promise" (FLE 2:348–49; V.68.6).

[13] Cf. Hooker: "The manner of ... divine efficiencie being farre above us, ... Only thus much is discerned, that the naturall generation and processe of all things receyveth order of proceeding from the setled stabilitie of divine understanding. This appointeth unto them their kinds of working, the disposition whereof in the puritie of Gods owne knowledge and will is rightly tearmed by the name of *Providence*. The same ... was woont by the auncient to be called *naturall destinie*" (FLE 1:68; I.3.4).

[14] Describing "the finall consummation of the world" (FLE 1:199; III.1.8), Hooker cites Romans 2:5, where Paul more sternly promises "*the day of wrath, and evident appearance of the just judgement of God*" to the unrepentant (FLE 3:57; VI.5.5).

[15] Hooker scandalized Walter Travers by the inclusiveness of his definition of church membership; Travers protested: "I thinck the like to this ... have not ben heard in publick places, with in this land, synce Quene Maries daies" ("A Supplication to the Privy Counsel," FLE 5:189–210 esp. 208; 638–40).

record. The historical participation of God in the creating of human texts underwrites the human history related therein as ontologically real and thus worthy of our epistemological trust. Conversely, the textualization of that history facilitates and underwrites the work of later continuators, interpreters, commentators, and — one may say — editors. It is in this sense that God is the "author" of Holy Scripture.

As human history moves purposively from the Creation to the Last Judgment, the thrust is toward a definitive, foreordained conclusion, one in which the world as we know it ceases to exist, the reprobate are deservedly punished and the righteous richly, if spiritually, rewarded. One consequence of this narrative is a privileging of earlier and, therefore, purer times of the Church's history. For the Elizabethan Church John Jewel had laid out the basic parameters: authentic tradition comprised the first four ecumenical councils, concluding with that of Chalcedon in 451, and the Church Fathers who wrote within the first six hundred years of the Christian era. Hooker shares Jewel's bias, but his authorities are not confined to those in the early church. Still, later writers are — in general — deemed less authoritative, as worldly corruption overtook the visible church, now identified with the imperial ambitions of the Church of Rome. Were it not for the efforts of the early Reformers, the triumph of Anti-Christ and his collaborators would have gone unchallenged. Still, the millenial expectations of the time were that things would get a great deal worse before they would get better.

Hooker's eschatology is not salient. He does not specify just what is to come in "the last daies," but his anxiety is evident, for example, in the elegiac tone of the famous first sentence of the Preface: "*Though for no other cause, yet for this; . . . that posteritie may know we have not loosely through silence permitted things to passe away as in a dream, there shall be for mens information extant thus much concerning the present state of the Church of God established amongst us, and their carefull endevour which woulde have upheld the same*" (FLE 1:1; Pref. 1.1); it is also evident in his allusions to what he takes to be the religious and political instability of the times: ". . . we have just cause exceedingly to fear, that those miserable times of confusion are drawing on, wherein *the people shall be oppressed one of another*" (FLE 3:263; III.18.12, citing Isaiah 3:5). Hooker preached his first two surviving sermons on the brief Epistle of Jude, verse 18 of which he sees as prophetic of the "*mockers in the last time, which should walke after their owne ungodly lusts*" (FLE 5:13).[16]

Hooker's repeated assertion that "the dayes are evill" (FLE 1:98; I.10.3)

---

[16] Jude 18 is cited in Book V as a warning "that the miserable tymes wereinto we are fallen should abounde" (FLE 2:24; V.2.2).

was evidently confirmed by his reading in the history of the early Church, threatened as it was by numerous and imbedded heresies.[17] It is not that the Disciplinarians are themselves heretics; rather, disputes within the Church render it vulnerable to attack, whether by heretics (whom Hooker associates with idolaters — i.e., unreformed, superstitious worshipers in the Church of Rome) — or by outright atheists (FLE 2:22–31; see V.2–4).

A historiographic dilemma thus arises: at any given moment, is the direction of history up or down? Is historical "progress" good or bad? is the "promised end" cited by King Lear to be welcomed or feared? One resolution was to invoke the Augustinian argument that the Old Testament is to be read typologically, in close conjunction with the New.[18] This view restores closure to the biblical narrative, seeing divine participation in the human as a cycle of prophecy and fulfillment, though at the expense of a drastically foreshortened sense of historical process.

This is *not* Hooker's view. He almost never reads Scripture typologically, and the Augustinian scheme is useless in post-biblical times. He favors the literal reading of scriptural texts (by which he meant non-allegorical, and hence non-typological) over the traditional fourfold explication that earlier humanist exegetes like Erasmus, Tyndale, and Colet had earlier rejected.

> I holde it for a most infallible rule in expositions of sacred scripture, that where a litterall construction will stand, the farthest from the letter is commonlie the worst. There is nothinge more daungerous then this licentious and deludinge arte, which chaungeth the meaninge of wordes as alchymie doth or would doe the substance of meatals, maketh of any thinge what it listeth and bringeth in the ende all truth to nothinge. (FLE 2:252; V.59.2)[19]

Hooker had more of a humanist faith in the texts of history, *as* history, and in the historical reading of Scripture, than a typological hermeneutics could sustain.

A second historiographic issue arises: what is the force of the "ancient examples" submitted by the Disciplinarians as authoritative precedents for

---

[17] Epiphanius Salamis distinguished eighty in his tract *Contra octaginta haereses*, cited seven times in the *Lawes*.

[18] Headley defines typology as "the exegetical practice of relating a thoroughly historical and concrete event in the Old Testament to one in the New Testament through the reference of both to the divine plan or framework within which both events or facts exist": *Luther's View of Church History*, 140.

[19] See W. Speed Hill, "Scripture as Text, Text as Scripture: The Case of Richard Hooker," *TEXT* 9 (1996): 93–110, esp. 100.

contemporary implementation? Well, it depends — on context, on circumstance, on "whether the example alleged be pertinent pregnant and stronge" (FLE 2:313; V.65.14). In an extended meditation on the rhetorical force of examples — the building blocks, after all, of narrative history — Hooker notes that men are persuaded by the force of a given example because of its concreteness. But he cautions: "In all perswasions which ground them selves upon example, wee are not so much to respect what is done, as the causes and secret inducementes leadinge thereunto" (FLE 2:318; V.65.19). Examples are neither laws nor commandments, "but of counsels onlie and persuasions not amisse to be followed by them whose case is the like" (FLE 2:64; V.17.5; cf. FLE 3:22; VI.4.5).

Hooker is thinking rhetorically, but the issue is historiographical: how does one deploy as authoritative precedent a history comprised of no more than a collection of discrete examples, chronologically ordered? How can one develop a historical intelligence that searches out "the causes and secret inducementes" to human actions? How can one confidently ascertain what lessons a divinely ordered history has to teach us? Trained to think abstractly, confronted by example after example cited by the Disciplinarians, each necessitating inquiry into context and circumstance, fitness and pertinence, Hooker loses patience with opponents fixated on finding a model of church polity in the scattered and incomplete historical records of the early Church. The beauty of "rules" is their economy: "Although tenn thousand such examples shold bee brought, they overthrow not this one principle, ..." (FLE 3:88; VI.6.11).

The ultimate historical "cause" is divine providence, which Hooker subdivides into ordinary oversight and "speciall"[20] or "extraordinarie" intervention, the latter working through the agency of the Holy Spirit. Its "inducementes" are "secret," however, for the ways of God to men remain finally unknowable. A skeptic might urge that such a providence is no more adequate a foundation for a concept of historical causation than the pagan concept of "*naturall destinie*" it was meant to replace. Still, its ultimate directionality is assured even if its intermediary meanderings are obscure.

For Hooker, the relevant historical "rule" is that the Church in each of its "distinct societies" enjoys a separate and distinct existence. He famously compares individual churches to "divers precinctes" within "the maine body of the sea" (FLE 1:205; III.1.14). Each such church, as a "politic societie,"[21]

---

[20] It is this "special" providence that Hamlet invokes even "in the fall of a sparrow" (V.ii.220).

[21] W. D. J. Cargill Thompson, "The Philosopher of the 'Politic Society'," in *Studies in Richard Hooker*, ed. W. Speed Hill (Cleveland: Press of Case Western Reserve Univ., 1972; repr. 1992), 3–76.

is entitled to determine the form of its "politie" by the reasonable use of the
human resources available to it. There are certain historical precedents Hooker
claims as authoritative: government by bishops; ceremonial practices as set
forth in the Book of Common Prayer; the co-mingling of secular and ecclesiastical jurisdiction in the person of the queen. These precedents have the
rhetorical authority of a "rule," which mutates into the political authority of
the "rule of law." Hooker is prepared to argue passionately the "fitness" and
pertinence of the examples he urges as precedents. But it is not the isolated
example that commands assent so much as the *series* of examples that, over
time, come to constitute the substance of history itself as they cohere into
"custome,"[22] an explicitly legal authority "by silent allowance famously noti-
fied ... reach[ing] beyonde the memorie of man" (FLE 3:340; VIII.3.3).

§

Hooker's history of the English Reformation is particularly instructive. He
rarely uses the term "reformed" in addressing his opponents without its being
dismissive in diction or tone. The first title the reader encounters is addressed
to "*them that seeke (as they tearme it) the reformation of the Lawes, and orders ecclesiastical, in the Church of ENGLAND*" (FLE 1:1; Pref. 0.1). He refers to "*this
reformation* [in which] *there will be though little wisedome, yet some indifferencie*"
(FLE 1:23; Pref. 4.3; cf. FLE 1:295; IV.7.4). Yet Hooker is not dismissive of
reformation itself. It is simply a normal process of ongoing institutional self-
correction. It is not a rupture with — or wholesale repudiation of — the historical Church. "To reforme our selves, if at anie time we have done amisse,
is not to sever our selves from the Church we were of before. In the Church
we were and we are so still." Referring to "the indisposition ... of the
Church of Rome to reforme hir selfe" (FLE 1:201), its maintaining of "extremely most hurtfull corruptions," and its "tyranny and superstition" (FLE
1:341), Hooker praises Henry VIII as "the first that with us made way to re-
paire the decayes thereof by beheading superstition" (FLE 1:343; IV.14.7).
The appropriate model of reform is thus not the radical polities of the French
and Scottish Churches (cf. FLE 1:11; Pref. 2.8; FLE 1:264; III.11.16) but
"such, as we see in Juda, which having some time beene idolatrous became
afterwardes more soundlie religious by renouncing idolatrie and superstition"
(FLE 1:201–2).

Hooker's historical synopsis of the English Reformation (FLE 1:343;
IV.14l; see esp. FLE 6:651–52) stresses its providential benignity. Henry VIII

---

[22] Lawrence Manley, *Convention: 1500–1750* (Cambridge, MA, and London: Harvard Univ. Press, 1980), esp. chaps. II.1–2.

was its inaugural agent; the saintly Edward VI its divinely ordained advocate; Mary Tudor (unnamed) the "overthrow[er]" of the "worke" Henry had begun and Edward continued; and Elizabeth its miraculous but providential culmination, whom "God . . . caused in the depth of discomfort and darknes [as] a most glorious starre to arise, and on hir head setled the Crowne, whome him selfe had kept as a lambe from the slaughter of those bloudie times."

"The state of reformed religion," the nominal subject of the *Lawes*, "the present matter we treate of," is

> . . . a thing at hir comming to the Crowne even raysed as it were by myracle from the dead; a thing which we so little hoped to see, that even they which beheld it done, scarcely believed their own senses at the first beholding. Yet being then brought to passe, thus many years it hath continued, standing by no other worldly meane but that one only hand which erected it, that hand which as no kind of imminent daunger could cause at the first to withhold it selfe, so neyther have the practises so manie so bloudie following since bene ever able to make wearie. (FLE 1:343–44; IV.14.71)

The vagueness of the grammatical subject — is it Elizabeth? or "the state of reformed religion" in England? — is Hooker's: Queen and Church merge so that we read of God's providential subvention of both, the one embodied in — embedded in — the other. Only at the closing two sentences is it finally clear that "it" is "the veritie of religion established" and that the "glorious and sacred instrument" is Elizabeth:

> Which grace and favour of divine assistance having not in one thing or two shewed itself, nor for some few dayes or yeares appeared, but in such sort so long continued, our manifold sinnes and transgressions striving to the contrarie, what can we lesse thereupon conclude, then that God would at leastwise by tract of time teach the world, that the thing which he blesseth, defendeth, keepeth so strangelie[23] cannot choose but be of him? (FLE 1:344; IV.14.71)

The "myracle" is all the more stunning in the larger European context that precedes his account. Hooker divides reformation into two "kinds": "this moderate kind, which the church of England hath taken," and "that other more extreme and rigorous which certaine Churches elsewhere have better

---

[23] The sense must be: "remarkably, astonishingly" (see *New Shorter Oxford Dictionary*, s.v. "strange").

liked" (FLE 1:343; IV.14.6). Faced with the self-destructive civil wars provoked by continental variants of more extreme reform, "Christendome flam-
ing in all partes of greatest importance at once" (FLE 1:342), Hooker endorses
as literally "providential" England's more moderate course. History's *telos* is
manifest in "the tract of time" — in hindsight — "for so by the event we
may gather." It has a heroine in distress who fashions herself into her people's
divinely sustained savior. And its authenticity is not to be gainsaid by extrem-
ists masquerading as "pretended" reformers.

§

It took a remarkably strong faith to sustain one's conviction that, behind the
clashing polities within and without the Church of England in the sixteenth
century, there was a sustaining, beneficent, interventionist deity. Hooker's
view of the English Reformation is not so overtly nationalistic as John Milton's,[24] but he insists on its "reasonable moderation," its good order, and its
"calme."[25] Ratification of the established "Lawes of Ecclesiasticall Politie,"
the announced aim of his treatise, is crucial to maintaining that good order.

Hooker's *Lawes* is an undeniable source of that note of self-congratulation
that long since entered into "Whig" readings of the English Reformation,[26]
in which the transformation of England under Elizabeth from medieval to
modern flourished thanks to her resolutely secular moderation.[27] But what
latter-day Whigs forget is that it is Hooker's explicitly *religious* sense of history,
historical change, and historical causation that underwrites what they see as
secular or nationalistic progress. But to secularize Hooker is to drain his
historical discourse of its core agency, its foundational belief in God's providential care for the actual, historical church, the visible church in England
— the subject of his treatise and the object of his protective care.

---

[24] W. Speed Hill, "Richard Hooker in the Folger Edition: An Editorial Perspective," in *Richard Hooker and the Construction of Christian Community*, ed. A. S.
McGrade, MRTS 165 (Tempe, AZ: MRTS, 1997), 3–20, here 14.

[25] As compared to its continental (and Scottish) counterparts (see esp. IV.14.6;
FLE 1:342–43).

[26] Robert B. Eccleshall describes Hooker as providing "window dressing for the
command structure of Elizabethan society" and as exhibiting "a peculiarly English
brand of national smugness with regard to the native political system": cited from
A. S. McGrade, "Foreword," in *Richard Hooker and the Construction of Christian Community*, xi–xxii, here xiii; see R. B. Eccleshall, "Richard Hooker and the Peculiarities
of the English: The Reception of the 'Ecclesiastical Polity' in the Seventeenth and
Eighteenth Centuries," *History of Political Thought* 2 (1981): 63–117.

[27] William P. Haugaard, *Elizabeth and the English Reformation* (Cambridge: Cambridge Univ. Press, 1968).

Treacherous Accidents and the Abominable Printing of Katherine Philips's 1664 Poems

ELIZABETH H. HAGEMAN

O
N 14 JANUARY 1664, THE BOOKSELLER RICHARD MARRIOT AD-
vertised in the *London Newes* a book of "Poems of the incomparable
Madam Catherine Phillips." Four days later, on 18 January, he announced the cancellation of the book's sale, assuring readers, however, that he
had published the volume under the belief that the poems had come to him
with Philips's permission and that the manuscript he had published was a
"true" copy of her poems. What Marriot says is this:

> Publication being made upon last Thursday of the Poems of Madam
> *Catherine Phillips* newly Printed for *Richard Marriot.* It is now the desire
> of the said *Richard Marriot* to Notify, that whereas he was fully per-
> suaded, both of the Correctnesse of the Copy and of that Ingenious
> Lady's Allowance to have them Printed, that now he finds neither the
> One, nor the Other, according to his Expectation; which is a double
> Injury, and that he intends to forbeare the sale of them, being not
> without hope, that this false Copy, may produce the true One.[1]

---

[1] Both the *London Newes* and the *Intelligencer* were printed by Roger L'Estrange —
the *Newes* each Thursday, and the *Intelligencer* on Mondays. The edition of Philips's
poems had been listed in the Stationers' Register on 25 November 1663, and the octavo bears the imprimatur of Roger L'Estrange with the date "Nov. 25. 1663" on the
page facing its title page.

Within the next eleven days, Katherine Philips, who was then in Wales, wrote to London friends expressing dismay that her poems had been published and asking their help in extricating her from the disaster into which she had been plunged by the publication of the edition. Apparently having heard first from John Jeffries (Philaster in the poems), who wrote soon after the book was first published but before Marriot withdrew it from sale, on 22 January she closed a rather long letter to Lady Dorothy Temple with hopes that she would offer advice on "how I may best get this impression suppressed & myself vindicated." Philips has written, she says, "to Coll. Jeffreys (who first sent me word of it) to get the Printer punish'd the book call'd in, & me some way publickly vindicated, yet I shall need all my friends to be my Champions to ye Critticall & malicious." Complaining of "this pittifull design of a Knave to get a Groat," Philips "utterly disclaim[s] whatever he hath so unhandsomly expos'd."[2] By 29 January, she had heard from Sir Charles Cotterell (Poliarchus in her letters) as well, and she wrote to thank him for working with Jefferies in "doing what I see your Friendship had urg'd you both do without that Request [i.e., her appeal to Jeffries]" (125). Philips sent in fact two letters to Cotterell on the 29th. One is the private letter from which I quote; the other is a public letter, written, she says, "to the end that you may, if you please, shew it to any body that suspects my Ignorance and Innocence of that false Edition of my verses" (125). Although no known evidence indicates whether Cotterell circulated the latter in 1664, it was published twice soon afterwards: first within the Preface to the 1667 posthumous edition of Philips's poems and plays issued by Henry Herringman (and in the 1669, 1678, and 1710 reprints of that volume), and also immediately following the private letter in the 1705 edition of *Letters from Orinda to Poliarchus* published by Bernard Lintot.

Some time ago, Lucy Brashear suggested that "Considering the remarkable excellence of the pirated edition and the advantages it offered to Orinda's career, it is tempting to speculate that she herself engineered the entire incident"; the fact that some copies of the octavo had been sold before Marriot withdrew them from his shop was "a situation which virtually required a corrected edition."[3] Germaine Greer's theory is that Philips (or her husband or a friend of theirs) sold the poems to Marriot. When they saw the book, Greer argues, Jeffries and Cotterell convinced her that the "publication [was]

---

[2] *The Collected Works of Katherine Philips, "The Matchless Orinda,"* Vol. 2, *The Letters,* ed. Patrick Thomas (Stump Cross, Essex: Stump Cross Books, 1990), 142. All subsequent references to the letters are from this edition.

[3] Lucy Brashear, "The Forgotten Legacy of the 'Matchless Orinda'," *Anglo-Welsh Review* 65 (1979): 71.

an injury to her self and her reputation"; in the face of their argument, Philips's only possible response was "to clamor for the book's withdrawal." Her friends' real concern about the book, Greer believes, is its public nature. As she says, headings of the poems often identify Philips's friends, telling the world, for example, that Jeffries had been rejected in an early courtship of Mary Carne and that Cotterell's friend Mary (Aubrey) Montague had betrayed the poet's friendship.[4]

Noting a frantic tone in Philips's letters, one might well explicate them in terms of cultural strictures that would make a seventeenth-century woman genuinely fear public "exposure" of her poems — and fear, too, the exposure of her own name (or rather her initials — Philips's name appears in Marriot's advertisement, but not in the book itself) on a book to be sold — and then inspected, handled, and discussed by others. As Philips writes in the public letter she sent to Cotterell, with this edition she has been "expos'd to play the Mountebanks and dance upon the Ropes to entertain the Rabble, to undergo all the Raillery of the Wits, and all the Severity of the Wise, to be the Sport of some that can, and Derision of others that cannot read a Verse" (144). "[S]ometimes," she continues, "I think that to make Verses is so much above my Reach, and a Diversion so unfit for the Sex to which I belong, that I am about to resolve against it for ever" (145).[5] But then Philips turns away from issues of gender and social class to focus on "the careless blotted Writing" in the copies on which the volume was based, on the poems having been "abominably printed," on the fact that the volume contains some poems "that are not mine," and on her concern that "worthy Persons ... whose Names are without their leave expos'd to this Impression." The event, she says, is a "treacherous Accident" (145).

I have commented elsewhere on Philips's discomfort at making her friends' names public, and I have noted as well that when Philips complains that some of the poems in the volume are not hers, she is correct, for excerpts of poems by Henry More and Edward Dering are printed in *1664*. Eight lines by Dering (from a poem that does not otherwise survive) are printed before her

---

[4] Germaine Greer, *Slip-Shod Sibyls: Recognition, Rejection and the Woman Poet* (London: Viking, 1995), 160, 163–64.

[5] As Peter Beal says, "By reaching an untargeted, indiscriminate, 'vulgar' audience, the publication of a body of verse which celebrated the feelings, activities, and relationships of a 'private' circle of genteel friends could only lower, not enhance her prestige in the eyes of tht social class whose approbation alone she sought. Least of all did she need Cotterell or Jeffreys to warn her of the dangers": *In Praise of Scribes: Manuscripts and Their Makers in Seventeenth-Century England* (Oxford: Clarendon Press, 1998), 164.

poem responding to him — and labeled "Thus far Sir Edw. Deering." Eighteen lines from More's "Cupid's Conflict" preface Philips's poem beginning "Eternal Reason, Glorious Majesty" (called "God" in Sir Edward Dering's manuscript copy and "A Prayer" in the 1667 folio of her writing). Although More's and Philips's poems are in different verse forms, no heading or other indication marks Philips's poem off from More's, which is headed and listed in the book's Table "Out of Mr. More's Cop. [sic] Conf."[6] I take seriously, too, Philips's concern at the report that the poems are "abominably printed" (145),[7] for there are problems with the octavo that even a cursory glance by a friend of Philips would quickly reveal. In three poems, asterisks replace lines perhaps indistinct or absent from the base text; in the heading of the elegy on Philips's stepdaughter Frances (and also in the Table of poems), the girl's initials are given as "T. P." rather than "F. P."; and Philips's relatives John Collier and his daughter Regina are said to be buried in Bedlington (which is in Northumberland), rather than Beddington (which is in Surrey).

What I want to do here is to show that three extant manuscript texts of poems by Philips suggest the nature of the "treacherous Accident" that lay behind the "abominabl[e] print[ing]" of the poems; they indicate that indeed the copy of Philips's poems from which John Grismond[8] printed the volume for Richard Marriot was not, to use again Marriot's word from his 18 January advertisement, "true." What I argue is that a manuscript of seventy-three of Philips's poems now in the Clarke papers at Worcester College, Oxford (when examined alongside two other early transcripts of her poems) can be seen to be not the base text for the 1664 octavo edition, but a witness to that base text. What Worcester College MS. 6.13 shows is that the base text for Marriot's edition was — and I use the following terms with bibliographical but not moral meanings — corrupt, false, not true. At the same time, examination of the Clarke manuscript clarifies some otherwise puzzling aspects of

[6] E. H. Hageman, "Katherine Philips: The Matchless Orinda," in *Women Writers of the Renaissance and Reformation*, ed. Katharina M. Wilson (Athens, GA: Univ. of Georgia Press, 1987), 578–79, and Hageman, "Making a Good Impression: Early Texts of Poems and Letters by Katherine Philips, the 'Matchless Orinda'," *South Central Review* 11 (1994): 55.

[7] This phrase is from the 1705 version of the letter Philips asked Cotterell to circulate among their friends. The version of this letter printed within the Preface of the 1667 folio of her poems says that the poems were "abominably transcrib'd" (130).

[8] Nathan P. Tinker has established that the J. G. named on the title page of Marriot's book was the "successful, reputable printer" John Grismond: "John Grismond: Printer of the Unauthorized Edition of Katherine Philips's Poems (1664)," *English Language Notes* 34 (1996): 30–34.

Philips's own autograph manuscript of some fifty-five of her poems (now National Library of Wales, MS. 775B) and also of a collection of poems transcribed by Philips's friend Sir Edward Dering in the manuscript now catalogued as Misc *HRC 155 (formerly Phillipps MS. 14,937) in the Harry
Ransom Humanities Research Center of the University of Texas at Austin.

Less directly related to my discussion, except by way of contrast, is the so-
called *Rosania* manuscript, now National Library of Wales, MS. 776B. Dedicated to Rosania (Philips's sobriquet for Mary Montague) by one Polexander,
Rosania is a memorial volume transcribed not long after Philips's early death
from smallpox on 22 June 1664. If we knew the textual history of the ninety-
six *Rosania* poems (and indeed some day we may), we might, as Germaine
Greer has suggested, use them as base texts for future editions of Philips. As
things stand now, however, there is as yet no way to trace their variants to
the poet herself — no firm reason to accept Greer's intriguing theory that
they represent Philips's own revisions of texts she earlier wrote in the autograph book to be discussed below.[9]

Of prime interest to all students of Philips — and to the argument of this
essay — is the autograph book of fifty-five of her poems (three of them frag-
ments) and two additional titles.[10] Sold by Philips's early-twentieth-century
publisher, J. R. Tutin, to the National Library of Wales in 1913, MS. 775B
is stamped on both front and back covers of its contemporary binding with
the initials "KP." In this book Philips transcribed copies of her poems (almost
always) on the rectos of pages — copying out poems on individual friends and
family members at one end of the volume and philosophical verse essays on
topics such as "Happyness," "Death," and "The World" at the other. That
the poems cross in the middle of the book demonstrates that the volume is
not made up of gatherings bound together after the fact. That the poems are
crowded together at the end of the "personal" section of the book affirms that
Philips thought those poems belonged there rather than on blank pages elsewhere in the manuscript. Similarly, that she turned the book over to tran-

---

[9] For Greer's masterful argument that the *Rosania* poems are carefully edited "by
Orinda or with her consent," see *Slip-Shod Sibyls*, 166–67.

[10] As I note below, two stubs in the NLW MS. 775B represent pages of the poem
on Alice, Countess of Carberry, and "La Grandeur d'esprit" now missing from the
manuscript. The third incomplete poem is "On the death of my first and dearest
childe": after transcribing the first two stanzas of the poem on page 111, Philips wrote
on pages 111 and 113 the numbers 3, 4, and 5 for the remaining stanzas and left blank
spaces for the lines. In the middle of page 113 she wrote in the title of "To my dearest friend, on her greatest loss, which she suffer'd the 27th. December 1655" and left
space for the poem itself. On page 135, she transcribed only the title "To ye Rt:
Honor: ye lady E.C.," again leaving space for the poem.

scribe "To my Lucasia in defence of declared friendship" on the versos of pages 109–10 within the section of "personal" poems shows her sense that this poem should come after "To my Lucasia" and before the elegy on her son. All of the poems within the Tutin manuscript that can be dated are from 1658 or earlier — well before the Restoration of the English monarchy in the spring of 1660 and before Philips left Wales for Ireland in June of 1662.

The Tutin manuscript now contains twenty-eight stubs. Five in the middles of poems represent leaves perhaps torn out before Philips wrote in the book, or perhaps torn out when she made a serious error and wanted to discard a page and start over. Other stubs represent pages torn out after Philips inscribed the poems: the second page of her poem to the Countess of Carberry is missing, for instance, as is a page on which the final fourteen lines of "La Grandeur d'esprit" were surely once transcribed. As I demonstrated for an article Andrea Sununu and I published in volume four of *English Manuscript Studies*, at some time before the book was paginated, Philips's "Sea-voyage from Tenby to Bristol" was torn out of the volume. The ragged edges of the two-page autograph copy of that poem now in the University of Kentucky Library match the second and third of three stubs between "Content: To my Dearest Lucasia" and "To my deare Sister Mrs. C: P. on her nuptialls" — as the paper, ink, chain lines, and foxing of the Kentucky poem match those in that part of *Tutin*.[11]

It was my examination of the Clarke manuscript now at Worcester College that led me to guess that the Kentucky "Sea Voyage" was transcribed before page 89 — before "To my deare Sister Mrs. C: P: on her nuptialls" in *Tutin*. Described by Peter Beal as written in "a single, neat, nonprofessional hand,"[12] *Clarke* is a transcript of seventy-three of Philips's poems on the first eighty-eight folios of Worcester College, MS. 6.13. This manuscript was once owned by George Clarke (1661–1736), whose father Sir William Clarke (1623?–66) was Secretary of the Army under both the Commonwealth and Charles II and thus a colleague of Philips's stepfather, Philip Skippon. An even closer connection to the poet is clear from the fact that Sir William gave evidence in the 1661 trial of her husband James Philips (B.L., Egerton MS. 2979, fol. 116v). That Sir William obtained this collection of poems while Philips was in Dublin is suggested by Beal, who observes that Sir William had business in Ireland in the early 1660s (*In Praise of Scribes*, 163). And yet it is also possible that George Clarke obtained the manuscript from his stepfather, the

---

[11] E. H. Hageman and A. Sununu, "New Manuscript Texts of Katherine Philips, the 'Matchless Orinda'," *English Manuscript Studies, 1100–1700* 4 (1993): 175–80.

[12] *Index of English Literary Manuscripts*, Vol. 2: *1625–1700*, Part 2: *Lee-Wycherley* (London: Mansell, 1993), 130.

physician Samuel Barrow (1625–82), whose name is written on the front fly leaf of the manuscript.

A note in *Clarke* indicates that Louise I. Guiney identified the poems as Philips's in 1907, three years after she edited the collection of poems by Philips that J. R. Tutin published in 1904. Although the *Clarke* poems appear in a different order from the 1664 octavo, they are the same poems as the first seventy-three of the seventy-five poems in *1664*. (The other two poems in *1664* are "To the Queen's Majesty, on her late sickness and recovery" of November 1663 and "Upon Mr. Abraham Cowley's Retirement," first printed in March 1663 in *Poems, by Several Persons*, the same volume that includes the first printing of Cowley's ode on Philips's poems, with which both *Clarke* and *1664* open.)

While the order of the *Clarke* poems is different from that of *1664*, it is very similar to the order of the fifty-five poems in *Tutin*. Of the first sixteen poems in Clarke, all but "The Country Life" are in the "philosophical" end of *Tutin* as well. Beginning with "Happyness" (the third poem in that section of *Tutin*) and ending with "Friendship" (the seventeenth poem in that section), the *Clarke* transcripts are in the same order as the copies in Philips's autograph. The next forty poems in *Clarke* are in the same order as poems in the "personal" end of that same manuscript, beginning, as in *Tutin*, with Philips's poem on Antenor's parting and ending with "To Lucasia in defence of declared friendship." The next eleven poems in *Clarke* are distinctly later than the *Tutin* poems. Nine treat events of 1660–62 concerning the restoration of Charles II and his family to England; one is the elegy in memory of young Frances Philips, who died on 24 May 1660, the same month as the return of Charles II; the other is "The Enquiry," which one might thus surmise is also from the early 1660s. At the end of *Clarke* are six more poems, all of which are also in *Tutin*, though the *Clarke* collection ends with a complete copy of the poem to Lady Elizabeth Carre, one of two poems represented by only its title in *Tutin*. (I should note, too, that two *Tutin* poems — the epitaph for John Lloyd's funeral monument in Cilgarron and "Twice forty months" on the death of Philips's own son Hector — are not in *Clarke* at all.)

As I noted above, it was *Clarke*'s placing "A Sea Voyage" between "A Dialogue between Lucasia and Orinda" and "To my deare Sister Mrs. C: P." that first led me to realize that the Kentucky poem might have once been torn out from before the page now numbered 89 in *Tutin*. A third stub between "Content to my dearest Lucasia" and "To my deare Sister Mrs C: P. on her nuptialls" surely represents a now-lost copy of "A Dialogue between Orinda and Lucasia" that the *Clarke* order would lead one to expect to find there. Other stubs represent "To Mrs. M. A. at parting" (two stubs before p. 19), "To Antenor on a paper of Mine" (one stub before p. 39), and "Upon the double Murther of K. Charles" (one stub before p. 67). Three stubs before page 137 might seem to allow space for the 88-line "A Country Life," but the first of the missing pages there is surely the leaf on which the last fourteen lines of "La Grandeur d'esprit" were first written. Noting, however, that Dering writes out "A Country Life" in double columns on page 93 in the manuscript to be discussed below, one might speculate that his format emulates Philips's: if she transcribed the poem in double columns, it would have fit onto two pages. Alternately, Philips may have used both the rectos and versos of the two leaves immediately before page 137 — or she may have written three or four stanzas of "A Country Life" below the ending of "La Grandeur d'esprit" and then transcribed the rest of the poem on the next two now-missing leaves. The only problem that arises from this observation of the close relationship between materials in *Tutin* and in *Clarke* (and it is a problem) is that just as the *Clarke* scribe used a different source for the eleven later poems and for the text of the poem on Lady Elizabeth Carre, so too did he or she need a different source for two poems — "To Regina Collier on her Cruelty to Philaster" and "To the Queene of Inconstancy Regina Collier in Antwerpe" — that do not appear where a reader of *Clarke* would expect to find them: in the personal section of *Tutin*.

The final manuscript to be treated here is the one in the hand of Philips's friend Sir Edward Dering (her Silvander), who married Philips's school friend Mary Harvey in 1648, served on the Court of Claims in Dublin while Philips was in residence there in 1662 and 1663, and in 1663 wrote the Epilogue for her play *Pompey*. The manuscript includes seventy-four complete copies of poems by Philips, as well as the title of "The Irish Greyhound" and the title "Song" and first line of "How prodigous is my fate." Now at the University of Texas, *Dering* is closely related to *Tutin*, though that relationship can be most easily seen by lining up its poems with the seventy-three poems in *Clarke*. The seventy-four poems in *Dering* begin not with philosophical poems, but with the forty personal poems that are transcribed together in *Clarke*, again starting with "To my dearest Antenor, on his Parting" (in *Dering* headed "To Antenor parting") and ending with "To my Lucasia in defence of declared friendship." Next come ten of the eleven poems from the early 1660s (the Restoration poems, the epitaph on Philips's stepdaughter, and "The Enquiry") that are also in *Clarke*. (Why he saves "To the Queen's Majesty on her Arrival at Portsmouth" for late in the manuscript is unclear; possibly he omitted it by mistake and inserted it toward the end when he realized his error.) After that collection of later poems, *Dering* transcribes the same sixteen philosophical poems as at the beginning of Clarke — from "Happyness" through "Friendship." Like *Clarke*, he then returns to personal poems by Philips: "In memory of . . . Mrs. Mary Lloyd," "Parting with Lucasia," "Against Pleasure," "Out of Mr. More's Cup. Conf." and Philips's response to the selection from More, and the poem on Elizabeth Carre. Then *Dering* picks up

"To the queen on her arrival at portsmouth" of May 1662 and adds to his collection the title of "The Irish Greyhound" (first printed in the 1663 *Poems, by Several Persons*); the heading "Song" and first line of "How prodigious is my fate"; "To the Lady Mary Butler at her marriage with ye Lord Cavendish"; and finally "Upon Abraham Cowley's Retirement" (also printed in *Poems by Several Persons* — and in *1664* as well). *Dering*'s transcripts are followed by eight stubs, which may represent copies no longer extant of additional poems or possibly other materials. A comparison of the poems in *Dering* with poems in *Clarke* clarifies discrepancies between the order of *Tutin* and *Dering* — discrepancies that led one scholar to conclude that *Dering* had copied from loose sheets of paper, shuffled to create a different order from the order of *Tutin*,[13] and another to use the word "garbled" to describe the *Dering* poems.[14]

Placing Dering's poems beside the *Clarke* manuscript shows that *Dering* did copy the poems in the same order as in *Tutin* — though he occasionally shifted the order to allow the transcription of a poem on facing pages in his rather elegant book. Thus, for example, *Dering* transcribes "L'Amitie. To Mrs Mary Awbry" on his page 3, saving "On the excellent Palaemon" for pages 4–5 — in the course of this change, however, disrupting Philips's cluster of seven poems on Mary Aubrey/Rosania.

Thinking only of the order of the poems, I at first assumed that *Clarke* and *Dering* were both copied directly from *Tutin*, one copyist beginning at one end of *Tutin* and the other copyist at the other — each adding to his manuscript the eleven poems from a second source, probably also an autograph manuscript, and each then completing his collection with a few more poems — *Clarke* copying out additional poems from *Tutin*, and *Dering* using another source or sources. But although there are variants in which *Clarke* and *Tutin* agree against *Dering* and in which *Dering* and *Tutin* agree against *Clarke*, variants in which *Clarke* and *Dering* agree against *Tutin* show that Philips's contemporaries did not copy directly from *Tutin*. Instead, *Tutin*, *Clarke*, and *Dering* all derive from yet another manuscript, either a book with poems written at both ends or two packets of poems. And then of course both Edward Dering and the Clarke copyist used as well an additional packet of eleven poems:

---

[13] Rebecca Lynn Tate, "Katherine Philips: A Critical Edition of the Poetry" (Ph.D. diss., Texas Tech University, 1991), 1: 86–87. On page 87, Tate suggests that *Dering* derives from a copy of 775B that Philips made before going to Dublin. As will become clear below, my argument is just the opposite: that 775B and *Dering* both derive from an early manuscript of Philips's poems.

[14] Claudia A. Limbert, "The Poetry of Katherine Philips: Holographs, Manuscripts, and Early Printed Texts," *Philological Quarterly* 70 (1991): 181–98, here 185.

the poems on the royal family, on the death of Frances Philips, and "The Enquiry." Two of the three copyists — Philips and Dering — added at the end of their collections a few additional poems from another source. And as she copied out her own poems, Philips omitted the two in which she had criticized John Collier's widow.

Dering's copies of Philips's poems are quite different from her own transcripts in a number of ways, some of which seem to be casual changes, some careful alterations. As he wrote, Dering often imposed his own rhetorical patterns of punctuation on her poems. Unlike Philips, he sometimes uses minuscules at the beginnings of lines. He typically uses forms such as "thy, "thee," and "doth" where she writes "your," "you," and "doeth." And in his copies the poems' headings often vary from Philips's, quite often substituting sobriquets for names or initials. At least once, *Dering* transcribes a variant that may suggest an attempt at improving Philips's poem: in "A Sea Voyage," his copy reads "Let it be Dutch," rather than, as in *Clarke* and *Tutin*, "Let it be Spanish." Even so, in most regards, *Dering*'s copies are closer to Philips's than are the copies in *Clarke*. For while some of the *Clarke* variants can be, like *Dering*'s, attributed to the vagaries of coterie circulation of texts, the fact is that the *Clarke* poems contain a great many manifest errors.

What my collation of *Clarke, Dering, Tutin,* and *1664* shows, then, is that when *Clarke* lines make sense, they appear also in *1664*. But when *Clarke* variants are manifest errors, they are corrected, possibly by the same person who rearranged the order of the poems for the Grismond–Marriot edition, a person who did the best he or she could to mend a defective manuscript and to create a respectable text of Philips's poems. Part of that respectability is the *1664* use of asterisks to mark the three lines omitted from Philips's poems — all three absent from *Clarke* but with no indication that the *Clarke* copyist realized that his versions of Philips's stanzas were one line too short. When manifest errors involve only a word or two, the *1664* editor emends them. For example, *Tutin* and *Dering* copies of "Friendship's Mysteries" say that Orinda and Lucasia's "Captivity" is "Than thrones more great and innocent." In *Clarke* the line is mangled by the omission of "and" to read "Than thrones more great Innocent." *1664* reads,"Than greatest thrones more innocent," a line that scans but doesn't employ Philips's characteristic compound structure.

In "To the Noble Palaemon" Philips praises Francis Finch for defending Friendship, "At which the politician still had laughed" — this line in both *Tutin* and *Dering*. Noting that *1664* (and also *1667*) prints "Great Physician" rather than "politician" and observing Finch's close association with Dr. William Harvey, Mary Harvey's uncle and the physician who first described the circulation of the blood, Patrick Thomas proposes that Philips altered her poem to please Finch. He declines, however, to speculate which variant is earlier, which later.[15] Noting the common practice in coterie poetry of copyists using variants such as this to "improve" poems or to make them fit different circumstances, one might speculate that one line or the other derives from a variant consciously introduced by a contemporary of Philips. *Clarke*, however, provides a different explanation. In *Clarke* the line is "At which the phisition still had laughed," perhaps because the copyist inadvertently substituted one polysyllabic noun beginning with a "p" with another. *1664* adds "Great" to make the line metrically regular: "At which the Great Physician still had laughed."

Whether it was someone in Grismond's or Marriot's shop or a member of Philips's own coterie who used a defective manuscript to create the base text for the octavo edition I am not at all sure. What I will say with confidence is that Marriot was correct in saying that his publication was based on a "false Copy" of Philips's poems. It was, if not a "treacherous Accident," an "Accident" nonetheless that led the *Clarke* versions of Philips's poems to be printed by Grismond. Lines that thus entered Philips's canon — for some of them are repeated in the folio edition of 1667 and in later manuscript and printed copies derived from it — are perhaps not abominable, but they are not hers. Given the intrusive (if friendly) nature of Dering's variants in the poems, one could hardly wish that the 1664 editor had worked instead with a manuscript derived from his copy of Philips. I, at least, am left wishing that Marriot had had a copy of the poems in Philips's own hand — or that the copyist of *Clarke* had been a more accurate scribe.

---

[15] *The Collected Works of Katherine Philips, "The Matchless Orinda,"* Vol. 1, *The Poems* (Stump Cross, Essex: Stump Cross Books, 1900), 266–67.

A Family Affair:
The Life and Letters of
Elizabeth Cary, Lady Falkland

HEATHER WOLFE

E VER SINCE RICHARD SIMPSON FIRST EDITED THE NINETY-SEVEN-
page manuscript of *Lady Falkland: Her Life* in 1861, scholars have
accepted his attribution of the text to one of Elizabeth Cary, Lady
Falkland's four Catholic daughters, as well as his assertion that some of the
deletions to the text belonged to her Catholic son Patrick, who thought the
passages "too feminine."[1] Simpson's ca. 1655 dating of the manuscript, which

---

[1] All four of Cary's Catholic daughters have been put forth as author in recent
years, but the evidence for these attributions is minimal. Donald Foster asserts that "it
is clear from a collation of the internal and external evidence that the biography cannot have been written by anyone but Anne Cary": "Resurrecting the Author," in
Privileging Gender in Early Modern England, ed. Jean Brink (Kirksville, MO: Sixteenth
Century Journal Publishers, 1993), 145–46, n. 8. Barbara Lewalski proposes Anne as
the probable author, or perhaps Lucy, in *Writing Women of Jacobean England* (Cambridge, MA: Harvard Univ. Press, 1993), 180, 384 n. 9; Louise Schleiner proposes
Anne or Elizabeth, based on reported dialogue, in *Tudor and Stuart Women Writers*
(Bloomington and Indianapolis: Indiana Univ. Press, 1994), 190; Isobel Grundy
proposes Anne, maybe Mary, in "Women's History? Writing by English Nuns," in
Women, Writing, History: 1640–1740, ed. Grundy and Susan Wiseman (London: Bats-
ford, 1992), 126; Diane Purkiss proposes Mary, in *Renaissance Women: The Plays of
Elizabeth Cary, The Poems of Aemilia Lanyer* (London: Pickering and Chatto, 1994), ix;
Barry Weller and Margaret Ferguson propose Anne, or maybe Lucy, or neither in *The*

he suggests was originally written sometime between 1643 and 1650, has also been recycled. Because it makes one too many references to the workings of divine providence, *Lady Falkland: Her Life* has been perceived as a biased and therefore untrustworthy biographical account rather than as a valuable example of early modern life writing. These vague assumptions about *Life*'s authorship and dating have been perpetuated, and its usefulness underestimated, largely because Simpson's edition and the two other editions since then have placed the text in a privileged position over the document, and not edited it in the context of other available documentary evidence.

I first began transcribing *Lady Falkland: Her Life* for a project on the production and circulation of manuscripts among the English Benedictine communities of monks and nuns on the continent in the seventeenth century, particularly the communities at Cambrai and Paris, to which Cary's daughters belonged. It soon became apparent that an understanding of the manuscript's multiple hands, emendations, deletions, and marginal annotations was essential for an understanding of the *Life* as a literary, biographical, autobiographical, familial, and monastic text. I have just edited the *Life* for a series started by the late Jeremy Maule, called Renaissance Texts from Manuscripts.[2] The goal of this series was to provide affordable semi-diplomatic editions of early modern manuscripts for use by undergraduates and academics alike. In addition to the *Life*, this edition includes one hundred and thirty-seven letters and other documents relating to Cary's conversion to Catholicism and its aftermath. These documents, many of them interesting in their own right as literary texts, also serve as a form of reality check when read against the *Life*, assisting in the distillation of truth from fiction in Cary's *lived* life (to the extent that this is possible or indeed, necessary) by providing a three-dimensional view of the nature of her Catholicism and the consequences of her actions.

Tragedy of Mariam The Fair Queen of Jewry with The Lady Falkland her Life by one of her Daughters (Berkeley: Univ. of California Press, 1994), 1–2, 51–53; Dorothy Latz proposes Lucy in *"Glow-Worm Light": Writings of Seventeenth Century English Recusant Women from Original Manuscripts* (Salzburg: Institut für Anglistik und Amerikanistik der Universität, 1989), x. Richard Simpson proposed Lucy with increasing uncertainty. In "A Conversion from the Time of Charles I," *Rambler* 8 (1857): 188, he wrote: "it was written by Lucy . . . which accounts for the intimate knowledge she shows of all this passage with Chillingworth." In the second part of the *Rambler* edition he wrote: Lucy "was in all probability the author of the biography" (271). In *The Lady Falkland, Her Life, from a Manuscript in the Imperial Archives at Lille* (London: Catholic Publishing and Bookselling Company, 1861), he proposed "one of Lady Falkland's four daughters."

[2] Heather Wolfe, ed., *Elizabeth Cary, Lady Falkland: Life and Letters*, MRTS 230 (Tempe, AZ, and Cambridge, England: MRTS and RTM, 2001).

I. Previous Editions

Jerome McGann's observation that "Every new edition, including every critical edition, is an act of reimagining and redefining a text's audience(s) and its ways of interacting with those audience(s)"[3] is certainly true of the editions of *Lady Falkland: Her Life*. Its rediscovery in the 1850s was the result of the search of the Catholic convert, historian, and polemicist Richard Simpson for documents representing the history of English Catholics, a search undertaken because he believed that English Protestant historians had misrepresented the religious heritage of the sixteenth and seventeenth centuries. In October 1857, Simpson took over the editorship of the *Rambler*, a controversial periodical which sought to unite "implicit faith with free enquiry";[4] and in February 1858, Simpson and another convert, Lord Acton, the unofficial spokesmen for an increasingly radical part of the English liberal Catholic movement, became proprietors of the journal. One of Simpson's first articles as editor was an abridgement of *Lady Falkland: Her Life*, which appeared in two consecutive issues in 1857.[5] Titled "A Conversion in the Time of Charles I," it was the first of a series of historical articles about Catholic "martyrs" of the sixteenth and seventeenth centuries which were written "to make some amends" for his recent articles on Catholic education criticizing the intellectual timidity of the Catholic hierarchy.[6] Simpson omits almost all of the references to divine providence, as well as to Cary's reading, writing, and absent-mindedness, focusing instead on the passive persecution of Cary for her beliefs after she converted, something with which Simpson himself could identify. Simpson's introductory paragraphs and editorial interjections evoke a religious climate

---

[3] Jerome McGann, *The Textual Condition* (Princeton: Princeton Univ. Press, 1991), 66.

[4] Josef Altholz, Damian McElrath, and James Holland, eds., *The Correspondence of Lord Acton and Richard Simpson*, 3 vols. (Cambridge: Cambridge Univ. Press, 1971–75), 2: 181. See also Josef Altholz, *The Liberal Catholic Movement in England: The "Rambler" and its Contributors, 1848–1864* (London: Burns and Oates, 1962). Simpson (1820–76) was a frequent contributor of theological and polemical articles and literary reviews to the *Rambler* from 1850 to 1864. He officially edited the *Rambler* from February 1858 until February 1859 (when he was asked by the Catholic bishops to resign his editorial post), but served as editor or sub-editor in an unofficial capacity from 1856. It evolved into the quarterly *Home and Foreign Affairs* in 1862, and ceased publication altogether in 1864. Simpson's progressive ideas about the importance of historical and scientific enquiry regardless of whether it challenged Catholic doctrine were not embraced by the Catholic bishops or by the less intellectual "old" Catholics.

[5] R[ichard] S[impson], ed., "A Conversion from the Time of Charles I," *Rambler* 8 (1857): 173–89, 258–72.

[6] Altholz, *Liberal Catholic Movement*, 39.

which resembles England in the 1850s as much as it does England in the 1620s. According to Simpson,

> The affairs of Catholics were now more smooth than they had been since the beginning of the persecution. . . . They were looked upon as good subjects at court, and as good neighbours in the country; all the restraints and reproaches of former times being forgotten. But they were not prudent managers of this prosperity . . . [and] provoked the rage and destroyed the charity of great and powerful families which longed for their suppression.[7]

Behind Simpson's observations of the status of English Catholics under Charles I was his concern that divisions among his own Catholic contemporaries — between the bishops and the laity, and among "old" English Catholics, new English converts, and a large influx of Irish immigrants — would undermine the efforts of his fellow liberal Catholics to gain the respect of Protestants for English Catholicism through a fearless embrace of scientific and historical enquiry.[8] Penal laws against English Catholics had only been lifted in 1829, and in 1850 (the same decade as Simpson's abridgement of *Life*), the Catholic diocesan hierarchy had been restored after nearly three hundred years of suppression.

While Simpson's mildly topical abridgement of *Life* was meant to appease his critics, his next major biographical project was a direct challenge to them. In his most famous work, an eight-part biography of Edmund Campion, which first appeared in the *Rambler* in 1861, Simpson alienated Roman authorities by comparing the current Pope's (Pius IX's) defense of temporal power to that of Pius V in the sixteenth century, whose insistence on temporal power "lost England to the faith."[9] Simpson's analogy greatly distressed Roman authorities, who threatened to censure the *Rambler* unless it came out in favor of temporal power, and it was rumored that a Dominican priest had

---

[7] Simpson, ed., "A Conversion," 173.

[8] Damian McElrath, *Richard Simpson, 1820–1876: A Study of 19th Century English Liberal Catholicism* (Louvain: Publications Universitaires de Louvain, 1972), xiv. Between 1800 and 1851, the number of Catholics in England increased from 60,000 to 700,000.

[9] R[ichard] S[impson], "Edmund Campion," *Rambler*, n.s. 5 (1861): 91. Only the first eight chapters appeared in the *Rambler*. The Campion biography was printed in full in 1867 as *Edmund Campion: A Biography* (London and Edinburgh: Williams and Norgate, 1867).

said "that he would like to have the burning of the author."[10] Fortunately, Simpson received only a metaphorical burning. The *Rambler*'s Catholic publisher, Burns and Lambert, refused to print any further issues until the *Rambler* was under new management (Simpson was acting editor at the time). Instead of resigning, Simpson and Acton simply switched to a Protestant publishing house, Williams and Norgate.[11]

The appearance of a new edition by Simpson of *Lady Falkland: Her Life* immediately after the Campion controversy is not suprising. Simpson's full transcription of *Life*, promised to his readers in the second installment of his abridged version,[12] was published by the Catholic Publishing and Bookselling Company in the second half of August 1861.[13] Its publication only six weeks before the repeal of the paper tax, which led many other publishers to curtail publication of forthcoming books until after 1 October, suggests that Simpson's publishers could not wait for a more economical publication because of the immediate need to placate the enemies of his Campion biography. In contrast to Simpson's 1857 abridgement, Simpson's 1861 version altogether eschews polemical editing. Simpson's Introduction locates *Life*'s value both in its illumination of Cary's son Lucius, whose "talents and his temper" resembled those of his mother, and as a study of an individual Roman Catholic character. It is supplemented by a useful appendix of letters relating to Cary's conversion, and a series of letters concerning the life of Father Francis Slingsby.[14]

In keeping with other Victorian editors of Renaissance texts, Simpson did not aspire to remain faithful to the manuscript. He sometimes inserted the manuscript's marginal additions in the main text (in square brackets for the most part, but occasionally silently) and sometimes dropped them to footnotes.[15] Passages deleted in the manuscript are sometimes bracketed in the main text with footnotes stating they were "erased," or else are entirely set

---

[10] Altholz et al., eds, *The Correspondence*, 164, 166 (Acton to Newman, 19 June 1861; Newman to Acton, 7 June 1861).

[11] Altholz, *Liberal Catholic Movement*, 172. Williams and Norgate also published his biography of Campion in book form in 1867.

[12] Simpson, ed., "A Conversion," 272.

[13] R[ichard] S[impson], ed., *The Lady Falkland, Her Life* (above n. 1).

[14] See Jesse Swan's discussion of the influence of the Munich method of objective enquiry and explanation which Simpson employed in the preface and appendix to the 1861 edition, in "A Woman's Life as Ancillary Text: The Printed Texts of the Biography of Elizabeth Tanfield Cary," *Journal of the Rocky Mountain Medieval and Renaissance Association* 18 (2000 for 1997): 211–36.

[15] Simpson, ed., *The Lady Falkland, Her Life*, vi.

into footnotes. Sometimes Simpson included his own editorial comments in brackets within the text without indicating that these additions belonged to him. This loose editing was not so much the result of Simpson's carelessness as it was the result of different priorities. His appendix of letters and notes indicates that he had thoroughly and carefully researched his subject, and that this historical contextualization was of greater value than a faithful transcription.

Some of the letters in Simpson's appendix were silently incorporated by Lady Georgiana Fullerton, the prolific liberal Catholic novelist, playwright, poet, and biographer, into her adaptation of Simpson's edition of *Lady Falkland: Her Life*, published in 1883 by Burns and Oates. Fullerton's preface, like Simpson's abridgment, situates the text in late nineteenth-century English religious controversy, offering the example of Cary "to the imitation of all who suffer for justice's sake."[16] Lady Fullerton had originally intended to make her biography of Cary part of a trilogy of biographies of Catholic women from different periods in history who fought to defend their faith, but she died before completing the project.[17] Fullerton empathized with her source material so passionately that she could not resist taking creative liberties with the text, which consequently reads more like one of her popular novels than a biography. Imagining Lord Falkland's installation ceremony at Dublin Castle, in which James Ussher gave a sermon entitled "He beareth not the sword in vain," she interjects:

> Poor Lady Falkland had to sit and hear, with what patience she could, her husband exhorted and adjured not to tolerate the exercise of the Catholic religion. ... If up to that moment she had witnessed with pleasure the pageantry of the semi-regal progress ... a depressing heart sickness must have deprived her of all enjoyment during the ceremonies which followed the Protestant Prelate's ghastly sermon. When the sword was delivered into the hands of her lord, could she refrain from thinking of the words of Scripture so hatefully perverted?[18]

---

[16] Georgiana Fullerton, ed., *The Life of Elisabeth Lady Falkland 1585–1639*, Quarterly Series 43 (London: Burns and Oates, 1883), viii. Lady Fullerton (1812–85) was acquainted with Simpson and was the step-niece of his colleague Lord Acton. She converted in the same year as Simpson, and like him, was a prolific writer largely shaped by the Oxford Movement. Her biographies included the lives of eleven women.

[17] Henry James Coleridge, *Life of Lady Georgiana Fullerton. From the French of Mrs Augustus Craven* (London: Richard Bentley and Son, 1888), 465. Lady Buckingham and Lady Lothian were the other two intended subjects.

[18] Fullerton, ed., *The Life of Elisabeth Lady Falkland*, 34–35.

This version of *Life* deserves attention as the product of pious and politically motivated liberal Catholic editing; however, it does not attend to the manuscript itself, and not at all to its Benedictine context.[19]

The most recent version of *Life* was edited in 1994 by Barry Weller and Margaret Ferguson and is appended to their edition of *The Tragedy of Mariam*.[20] This modernized clear text edition of the manuscript was a timely and important contribution to Cary studies: Weller and Ferguson made *Life* widely available for the first time, since nineteenth-century editions are now quite rare, and they produced a text of *Life* which complements their main interest, *The Tragedy of Mariam*. However, by implicitly linking the protagonist of *Life* to the play's tragic heroine and not delving into the circumstances of *Life*'s production or referring to other contemporary documents for contextualization, they perpetuate the text's function as a rather unsatisfactory "decoding device" for the play.[21] Arguing that "stylistic nuance seems less crucial to its [*Life*'s] value," they decided not to provide "a full commentary on editorial procedure." Thus, while encouraging readers to "use their own interpretive skills to trace, and appreciate the talents of, the elusive daughter of Elizabeth Cary," they in fact contribute to her elusiveness by denying us access to critical bibliographical evidence.[22] In the process of recovering one woman writer, Elizabeth Cary, they inadvertently place a greater distance between the modern reader of *Life* and another woman writer, Cary's daughter.[23]

An example of this distancing occurs in the omission of a marginal addi-

---

[19] Fullerton's version of *Life* is not error-free. For example, she identifies Great Tew as "Few," most likely because she misread the word in a letter written by Cary's son Patrick (see *Life and Letters*, ed. Wolfe, 422), and she identifies Anne, not Mary, as the daughter who was offered as a nun to the Virgin Mary at birth (see *Life and Letters*, ed. Wolfe, 119).

[20] Weller and Ferguson, eds., *The Tragedy of Mariam* (see above, n. 1).

[21] Weller and Ferguson, eds., "Introduction," *The Tragedy of Mariam*, 50; Stephanie Wright, "The Canonization of Elizabeth Cary," in *Voicing Women: Gender and Sexuality in Early Modern Writing*, ed. Kate Chedgzoy, Melanie Hansen, and Suzanne Trill (Keele: Keele Univ. Press, 1996), 58.

[22] Weller and Ferguson, eds., "Introduction," *The Tragedy of Mariam*, 48, 50.

[23] In general, Weller and Ferguson place both marginal additions and their own editorial notes in footnotes, while interlinear insertions are silently incorporated into the main text and deletions are bracketed within the text. There are many exceptions, however. Square brackets in the main text serve the double duty of marking editorial notes and making conjectures about struck-through or cropped words. Though they supply missing letters to words, Weller and Ferguson sometimes introduce these letters silently, and sometimes place them in square brackets.

tion which identifies three of Cary's four daughters by name, as "Mother Clementia, Dame Augustina, Dame Magdalena" (Anne, Elizabeth, Lucy).[24] The Constitution of Our Lady of Consolation, Cambrai, where they were nuns, states that the nuns are to refer to themselves in speech and writing as "Sisters," to each other as "Dames," and to the prioress and sub-prioress as "Mother."[25] If one of the three named daughters had written this addition, she would have identified herself as "Sister." The only daughter not mentioned in this annotation is Mary, and from this, and another annotation like it, in which three of the sisters are identified as "Mother Clementia, Dame Magdalena, and Sister Maria" (Anne, Lucy, Mary), we can deduce that Mary was the writer of these two annotations as well as twenty-nine others. Mary's hand appears in other manuscripts which were produced at Cambrai as well, as do each of her sister's hands.

II. A New Edition

While previous editions unintentionally obscured the habits and identities of *Life*'s multiple contributors by smoothing over the peculiarities of the manuscript, it was not my aim to transform *Life* into an artificially polished text, but to set forth the meanings in and of its imperfect state.[26] I wanted to represent the different hands and the different kinds of additions and deletions to the text without making it overly difficult or tedious to read, and I wanted to annotate it so that the modern reader could be armed with background information that would have been known or obvious to the manuscript's original writers, correctors, and readers. Of course, this was not nearly as straightforward a process as it would seem.

Handwriting evidence suggests that Lucy was most likely the main scribe and author of *Life*,[27] with Mary supplying the marginal annotations noted above and her brother Patrick clarifying, correcting, and expanding upon *Life*'s narrative in eight places, in particular concerning his father's time in Holland

---

[24] *Life and Letters*, ed. Wolfe, 146 (fol. 20r).

[25] Archives Départementales du Nord, Lille, MS. 20H1.

[26] G. Thomas Tanselle has written of the "false starts, cancellations, insertions, and slips of the pen [which] are important characteristics" of manuscripts, and argues that eliminating or misrepresenting them alters "the nature of the document" and obscures "the evidence of motivation"; see Tanselle, *A Rationale of Textual Criticism* (Philadelphia: Univ. of Pennsylvania Press, 1989), 65.

[27] See Heather Wolfe, "The Scribal Hands and Dating of *Lady Falkland: Her Life*," *English Manuscript Studies* 9 (2000): 187–217, here 192–98, for discussion and examples of the hands of Anne, Mary, Elizabeth, and Lucy.

and his own "kidnapping" from Great Tew. By reading *Life* in the context of its production at Our Lady of Consolation, Cambrai, it is possible to date it between February and August 1645, with Patrick's emendations being made between March and May 1649. These dates can be established through references within the manuscript to historical events and to the current posts of members of the English Benedictine Congregation, and by tracking Patrick's travels after he left Rome and before he began his novitiate at Douai.[28]

In a sense, the manuscript was first edited in the seventeenth century: instead of footnotes, the original editors added marginal glosses placed near the text being explicated. I felt that this original textual apparatus needed to remain in the margins rather than being sunk to footnotes or absorbed into the linear text, both in order to retain its original meaning and to prevent the modern reader from confusing it with my own footnotes at the bottom of the page or from thinking that it was a seamless part of the narrative.[29] I identified the individual marginal annotators because their additions, clarifications, and, occasionally, contradictions remind us of the multiple and sometimes competing intentions of the author and her sibling-editors.[30]

Deletions in the manuscript are struck through uniformly in the edition, leaving them still legible and allowing the modern reader to follow the process of composition and revision with a minimum of effort. I would have liked to represent the different types of deletions with different types of strikethroughs, but this was too difficult to do typographically, and I didn't want to burden a modern reader with any extra symbols or apparatus. One kind of deletion, however, seemed important to draw attention to in the footnotes. In a few cases, entire passages are casually marked for deletion with broad slash marks, but the text is for the most part completely unaffected. This style of

---

[28] See Wolfe, "Scribal Hands and Dating," 199, 203–4.

[29] Early modern readers were accustomed to both printed and manuscript marginal annotations, which formed an intrinsic part of the reading process. See Evelyn B. Tribble, *Margins and Marginality: The Printed Page in Early Modern England* (Charlottesville: Univ. Press of Virginia, 1993).

[30] Jack Stillinger writes of each contributor of a collaborative text as having an "intrinsic . . . place in the text," and stresses the importance of recognizing the "harmonious or discordant network of many separate intentions": "Multiple Authorship and the Question of Authority," *Text* 5 (1991): 283–93, here 292. I maintained original spelling (including i/j and u/v graphs), capitalization, and punctuation, and expanded abbreviations with supplied letters in italics. Lineation is not maintained, but foliation is indicated in the outer margins with a vertical line in the text indicating the location of each page break. I decided to represent scribal errors such as false starts and spelling corrections, as well as the more substantive alterations to the text, since I felt that both types would give the reader a sense of the habits and tendencies of each contributor.

deletion, which could have been made by any one of Cary's Catholic children
or the anonymous Benedictine emender, is applied to passages referring to
Cary's forgetful, distracted, and sometimes manic–depressive behavior. The
style of these deletions suggests that the manuscript was being prepared for
wider scribal publication or, possibly, printing. The slash marks were not
meant to obfuscate the text in this particular copy, which belonged to the enclosed nuns, but were perhaps intended to signal that future copies, the circulation of which they could not control, should not include these lines. The
deleter might have been concerned that an outside reader would interpret
Cary's eccentric behavior as a sign of God's punishment, as in Foxe's *Book
of Martyrs*, or a symptom of religious doubt and pre-conversion anxiety, as in
St. Augustine's *Confessions* or in Puritan conversion narratives. When one reads
the text without these deleted passages, Cary's conversion seems less like the
passing fancy of an impressionable, weak-minded woman and more like the
informed and clear-headed decision that it was. This type of deletion allows
for two sets of readers, then: a general audience seeking an exemplary, formu-
laic text, and a family and monastic audience, who would prefer an edifying
and personal memorial of Cary, warts and all. In a sense, the marginal glosses
and pseudo-deletions are a form of hypertext meant to please a variety of audiences, and indeed, the biography would be a prime candidate for an online
hypertext edition that would represent the text as both a "private" document
and a "public" text.

So, how does a representation and description of the physical layout help
in the interpretation of *Life*, and how exactly does the inclusion of the *Life*
and letters in a single volume increase our understanding of Cary's lived life,
as well as contribute to our understanding of her children as authors, editors,
and Catholics? I can provide a few brief examples here, of features that are
not fully described in earlier editions. First, one of the leaves in the manuscript of *Life* is tipped-in and smaller in size than the other leaves.[31] While
the narrative flows continuously without this leaf, its presence greatly changes
the nature of Cary's conversion. The leaf concerns the dying moments of
Cary's eldest daughter Katherine, who had married a "Scotch puritan" and
thus had little exposure to Roman Catholicism. Katherine is described as having had a deathbed vision of "a bright woman cloathed in white having a
Crowne on her head," and Cary, who was at her daughter's side, unsurpris-
ingly convinces her that this was the Virgin Mary. Without the inserted leaf,
the reader would have been unaware that Katherine harbored any Catholic
sympathies. With the leaf, not only is she revealed as a closet Catholic, but
her vision of the Virgin Mary also becomes the main impetus, or trigger, for

---

[31] *Life and Letters*, ed. Wolfe, 126–27 (fol. 12r).

her mother's conversion, which might otherwise appear motivated mainly by intellectual reasons. The placement of this tipped-in leaf describing the role of divine providence in her conversion is crucial, since on the following page Cary is reconciled to the Church of Rome in the barn of a neighbor. Although I haven't been able to establish whether this leaf was added before or after the manuscript circulated among the other siblings, it does seem important that this significant plot-twist was not part of the original narrative.

Just as Katherine was posthumously "converted" in a tipped-in leaf, Lucius and Lorenzo, Cary's other two Protestant children, receive their Catholic crowns in the margins of the manuscript, in the hands of their siblings Patrick and Mary. According to the main text of *Life*, Lucius and Lorenzo were killed in the civil wars "without any signe of hope" of ever being Catholics.[32] After the word "any" is a dagger symbol directing the reader to a partially cropped marginal addition in Patrick's hand: "God be tha[nked] some [sign] there is hopes they died catholic." Perhaps because Patrick's addition was cropped, Mary copies it into the inside margin, improving upon its sense at the same time: "God be thanked there is great hopes they both dyed Catholickes." In this series of corrections, Lucy has been edited by Patrick, and Patrick has in turn been edited by Mary. This crescendo of hope, from *none* to *some* to *great*, exemplifies the purposefulness of Lucy's narrative, which is further framed by her siblings.[33]

Some details in *Life* which we might be inclined to relegate to hyperbole or hagiography are supported by evidence in the letters (although letters, with their own set of rhetorical conventions, should be treated with the same caution when trying to separate "truth" from rhetoric). Both *Life* and the letters provide surprisingly similar accounts of Cary's dalliances with Arminianism; the reaction of the king, her husband, her mother, and others to her conver-

---

[32] *Life and Letters*, ed. Wolfe, 212 (fol. 45r).

[33] The timing of Patrick's corrections is interesting. During the same period, he also wrote to his late brother Lucius' close friend, the earl of Clarendon, discussing the possibility of leaving the Catholic church. Patrick's involvement in creating a Catholic genealogy for his family in the *Life* of his mother must be read against his carefully-worded account of his conversion, which differs greatly from the account of his conversion in *Life*. He explains to Clarendon that at the time of his secret conversion, aged 12, "he knew noe other distinction then, betweene the Catholicke, and Protestant one but that my Mother was of that, my father of this." In order to "bee taught whatt itt was," he "was stolen into france." As a result, his brother Lucius retained his portion, leaving Patrick "to a strange likely-hood of staruing" (*Life and Letters*, ed. Wolfe, 428). The inclusion of the letters and *Life* in a single edition allows the reader to confirm or challenge certain claims in each, and to determine the extent and nature of their literary manipulations.

sion; her friendship with the duke of Buckingham's female relatives; the kidnapping of her sons; the meddlesomeness of her husband's servants; details of
her allowance and other sources of income; the account of her husband's
death; her tendency to travel by foot rather than coach after her husband's
death; and William Chillingworth's deceptive attempts to return Cary's daughters to the Protestant church.

The letters and documents also provide details not mentioned in *Life*, and
their exclusion is noteworthy. A series of letters between the papal emissary
to England and Cardinal Barberini's secretary in Rome discuss Cary's plan to
move to Rome with her Catholic children, of which the Cardinal strongly
disapproved.[34] A few letters from the priest Francis Slingsby discuss his attempts to discourage his brother Henry from joining the Cary caravan to
Rome, and one letter in particular alludes to the fact that Henry was in fact
in love with "some" of Cary's daughters.[35]

One of the more interesting contradictions concerns Cary's claims in her
letters, and her daughters' claims in *Life*, that she was in dire financial straits in
the months after her conversion. Against these claims of starvation and poverty
we have Conway's docket on a pleading letter from Cary which summarily
states, "Doubteth much she is neglected," as well as a note to Lord Falkland
from his agent in London, who had the unfortunate task of keeping tabs on
Cary's comings and goings.[36] He writes: "my Lady keepes a plentifull Table
att hir Lodginges in drury Lane where hir ladyshipps dayly guiestes are 2
Priestes with other Romish Catholiques, the supply ʌ^by way of loaneʌ as I am
informed Cometh from the dutchesse & Countesse of Buckingham with other
ladies of that Religyon."

This edition of *Life* is in no way the final word on the manuscript. There
are still a number of outstanding questions regarding the text, which I hope
readers of my edition will be able to take up. Can the reader recreate the
manuscript from my edition, or is this even necessary? Probably not, but I
hope it faithfully represents the complexities of the manuscript as well as the
type of information that will be useful to its anticipated audiences: students of
women's history and writing, Catholic history and writing, and life writing
and letter writing in general. Editing collaboratively written manuscripts is
always a dangerous balancing act, but as textual criticism continues to become
less focused on the author's original or final intentions, and more focused on
the representation of meaningful ambiguities and multiple intentions, I hope
that this edition is at least tipped in the right direction.

---

[34] *Life and Letters*, ed. Wolfe, 400–1, 404–6.
[35] *Life and Letters*, ed. Wolfe, 206n, 405n.
[36] *Life and Letters*, ed. Wolfe, 291, 307.

"But a Copie":
Textual Authority and Gender
in Editions of
"The Life of John Hutchinson"

DAVID NORBROOK

"THE HEAT OF HIS YOUTH A LITTLE INCLINED HIM TO THE PASSION of anger, and the goodness of his nature to those of love and grief, but reason was never dethroned by them, but continued governor and moderator in his soul." Thus, generations of readers believed, did Lucy Hutchinson conclude the introduction to her celebrated biography of her husband.[1] A firm distinction is made between reason, government, and masculinity on the one hand and passion on the other. This is one of a number of passages which can be marshalled in support of a reading of Hutchinson as conservative and patriarchal in mentality when compared with bolder contemporary women writers such as Margaret Cavendish. The lack of a distinctively gendered authorial voice has been much remarked: where Lucy Hutchinson writes of herself in this text, it is always in the third person.

But readers of the *Memoirs of the Life of Colonel Hutchinson* must beware of textual pitfalls. The passage with which I began appeared in most editions from 1846 down to 1968. But what Lucy Hutchinson actually wrote was that

---

[1] Lucy Hutchinson, *Memoirs of the Life of Colonel Hutchinson*, ed. Margaret Bottrall (London: J. M. Dent & Co.; New York: E. P. Dutton, 1968), 28; hereafter *Memoirs*.

"reason was neuer dethrond by them but continued governesse and moderator in his soule": she personifies reason as feminine, consistently with a later passage in which she writes that "it booted him not to be angrie at himselfe, nor to sett wisdome in her reprooving chaire, or reason in her throne of councell; the sick heart could not be chid nor advizd into health."[2] Too much should perhaps not be made of such gendering of personifications, a practice in which Hutchinson was not consistent; but in this case it is interesting that the female reason emerges at virtually the only point where she acknowledges her husband to have had a fault, with an oblique suggestion that she helped to modify it. The gendering of reason as masculine here was the work not of Hutchinson but of a nineteenth-century editor.

This change is a particularly striking example of the editorial reshaping that Hutchinson's manuscript has undergone over the years, by editors who have overruled or simplified her own preferences, and subtly contributed to the impression of a specially "masculine" woman writer. The Everyman text reprinted an 1846 version that severely reworked and reworded an earlier printed text which itself reworked and reworded the manuscript. Although the manuscript, which went missing during the nineteenth century, has been available again since the 1920s, no edition has yet fully recovered the manuscript version. In the light of current textual theory, that need not particularly surprise us: editions mediate between documents and audiences, and until fairly recently what audiences have most demanded of the *Memoirs* has been a readable history of the Civil War in a local setting, not close engagement with the author. With the emergence of a strongly feminist literary history, however, it has been increasingly assumed that what the editors gave us was indeed a minutely accurate account of what the author wrote, and the result has been a misunderstanding of Hutchinson's own engagement as a writer. I hope to be able to provide a fuller understanding in the new edition on which I am currently working with Martyn Bennett, as part of an Oxford English Texts edition of her complete works. Earlier editions, as I shall try to show, have had their own priorities and value, but they did not pay the kind of attention to the author and her processes of composition which the manuscript evidence does in fact make possible.

Lucy Hutchinson (1620–81) composed her life of her husband John as a response to his death in prison 1664. Despite his liability to the death penalty in 1660 as a signatory of Charles I's death warrant, his life had been spared,

---

[2] Nottinghamshire Archives, MS. DD/HU4, pp. 21, 53. This and other Hutchinson manuscripts are on loan and I am grateful to Mrs Hugh Priestley and to the Principal Archivist of the Nottinghamshire Archives for permission to edit the manuscript. Further page references to this manuscript are given in parentheses.

partly through the tactical support of his wife and her royalist relatives. In 1663, however, he was imprisoned without trial for alleged complicity in a republican rising. His name was thus tarnished not only amongst royalists but amongst republicans who had accused him of time-serving, and Lucy Hutchinson aimed to redeem his honor as a consistent and noble public servant. In doing so, she refused any political compromise, and in insisting that he never wavered in believing that Charles had been justly executed, she placed her text far outside the boundaries of acceptable public discourse. Parts of the opening were addressed specifically to her children, which has been taken by some critics as relegating it to a private sphere; but a comparable familial address can also be found in the writings of Clarendon and Bulstrode Whitelocke, which were inextricably bound up with the public consequences of personal actions. Clarendon writes of himself in the third person, indicating the distance appropriate to public occasions, so that Lucy Hutchinson's adoption of the same convention need not be seen as specifically gendered. As with these contemporary narratives, the bulk of Hutchinson's subject-matter is political. If the text remained largely within her family, it was because it would have been politically dangerous to circulate it further. And indeed its central portion was derived from a document with a public purpose, a narrative of her husband's actions as Governor of Nottingham Castle during the 1640s and probably designed to serve in his legal defense during a barrage of charges and counter-charges between rival Parliamentarian factions.

Composed twenty years earlier, this document is often called a first draft, but it had a different rhetorical purpose, and there are innumerable differences, from minutiae of phrasing to the inclusion of different episodes. Sir Charles Firth's editions of 1885 and 1906 offered substantial excerpts, but adequately to represent all the variations would require a hugely unwieldy textual apparatus, and would imply a misleading teleology in which the narrative of the 1640s was no more than a preparation for the later text.[3] The Oxford edition plans to present the "Defense of John Hutchinson" as a separate text. From the point of view of gender and editing, the most significant aspect of this narrative is that it was written as a brief for John Hutchinson and probably based very heavily on his own notes; she tells us that she was

---

[3] The manuscript was fragmented during the nineteenth century, and the surviving parts are now British Library Additional MSS. 25,901, 39,779, and 46,172N. The only extensive discussion the manuscripts have received is Sydney Race, "The British Museum MS. of the Life of Colonel Hutchinson and its Relation to the Published Memoirs," *Transactions of the Thoroton Society* 18 (1914): 35–66, who reproduces part of a leaf then in Nottingham Castle Museum and now missing; it followed on from Additional MS. 25,901, fol. 87v.

"us'd sometimes to write the letters he dictated, and her character not much different from his."[4] This version includes some vivid touches which seem to have been omitted from her later version in the name of literary decorum. For example, she notes in recording a speech by one of her husband's adversaries that he referred to him as "John (for soe in a iesting way he vsed to call Lft Coll Hutchinson)." This disrespect was evidently considered better suppressed (it throws interesting light on what she would think about the common habit of referring to her as "Lucy").[5] Critics have argued that Lucy Hutchinson shows two different voices, one personal and gendered female, the other more conventionally "masculine," but it has not often been recognized that for portions of the text the wording may indeed derive from a specifically masculine voice.[6] Nonetheless, there is no reason to doubt her own deep interest in writing a narrative of public affairs; the changes in later versions show hesitations between different literary solutions to a problem of exposition rather than any kind of shift from a "masculine" to a "feminine" style. Such distinctions may inhibit — rather than encourage — the exploration of writing by early modern women by prematurely limiting their range. And it is interesting to note that pages from this early, much more public narrative became a source of inspiration for later women writers. In the 1820s the manuscript came into the possession of Anna Montagu, who headed what became a rather formidable female literary dynasty; she handed leaves to members of her circle, including the poet Adelaide Procter and the novelist Mrs Craik.[7]

The manuscript of the 1660s does at some points strike a more personal note than the "Defence," when Lucy Hutchinson chronicles her husband's marriage and some other aspects of his family life. These are the episodes that have attracted most attention from those seeking a female voice in her writings, and they have occasioned disappointment owing to their relative restraint in self-expression. Within the overall rhetorical aim of the "Life," however, the restraint is arguably appropriate, and there is no reason to believe that the

---

[4] *Memoirs*, ed. James Sutherland (London: Oxford Univ. Press, 1973), 230.

[5] British Library Additional MS. 25,901, fol. 14r; *Memoirs*, ed. Julius Hutchinson (London: Longman, Hurst, Rees, and Orme, 1806), 139.

[6] N. H. Keeble, " 'The Colonel's Shadow': Lucy Hutchinson, Women's Writing and the Civil War," in Thomas Healy and Jonathan Sawday, eds., *Literature and the English Civil War* (Cambridge: Cambridge Univ. Press, 1990), 227–47, here 244; Elaine Hobby, *Virtue of Necessity: English Women's Writing 1649–1688* (London: Virago, 1988), 79.

[7] Notes accompanying BL Additional MSS. 25,901 and 46,172N.

account of her courtship is more intrinsic to her identity than her incisive and original analysis of the causes of the Civil War, which immediately follows it. Hutchinson here draws on another masculine voice, that of Thomas May, but she significantly radicalizes his analysis; no edition has yet given a full account of the revisions which bring out how she struggled with and rejected May's more conciliatory view. To rebuke this writer, who after 1660 was blackened as the deepest-dyed of Satanic republicans, for showing "more indulgence to the King's guilt than can justly be allow'd" was hardly the action of a timo-rously conventional woman.[8]

The boldness of the manuscript is heightened if we take into account an element that has never been properly noted in previous editions. The life of her husband is followed by a long section headed "Psalmes he had markd when he first began to be pers[ecuted]." Lucy Hutchinson had gone through her husband's Bible and copied out all the verses he had marked, listing them under topics with clear political and religious resonance, such as "In reference to the Presbiterian party & other Apostates," "Applicable Scriptures to the Prelates," and "For the 30th of January" — the anniversary of the regicide. These quotations not only provide an intellectual portrait of her husband, leaving the manuscript a memorial to him in a further sense, but also bring out messages for the future: in defiantly linking her husband's particular po-litical positions with the prophets of the Old Testament, Lucy Hutchinson provides inspiration and guidelines for her children and other sympathetic readers of the manuscript. This raises a difficult question for the editor: should not an edition aiming at respecting the manuscript print these quotations, even though they are not strictly speaking part of Lucy Hutchinson's canon?

It is, in fact, in some ways difficult to be sure exactly where the earlier part of the manuscript does end. No edition yet printed takes full account of these complexities. The narrative of the Colonel's life as printed in the most recent editions ends with the triumphant sentence: "Lett us blesse the Lord for him, and for the signall and eminent mercy shew'd unto him, which made him in life and death victorious over the Lord's and his enemies." In the manuscript this is succeeded by a deleted passage which reads something like: "he hath not left yet one like him in the world nor able to make him a worthy epitap He lies withou[t] an Epitaph because my deaded spirites can."[9] This sentence was presumably written before she had erected a memorial for him in Ow-thorpe church, and it indicates her sense that the manuscript will be his only memorial. In a writer as self-conscious as Hutchinson, we can perhaps see the

---

[8] *Memoirs*, ed. Sutherland, 53.
[9] *Memoirs*, ed. Sutherland, 277; DD/HU4, 419.

impossibility topos as a deliberate rhetorical gesture, memorializing the impossibility of making a full copy of her husband.

The reverse of this leaf (whose lower half has been torn off) is blank; it is succeeded by another leaf containing a moving epilogue in which Hutchinson voices her sense of estrangement from the world and bids an anticipatory farewell to her children. The opening, "You will now confesse those feares I did not hide from you were not in vaine . . . ," indicates that it follows on from the rest. Hutchinson goes on to assert that "his memory will neuer perish while there ∧^are any good men surviving who desire to preseruer one of the fairest copies in the ~~book~~ examplary booke of honor & vertue by the gracious precepts he left with his children to transferre to their posterity he will preach truth and holinesse to succeeding generations." Here she takes up a metaphor she had used in her opening address to her children:

> What I shall write of him is but a Copie of [him]. The ~~orig~~ originall of all excellence is God . . . and god alone whose glorie was first transcri[bed in] the humanity of Christ and that Copie left vs faire in the written word wherein this pious soule exercisd himselfe day and night ~~so while~~ as the rule of his practise the power he had to approach it his delight in transcribing it and his finall perserverance in that laudable delight were all but extracts of Christ drawne vpon his spiritt by the spiritt of god. (DD/HU4, 2)

At that point she had expressed the fear that she might have delighted "more then I ought to haue done in the mirror that reflected the creators excell-l[ence] which I should haue allwayes admird in its owne fountaine." It was Christ's grace alone that "raysd that wretched fallen nature and changd it into such a blessed image of his owne glory." Her husband was an image, a copy, of the divine, and all such copies in a fallen world are fallible. Hutchinson takes the standard epideictic formula of *occultatio*, proclaiming her inadequacy to the subject-matter, and both gives it a reflexive colouring, drawing attention to her own activity as an author writing out a fair copy, and adds a strong Calvinist weighting. The concluding passage can be seen as a bridge into the biblical excerpts, the precepts which he had tried to copy in his life and which his children are to emulate in turn by reading her transcription. The passage ends abruptly: "A good mans death is a presage of succeeding miserie happie are you whom god giues time and ope." The incomplete word may be "opertunitie," a word which for early modern republicans had connotations of decisive action when the moment came — Machiavelli's *occasione*. We may wonder whether the broken word may be a version of *occultatio*: Lucy Hutchinson registers her sense of the impossibility of fulfilling her husband's legacy, yet hints to her children at an alternative outcome in a successful over-throw of the Stuarts. The biblical precepts she goes on to enumerate are full of denunciations of tyranny and warnings that idolatry will never go long un-punished.[10]

If the precise ending of Lucy Hutchinson's life of her husband is hard to establish, so is its beginning. The manuscript launches into an introductory ad-dress to her children; there follows a panegyric beginning with a section headed "His Description," which is succeeded by "His vertues," at the end of which she declares: "All this & more is true but I so much dislike the manner of relatiting it that I will att make another assay." It is interesting that she breaks off at the point where she is hinting at her husband's limitations, but in fact this new "assay" elaborates on his difficulty in controlling his temper. In general, however, this second version is more emphatic on his godly self-sacri-fice, playing down secular issues and becoming less vivid in style. This version seems likewise to have displeased her, for after a further seven pages she writes that his "absence so distracts my memory with iust woe that I cannot call things forth in their due formes & order . . . therefore to wind vp all I shall only say," and launches into a set of balanced phrases. She does not wind up all, however, at least as the manuscript stands, for this page ends in mid-sentence (DD/HU4, 1–21, 22–29). Sydney Race has argued that though "one or more sheets are here missing, there is no break in the numbering, which proves that the book was written under Mrs. Hutchinson's supervision" ("British Museum MS.," 11). The manuscript now continues with the head-ing "The Life of John Hutchinson of Owthorpe in the County of Notting-ham Esquire." Clearly more is at issue here than rhetorical formulae: Hutchinson was writing under great emotional strain and did find it hard to do justice to her husband. Her prose, nonetheless, has elements of great formality, and it is her sense of the need to achieve the highest possible level of artistry that pushes her to a new beginning. And the sense that incomplete-ness is also a tribute may explain her readiness to leave not one but two frac-tured encomia at the head of her biography.

In its combination of careful copying and self-conscious incompleteness, then, the physical presence of the manuscript offers insights into Hutchinson's meaning which have been lost in successive printed versions. Paradoxically, the loss was intensified by the fact that the very first printed edition made a great deal of its fidelity to the manuscript. Julius Hutchinson, the editor, was a direct descendant of Charles Hutchinson, John Hutchinson's half-brother, to whom the manuscript had passed along with the family estate at Owthorpe.

---

[10] DD/HU4, [421], 2–3, 419.

Julius had access to several other manuscripts by Lucy Hutchinson and made use of them in annotating his edition; he also reproduced an engraving of a page of her theological commonplace book. He had, then, some familiarity with seventeenth-century manuscript conventions. Noting that the "orthography was in Mrs. Hutchinson's time in a most unsettled state," he insisted that his edition was faithful to the original:

> Great care being taken to follow the orthography of the writer, the reader need be under no apprehension as to the correctness of the print, though he should find the same word spelt differently even in the same line: as unperfect, imperfect; son, sonne, &c. The only deviation we have made from the MS. is in putting the U and V in their proper places; they being written promiscuously.[11]

This procedure had its critics: one reviewer objected that the manuscript's punctuation was "altogether execrable, and such as to render nearly incomprehensible many sentences which, when properly divided, are not only distinct but elegant" (he compared her to Sallust for economy of style); the editor's "zeal for antiquity," he punned, "might have been less *pointed*."[12] A more sympathetic reviewer, while declaring that he did not "object to the old spelling, which occasions no perplexity," proposed that "when the work comes to another edition, we would recommend it to him ... to break his pages into more paragraphs, and to revise his punctuation."[13] However, when he issued a cheaper octavo edition four years after the first, handsomely produced quarto appeared, Hutchinson was unrepentant on questions of spelling and punctuation. "The Critical Reviewer," he objected, "in order to prove that he was guilty of faulty punctuation, extracted pretty large quotations, in which so considerable a variation was made from the original words as totally to alter

---

[11] *Memoirs*, ed. J. Hutchinson (1806), xiv, 18 [sig. D1v] (he refers in the latter passage to the autobiographical narrative). Sydney Race, "Notes on Mrs. Hutchinson's Manuscripts," *Notes and Queries* 145 (13th ser. 1) (1923): 3–4, here 4, argues that the punctuation, "a difficult task in this case, seems to have been left to the compositor." Sutherland, xxvi, agrees that "the printer appears to have taken charge of the punctuation," and argues that in view of "the many differences between the MS. and his edition of it one must suppose that the printer was instructed to set up the whole MS. (apart from a few passages marked for omission), and that JH then proceeded to edit it from the proofs" (xxiv).
[12] *Critical Review*, 3rd ser., 10 (1807): 66–89, here 73, 77.
[13] [Francis Jeffrey], *Edinburgh Review*, 13 no. 25 (October 1808): 1–25, here 25.

the sense." He presented the work "unmutilated and unchanged."[14] (There were in fact a few corrections, some of them carried over from the second quarto edition of 1808. Notably, in the famous passage where she compares herself to a "faithfull mirror" reflecting her husband until he was taken "into that region of light which admitts of none," 1806 had read "admitts of more."[15])

In many ways Julius Hutchinson's edition did Lucy Hutchinson justice: handsomely produced and extensively annotated, it was a labor of love. The greatest part of the manuscript is transcribed with a good standard of accuracy for one with no scholarly experience, and without the compromises of modernization, so that it is possible to gain a feel for her distinctive language and syntax. He reproduced at length one extract from the earlier narrative of the 1640s, where Lucy Hutchinson had experimented with a dialogue form, and offered some notes on annotations in the "Life" manuscript made by later members of the family (which may reflect an earlier attempt to prepare the manuscript for publication).[16] At one point, duly registered in all later reprints, he restored a passage which had been deleted from the manuscript.[17] The old spelling did not prevent the book from becoming a best-seller, with three editions within four years, immediately propelling her into fame as a highly significant literary voice of her time. His enthusiastic, discursive notes treated Lucy Hutchinson as a significant historian whose views deserved weighing against classic texts.

Unfortunately, he did not tell the full story about his editorial policy, with the result that generations of readers wrongly took his edition for a full and accurate transcription of the manuscript, long after comparison with the original had become a possibility. As James Sutherland has noted, Julius Hutchinson "omitted passages amounting to about 9,000 words" and "silently altered the wording in innumerable cases, either to improve the sense or correct the grammar, or to remove obsolete words that were felt to be impolite, or simply to indulge his preference for one word rather than another."[18] In some

---

[14] *Memoirs*, 3rd ed., ed. Julius Hutchinson, 2 vols. (London: Longman, Hurst, Rees, and Orme, 1810), 1: iv–v.

[15] *Memoirs* (1806), 45; DD/HU4, 56.

[16] *Memoirs* (1806), 82–88, 35, 148; Additional MS. 39,799, fols. 42v–47r. He also noted Lucy Hutchinson's comment about the jesting use of "John," 139.

[17] DD/HU4, 253; *Memoirs* (1806), 264.

[18] *Memoirs*, ed. Sutherland, xxiv. For a rare example of a change going beyond mere cutting and rewording, see the passage on p. 8 of the 1806 edition from "He detested all scoffes" to "so avoid persecution," which has been transferred, with slight rearrangement, from a later discussion of his sincerity to the section on religion (MS. 253; *Memoirs* [1806], 266). The comma is in the MS.

ways his very concern to make the text look authentic impeded his editorial fidelity. He — or his printer — would "antique" his spellings in a way he considered appropriate to the original context. Thus when Lucy Hutchinson baldly writes "When the Towne was full" (MS., 137), Julius Hutchinson adds an explanatory "of troops" and feels constrained to give his own word an archaic spelling: "When the Towne was full of Troopes" (135). Apparently motivated by a kind of Romantic antiquarian impulse, Julius Hutchinson actually modified the manuscript's spelling so that it would look more different: thus he transmutes the commonplace surname "Perkins" into the presumably more sonorous "Parkyns" (138, 136). His changes went further, however. In a sense his first act as an editor was to overrule Lucy Hutchinson's authorial preference, for he printed the version of the introductory tribute which she rejected and omitted its successor. His justification was that the new character "has the appearance of being much *more laboured*, and much *less characteristick*"; while there are literary grounds for preferring the first version, there is a worrying circularity in pronouncing on which is more characteristic. He also cut extensive passages from the version he did print and from the body of the narrative. He cut altogether the closing pages of the manuscript, in which she discussed her suspicions that the Colonel had been poisoned, and told the strange story that a ghost resembling herself had been haunting the place of his imprisonment. Not only were these pages silently omitted, but the 1808 and 1810 editions, for no clear reason, went further and cut the sentence that had stood last in the 1806 edition: "So was he brought lamented home, and layd in his owne vault, which he thrice before his death order'd he should be brought to."[19]

Some of Julius Hutchinson's changes to the manuscript may have been motivated by a certain caution about dealing with a highly politicized woman writer. His ancestors had been still more cautious, refusing the republican historian Catharine Macaulay access to the manuscript. Julius Hutchinson was Whiggish in politics but nonetheless strongly hostile to the French Revolution, and he announced in his prospectus that he withheld publication "till he saw the period arrive, when, the storms of Politics having subsided, the Public could dispassionately read, with information and improvement, the transactions of that eventful period which it describes."[20] He was concerned to draw a sharp distinction between Lucy Hutchinson's republicanism, which he saw as marked by an underlying reverence for English tradition and a female

---

[19] *Memoirs* (1806), 442. As an example of the minor tinkerings, p. 41 of the 1806 edition, 9 lines from the bottom, reads 'he remember'd the story was told him, when he came downe' (as MS, p. 53); the 1808 edition reads 'told him when he came downe'; the 1810 edition, p. 90, reads as in 1806. The comma is in the MS.

[20] Printed prospectus, bound with Hertfordshire Record Office D/EVF31/188.

deference for male authority, from that of contemporary republicans like Macaulay or Mary Wollstonecraft. His lengthy notes often laboured the contrast, to the point of arousing the derision of the Whig Francis Jeffrey, who saw his "alternate notes in laud of the English levellers, and in vituperation of the atheists and jacobins of France" as parts of a bid for preferment in the church. And yet Jeffrey himself made a similar contrast, celebrating her ultimately "domestic virtue" against the "intriguing ... brilliancy" of contemporary politicized women like Mme Roland whose talent was superior to their judgement or purity.[21] Before long, however, the French historian Guizot was placing Lucy Hutchinson on the other side of that divide, comparing her unfavourably with Charlotte Duplessis Mornay, wife of the Huguenot leader, precisely because, though less educated and brilliant, she had "a stricter sense of right and a simpler heart," whereas Hutchinson was "somewhat pedantic and vain." He contrasted the modesty of Duplessis Mornay's account of her marriage with the element of "vain complacency" in Lucy Hutchinson's narrative of John Hutchinson's courtship: she lacked "modesty ... a virtue unknown to revolutionaries."[22]

Against this background of post-revolutionary reaction, it is easier to understand why Julius Hutchinson should have made some cuts which would throw the emphasis on domestic virtue and subordination. While printing the passage where she describes herself as her husband's image, he cuts the passage cited above in which she writes that he was himself but an image of the divine and that she may have been guilty of idolatry in admiring him too much. His preference for the first version of the introduction may have been coloured by distaste for the greater religious "enthusiasm" of the second version — he had already omitted praise of Calvin from the first version. He makes no mention of the section of militant biblical precepts at the end of the manuscript and omits the concluding meditation, thus losing significant moments of both writerly self-consciousness and political engagement. The closing pages with their tales of ghosts and poisoning may have seemed too "enthusiastic" for Hutchinson's more rational Whiggism. To his edition he added one of her poems, a piece in praise of retirement which does have an anti-courtly edge

---

[21] Jeffrey in *Edinburgh Review* (above n. 13). For a discussion of the reviews as privileging romance and fiction over history, see Devoney Looser, *British Women and the Writing of History, 1670–1820* (Baltimore and London: Johns Hopkins Univ. Press, 2000), 47–52, though some of these reviewers paid more attention to political issues than Looser implies.

[22] *Memoirs* (London: J. M. Dent, 1908), xxiv, xii, xxvi; see *Mémoires de Mistress Hutchinson*, ed. and trans. François Guizot, 2 vols. (Paris: Béchet aîné, 1823; 2nd ed., Paris: Pichon-Béchet, 1827).

but lacks the fervent outspokenness on public issues found in much original verse to which he certainly had access.[23] There is a certain softening of the text's political edge in the title Julius Hutchinson gave it. The republican simplicity of the original title is wholly appropriate; Lucy Hutchinson repeatedly stresses that her husband took up arms only reluctantly and that he consistently opposed the Puritan zealots who put military victory above constitutional propriety, and her consistent emphasis on the emptiness of worldly titles is somewhat at odds with the canonization of her book as *Memoirs of the Life of Colonel Hutchinson*.

Julius Hutchinson did, nonetheless, offer a spirited defence of the Hutchinsons' public positions, and the *Memoirs* proved attractive to political radicals. A further edition of his old-spelling version in 1822 was succeeded by a series of cheaper versions, one of them offering itself as part of a series of works dating from the period of the Commonwealth which would demonstrate the "desire, the *will* of the people to be free."[24] With the rising political temperature of the 1840s, the *Memoirs* was an obvious choice as one of the first texts for Henry George Bohn's *Standard Library*, which began publication in 1846. Though Bohn's motives were commercial rather than political, he did encourage a growing interest in women's participation in politics by juxtaposing Hutchinson's narrative with a narrative of the Countess of Derby's defence of Lathom House, and he noted that the book was available "at about one-sixth of its original price." With Bohn's edition, however, the text of the *Memoirs* reached a further level of distance from the manuscript. The preface and other paratextual matter from Julius Hutchinson's 1808 or 1810 edition were retained, but there were differences in the text. Claiming the authority of Jeffrey's review, the editor declared that "the orthography and punctuation ... have in the present edition been carefully revised. A few obsolete words and minor defects of phraseology have been sparingly altered for those of modern usage."[25] This was an understatement: in fact this edition intervenes

---

[23] *Memoirs*, ed J. Hutchinson (1806), 225–26; contrast the "Elegies," printed by David Norbrook, "Lucy Hutchinson's 'Elegies' and the Situation of the Republican Woman Writer," *English Literary Renaissance* 27 (1997): 468–521.

[24] *Memoirs* (Edinburgh: William Oliphant, 1825); *Memoirs* ([London: W. Smith, 1839]), iii. The British Library catalogue lists Eliza Huskinson as editor of this modernized reprint of Julius Hutchinson's 1808 or 1810 edition, but I have been unable to find the reason for this ascription, the prefatory matter being anonymous. The edition proclaimed itself not to have "altered any word, or modernized any form of expression," and a provisional check indicates that it largely followed Julius Hutchinson's wording.

[25] *Memoirs of the Life of Colonel Hutchinson* (London: H. G. Bohn, 1846), vii.

more substantially in a text which Julius Hutchinson had already refashioned, drawing on some minor changes made in the earlier modernized editions but adding many more.

For a sense of the scope of these successive changes, it will be helpful to focus on a single episode from perhaps the most famous part of the work: the description of the beginnings of John Hutchinson's love for his wife (MS. 51–52):

There scarcely past any day, but some accident[,] or some discourse still kept awake **alive** his desire of seeing this gentlewoman, although the mention of her, for the most part, was enquiries whither **whether** she ~~was~~ had yett accomplisht the marriage that was in treaty. One day there was a greate deale of company [mett][**omitted Bohn, Keeble**] att Mr Colemans, the gentlemans house where he tabled, to heare ~~some songs~~ the musick, and a certeine song was sung, which had bene lately sett, and gaue occasion to some of the company to mention an answer to it, wch was in the house, and vpon some of their desires read,: **[and]** *A*a gentleman saying that twas **[saying 'twas]** [*saying it was*] belieud **that [1806, Sutherland, Keeble]** a woman in the neighbourhood had made it, ^{it} was presently enquird who? wherevpon a gentleman, there **then** present, ~~sayd~~ who had made the other **first [1806, Sutherland]** song, sayd, there were but two weomen that could be guilty of it, whereof one was a lady then among them, the other Mrs Apsley. Mr Hutchinson fancying something of rationallity in the sonnett, beyond the customary reach of a she witt, although, to speake truth, it signified very little, addrest himselfe to this **the** gentleman, and told him that **told him,** he could scarcely belieue it was a womans, wherevpon the gentleman himselfe, **this gentleman,** who was a man of good vnderstanding & expression, and inspird with some passion for her himselfe, which made him regard all her perfections through a multiplying glasse, told Mr Hutchinson, that though for civillity to the rest, he entitled another Lladie to the song, yet he was confident it was Mrs Apsleys only, for she had sence aboue all the rest, and fell into such high prayses of her, as might well haue begotten those vehement desires of her acquaintance, which a strange sympathie in nature had before producd; : *A*another gentleman, that sate by, seconded this com[m]endation, with such additions of prayse, as he would not haue giuen[,] if he had knowne her, . [which] Mr Hutchinson hearing **all this**, sayd to the first gentleman, I cannot be at rest till this ladies returne, that I may be acquainted with ^{her};. t*T*he gentleman replied, S^r, you must not expect that, for ~~it is not~~ she is of an humour, she will not be acquainted

with any of mankind, and howeuer this song is stollen forth, she is the
nicest creature in the world of ~~ma~~ suffering her perfections to be
knowne, she shuns the converse of men as the plague, she only liues in
the enioyment of herselfe, and hath **has** not **the [1806, Sutherland,
Keeble]** humanity **humanitie** to com[m]unicate that happinesse to
any of our sex;:. w*W*ell, sayd Mr Hutchinson, but I will be acquainted
wth her,; and indeed the information of this reserud humour, pleasd
him, more then all elce he had heard, and filld him now with
thoughts, how he should attaine the sight & knowledge of her, which
while he was exercisd in, **While he was exercised in this,** many
dayes past not, but a footeboy of my Lady her mothers, came to young
Mrs Apsley, as they were att dinner, bringing newes that her mother
and sister would in **a [1839, Bohn; Keeble]** few dayes returne, and
when they enquird of him whither Mrs Apsley were **was [1806, Kee-
ble]** married, having bene before **before bene [1806, Keeble]** instructed to make them belieue it, he smild and puld out some bride-
laces, which were giuen at a wedding in the house, where she was,
and gaue them to the young gentlewoman, and the gentlemans daughter of the house, and told them Mrs Apsley bade him tell no newes, but
giue them those tokens, and carried the matter so, that all the compa-
nie belieud she had bene married.[26]

Julius Hutchinson's changes can be seen to center on tidying up the syntax,
clarifying the somewhat awkward handling of the dialogue at Mr. Coleman's,
and opening a new sentence at "While he was exercised." The change of
"awake" to "alive" seems to be a mere slip. In general the claim to be following original orthography is accurate, though the spelling "humanitie" is an
example of his fondness for over-archaizing. The Bohn edition effectively per-
forms the same kind of operation on Julius Hutchinson's text as Hutchinson
had done on the manuscript, introducing new sentence breaks at "A gentleman," "Another gentleman," "The gentleman," and " 'Well,' said Mr. Hutchinson," and deleting or inserting further words or phrases in the interest of
smoother reading. At some points, the changes are more radical; the Bohn

---

[26] Bold type indicates changes by Julius Hutchinson, bold italic changes introduced
the modernized 1839 edition, italic changes introduced in the Bohn edition. Julius
Hutchinson's silent modifications of i/j and u/v, expansion of contractions, addition
of an apostrophe for past participles and of quotation marks are not recorded. The
Bohn edition follows Julius Hutchinson except where otherwise indicated. References
to Sutherland and Keeble will be explained below. The 1839, Bohn and Keeble editions have modernized spelling and the ensuing variants are not recorded.

editor is much more ready to substitute a different word to avoid glossing a change of meaning. For example, on being led to believe that Lucy Apsley has just been married, we are told in the manuscript that "the distemper of his mind had infected his body, with a cold sweate, and such a dispersion of spiritt that all the courage he could at present recollect, was little enough to keepe him alliue." Presumably taking the unfamiliar word "dispersion" to be a mistake, Bohn substitutes "depression"; this is much more readily intelligible, but in the process we lose the distinctiveness of Hutchinson the intellectual. "Disperst" and "dispersion" are words that recur very frequently in her translation of Lucretius's *De rerum natura*, rendering *dissolvere* and *dissolvi*. In Book III Lucretius describes how the soul's powers are "Disperst abroad" and that its parts, "disperst, To all the bodies sallieports", break loose.[27] This is part of an argument — heretical, of course, to Lucy Hutchinson — for the mortality of the soul. This is, then, an extremely strong word to have chosen to convey the intensity of her husband's passion; it is also, as with the song at Mr Coleman's, associated with her life as a writer. The Bohn text's tendency to homogenize her language produces a somewhat more conventional figure; and, as in the case of the metaphor of reason as governor discussed above, edits out elements that may carry an inflection of the author's gender (the earlier modernized version had retained "governess").

Bohn's edition — subsequently published by George Bell, who took over Bohn's copyrights in 1864[28] — held the field for many years, and its sales appear to have easily rebuffed the scholarly challenge of a new edition by C. H. Firth in 1885, which was limited to five hundred copies. The manuscript of the "Memoirs" had disappeared in the confusion surrounding Julius Hutchinson's papers after his bankruptcy and death, and family tradition held to the colorful explanation that it had gone down in an Atlantic shipwreck. However, sections of the earlier narrative had by now been deposited in the British Museum, and Firth printed substantial extracts from these. He followed Julius Hutchinson's text rather than Bohn's; in printing his modernized version, though he does not make it explicit, he presumably followed the revised 1808 or 1810 texts, for he omits the final sentence of 1806. Firth also continued the tradition of reprinting the majority of Julius Hutchinson's notes, though he added extensive notes of his own drawing on his much deeper knowledge of the period's history, often providing additional evidence to substantiate her

---

[27] *Memoirs*, ed. Sutherland, 30; *Lucy Hutchinson's Translation of Lucretius: De rerum natura*, ed. Hugh De Quehen (London: Duckworth, 1996), 99–100 (3:601–14).

[28] Francesco Cordasco, *The Bohn Libraries: A History and a Checklist* (New York: Burt Franklin, 1951), 15.

account.[29] However, the deference Firth paid to Julius Hutchinson's edition
may have blurred in many readers' minds the distinction between his text and
the Bohn version. The publisher's advertisement presented him as following
a middle ground:

> In the earlier editions the irregular and unfamiliar spelling of the
> original renders the book difficult for the general reader to enjoy. In
> the later ones the text has been modernised with more freedom than
> fidelity.[30]

In his Introduction, however, Firth — possibly because this was his very first
publication — was more circumspect, noting of the different editions merely
that they were "reprints of the edition of 1806," which, as the publisher's
note itself indicated, was not the whole truth. In the end, Firth's edition —
which was reissued in 1906 — continued the situation in which Julius Hutchinson became an authorizing figure supplanting Lucy Hutchinson, and his
name was felt to give authority even to editions which departed significantly
from his own as well as from her text. When Harold Child issued another
edition in 1904, he went further in reinstating the authority of Julius Hutchinson's text by going back to 1806 rather than 1808 or 1810, retaining the old
spelling because without it "a great part of the charm of the original narrative
is lost" (xxxi); he also presented part of Julius Hutchinson's engraving of a
manuscript (facing xxxii). He restored the final sentence lost in the later editions; but he also reinstated the conspicuous error of "more" for "none" in
the "mirror" passage.[31] These editions offered alternatives to the Bohn text,
but soon afterwards that text, which was still being reprinted every few years,
received a new lease of life. In 1908, two years after the last Bohn printing,
the text was reissued under the new imprint of Everyman's Library. The only
additions were a brief and not very helpful textual note and a translation of
Guizot's essay with its criticisms of Hutchinson's immodesty. This now stood
before Julius Hutchinson's preface as the reader's main guide to the book's
import.[32] Firth's and Child's versions had resumed Lucy Hutchinson's own

---

[29] *Memoirs*, ed. C. H. Firth, 2 vols. (London: John C. Nimmo; New York: Scrib-
ner & Welford, 1885); second edition, 1 vol. (London: George Routledge & Sons;
New York: E. P. Dutton & Co., 1906).

[30] *Publications of John C. Nimmo*, bound in with vol. 2 of Firth's 1885 edition, 6.

[31] *Memoirs*, ed. Harold Child, Dryden House Memoirs (London: Routledge, Ke-
gan Paul, Trench, Trübner & Co., 1904), xxxi, xxxii, 77.

[32] *Memoirs* (London: J. M. Dent & Co., New York: E. P. Dutton & Co, [1908]),
xxvii, rather misleadingly refers to Firth's 1906 edition, though not the 1885, as "ed.

gendering of reason as a governess, but the Everyman text firmly reinstated reason as a governor.

Remarkably, this patriarchal succession continued even after Lucy Hutchinson's own manuscript had been recovered. It went on sale in 1918 and was resold by Maggs Brothers in 1921; with the enthusiastic advocacy of F. E. Hutchinson, Julius Hutchinson's great-grandson, and Sydney Race, a local antiquarian, the manuscript was bought by the Nottingham Castle Museum.[33] There it languished for a further fifty years. Race published a series of papers drawing attention to its importance, and carefully noting passages missed in Julius Hutchinson's edition, but no editor took up his work.[34] As late as 1968 Everyman's Library brought out an edition which followed Bohn's 1846 text. The only concession to the manuscript was that the 1968 editor, Margaret Bottrall, reprinted from one of Race's articles the concluding pages which had been omitted by Julius Hutchinson; but this was done as a separate appendix, uniquely in Race's old-spelling version, and in describing it as "the original rejected ending" she may give the impression that it was Lucy, rather than Julius, Hutchinson who had rejected it. The final sentence

---

from the original manuscript"; on Firth's title page it is made clear that it was Julius Hutchinson who edited from the manuscript. Firth had cited Guizot in his 1885 edition, 1: 28–29, though he answered his censure only by emphasizing the modesty and humility of her later religious writing, 1: xxvii. The narrative of Lathom House was dropped from the Everyman edition.

[33] Race was unaware of the manuscript's provenance, but this can be traced in *Catalogue of Valuable Books and Manuscripts Comprising a Selection from the Library of George W. Fitzwilliam, Esq. . . . 29 April 1918* (London: Dryden Press, 1918), 18: "HUTCHINSON (Colonel John, Regicide, 1615–64) History of his Life, particularly of his conduct in the Great Rebellion, written by his Wife Lucy, MANUSCRIPT, on paper, neatly written on 237 leaves, last 29 ll. occupied by extracts from the Scriptures, old vellum, loose in covers"; *Rare Books, Manuscripts and Bindings* (London: Maggs Bros., 1921), catalogue no. 416, pp. 77–78 (priced £150); correspondence in Nottinghamshire Archives. The Fitzwilliams had family connections with the Hutchinsons, which Julius Hutchinson appealed to in his edition: "From him descends in a direct line the present Earl Fitzwilliam. Fortes creantur fortibus et bonis" (1806 edition, 25n.); that Earl subscribed for two copies, and it seems likely that he purchased the manuscript when it became available. More work remains to be done on the fortunes of the Hutchinson manuscripts in the nineteenth century.

[34] Race's articles include "Notes on Mrs. Hutchinson's Manuscripts," *Notes and Queries* 145 (13th ser. 1) (1923): 3–4, 26–28, and "Further Notes on the Hutchinson Memoirs," 165–66; "Colonel Hutchinson, Governor of Nottingham Castle, and Regicide," *Notes and Queries* 174 (1938): 39; 'Memoirs of the Life of Colonel Hutchinson,' *Notes and Queries* 183 (1942): 166; and "Colonel Hutchinson: Manuscript and Printed Memoirs," *Notes and Queries* 199 (1954): 160–63, 202–4.

omitted after 1806 was also placed in the appendix. The rest of the text remained unchanged from 1846, along with Julius Hutchinson's preface and
notes, though Bottrall provided a new introduction considerably more sympathetic than Guizot's. Bottrall was the first editor to mention the location of
the manuscript, but it is evident that she had not consulted it.[35] As had become customary since 1806, the "Life" was preceded by an autobiographical
narrative from which many leaves were missing, "torn out," claimed Julius
Hutchinson, "apparently by the writer herself." This manuscript has not been
recovered, but it is hard to see how he could have been so confident that it
was Lucy Hutchinson who did the tearing. This impression of self-censorship
could then be drawn on by a feminist critic to condemn Lucy Hutchinson's
subservience to patriarchal ideology: "Hutchinson abandoned her autobiographical project after describing her parentage and early years, and turned instead
to the biography of her husband . . . as if her own life story ended after ado-
lescence when marriage subsumed her identity in her husband's."[36] In fact
her reference to "my house at Owthorpe" strongly suggests that she was writing after her husband's death, when she was precisely not a *feme covert* but an
estate-owner.[37]

Not until 1973 was the editorial hegemony of Julius Hutchinson and of
Bohn finally displaced by a return to the manuscript. By this time Race's
work on the manuscript had so far faded from sight that James Sutherland
learned of the existence of the manuscript only from a scrutiny of the indices
of *Notes and Queries*.[38] His edition for the first time pointed out the inadequacy of earlier versions as guides to the manuscript and reprinted the substance of most of the original text. For the first time Julius Hutchinson's notes
were displaced, and the autobiographical narrative was placed at the end so
that it no longer appeared as an integral part of the narrative. And yet Julius
Hutchinson's legacy remained. On the question of the title, Sutherland writes
that after some hesitation "I have thought thought it best to avoid confusion
by retaining the title given . . . by her first editor." Sutherland followed Julius
Hutchinson in printing only the first version of the Introduction. Sutherland's

[35] *Memoirs*, ed. Bottrall (above n. 1), 387–90, xv.

[36] *Memoirs* (1806), 18 (D1v); Sidonie Smith, "Margaret Cavendish's *True Relation*
and the Heroics of Self-Disclosure," in Smith, *Poetics of Women's Autobiography*
(Bloomington: Indiana Univ. Press, 1987), repr. in Anita Pacheco, ed., *Early Women
Writers: 1600–1720* (London and New York: Longman, 1998), 111–32, here 115.

[37] *Memoirs*, ed. Sutherland, 287.

[38] James Sutherland, "Down Chancery Lane," in René Wellek and Alvaro Ri-
beiro, eds., *Evidence in Literary Scholarship: Essays in Memory of James Marshall Osborn*
(Oxford: Clarendon Press, 1979), 164–78, here 176.

edition, like 1806, appends Lucy Hutchinson's epitaph for her husband, reproducing the version printed in 1806 rather than the text of the epitaph in Owthorpe church, even though he provided a photograph of the latter. Like Julius Hutchinson, he omitted the epilogue and all reference to the ensuing biblical citations — despite Race's having drawn attention to the last two features fifty years earlier. Though the reworkings in the manuscript give interesting evidence of her processes of composition, Sutherland gave only a limited set of variants, "if they appeared to have some special significance," failing to mention, for example, the deleted final sentence.[39] The epilogue was not printed until 1995, when N. H. Keeble edited for Everyman's Library a modernized edition which took a fresh look at the manuscript.[40] Even now, however, the textual legacy of Julius Hutchinson and H. G. Bohn proved hard to displace. Returning to the sample passage quoted above, we can see that both recent editors sometimes follow Julius Hutchinson's text rather than the manuscript.

Three and a half centuries after the "Life" was composed, then, we still lack an edition that follows the language of the manuscript precisely. That will be the aim of the Oxford edition, but of course any edition will face the problem of some kind of negotiation between the physical artefact of the manuscript and the different conventions of the printed word. The Bohn/ Everyman edition may have gone to extremes in changing the text to open it up to readers, but its enormous sales testify to the effectiveness of the strategy, and the proportion of changes is small in relation to the length of the work. By comparison, a semi-diplomatic edition will certainly raise difficulties for readers. However, simply on the grounds of multiplying the available kinds of edition, the effort is worth making. And the desire to shelter readers from the defects of Lucy Hutchinson's manuscript may risk blurring issues of practical convenience with larger and more ideological factors.

Take, for example, the question of punctuation, which, as has been seen, has preoccupied readers from an early stage. Sutherland noted that "as far as punctuation is concerned Mrs Hutchinson's MS. might be almost a legal document" and claimed that unless punctuation were supplied the reader "would have been frequently at a loss; and, worse, he would have gained a totally false impression of mindless garrulity."[41] The generalizing "he" here seems to hint at a male reader who might believe that a long-winded female writer was reflecting the limitations of her gender. In the interests of avoiding

---

[39] *Memoirs*, ed. Sutherland (London, 1973), ix, 293–94, xxiv.

[40] *Memoirs*, ed. N. H. Keeble (London: J. M. Dent; Rutland, VT: Charles E. Tuttle, 1995; repr. London: Phoenix Press, 2000).

[41] *Memoirs*, ed. Sutherland, xxv.

such an imputation, Sutherland regularizes her sentences, in some cases more thoroughly than Julius Hutchinson, who is often closer to the original punctuation. As has been seen, some early reviewers did fault the punctuation, but they concurred in praising the text's style, and none found it garrulous. Sutherland's edition, however, revived concern on this issue. Keeble writes that "it is an idiosyncrasy of hers to use virtually no punctuation," while Devoney Looser has commented that "the *Memoirs* is notorious for its lack of punctuation."[42] These generalizations blur some important distinctions. In fact, as will have been observed, the part of the text cited above is very heavily punctuated; this punctuation begins with the start of the "Life" proper and peters out in the section soon after the account of her courtship, where attention turns to summarizing Thomas May's narrative of public affairs. By modern standards, this punctuation is striking by its heaviness rather than its absence, and Sutherland prunes rather more of it than Julius Hutchinson had done. This punctuation may, however, not have been Lucy Hutchinson's own, and in the opening and remaining pages of the manuscript there is indeed very little pointing, with capital letters alone indicating sentence breaks. But given the immense range of conventions within early modern manuscript culture, there is no need to see this as either an idiosyncratically personal or a gendered trait. Lucy Hutchinson used many different levels of punctuation in different manuscript works and sometimes within the same work.

Insofar as there is a case for seeing Hutchinson's style as idiosyncratic, it is arguably a reflection not of garrulity but her classical interests. A stylistic analysis of her poetry against a large database of seventeenth-century verse has shown her unusually frequent usage of the relative pronoun to introduce a clause, particularly in evidence in her translation of Lucretius — not surprisingly since this is a characteristic of Latin.[43] This kind of construction was generally widespread in the early modern period as humanists tried to imitate Latin style; the distinction between a new main clause and a relative clause was often uncertain.[44] There are two examples of this usage — "which Mr Hutchinson hearing," "which while he was exercisd in" — in the passage cited above. Their cumulative effect is indeed difficult for readers with different expectations, the more so because of the lack of paragraph breaks.

---

[42] *Memoirs*, ed. Keeble, xxxi; Looser, *British Women and the Writing of History, 1670–1820*, 38.

[43] John Burrows and Hugh Craig, "Lucy Hutchinson and the Authorship of Two Seventeenth-Century Poems: A Computational Approach," *The Seventeenth Century* 16 (2001): 259–82, here 271.

[44] Manfred Görlach, *Introduction to Early Modern English* (Cambridge: Cambridge Univ. Press, 1991), 126, and cf. example on 225–27.

Nevertheless, an argument can be made that regularizing the punctuation is different in degree rather than kind from Julius Hutchinson's reworking the syntax for the benefit of modern readers: in sheltering readers, it also denies them the opportunity of confronting as directly as possible the way Lucy Hutchinson wrote. In its combination of (regularized) old spelling and more modern punctuation, Sutherland's edition gives the illusory impression of being less modern than it is.

One way of telling this story would be as the steady displacement of a female voice by patriarchal authority, and the goal of a new edition would be to restore that voice. On the other hand, recent textual theory, sometimes with a feminist inflection, has presented any such quest for an original voice as itself dubious, implying an immaterial, Platonic archetype transcending material embodiments, and cautions against taking any manifestation of a text as definitive.[45] Lucy Hutchinson's case seems difficult to align with that kind of opposition, since she herself firmly endorsed a Puritan/Platonic belief in timeless absolutes. Her presentation of herself as an image, a shadow, implied a hierarchy in which the female was necessarily a poorer image of the divine than the male; and the quest for a divine "originall," a transcendental signified, made her unsympathetic to mere images. On the other hand, as we have seen, she was ready to identify reason as feminine; and the very intensity of her belief in the "original" had a leveling effect in implying that all images were to a large degree inadequate. John Hutchinson as well as his wife was an imperfect image or copy, and his life was an attempt to transcribe as far as he could a truth already set down in absolute form. Her manuscript aimed to provide a fair copy of his story, but it acknowledged a kind of infinite regress in which no copy could be fully fair.

To that extent, she might not have been too disturbed by the subsequent fate of her manuscript. She would very likely have wished it to be printed when political circumstances made it possible, though its seditious contents would have made this impossible in her lifetime. We may compare the case of the fellow-republican Edmund Ludlow, whose unrepentant narrative of his life likewise could not be published, but who asked that some judicious person should do so when circumstances changed, and if necessary illustrate it with similes and examples. Ludlow had no special investment in the material state of his manuscript; what counted was the political message, and he was ready for the text to be altered not just in accidentals but even in major points

---

[45] For a critique of much "gynocritical" literary history see Jonathan Goldberg, *Desiring Women Writing: English Renaissance Examples* (Stanford: Stanford Univ. Press, 1997).

of style provided this end was achieved.[46] Hutchinson was a much more conscious artist than Ludlow and it is unlikely that she would have been so willing to allow alterations in her style, but there is evidence that in her last years she was increasingly anxious for her voice to be heard in public. The first five cantos of her *Order and Disorder* were printed in 1679 with a preface indicating a strong desire to influence public opinion. Had the "Life" been printed in her own time, its spelling and punctuation would have been regularized for the press. Its eventual printing in the nineteenth century, with progressively more radical alterations, made possible its emergence as a classic of biographical and personal writing, making her probably the best-known and most highly-praised early modern woman writer. Both Julius Hutchinson and Firth took her very seriously as a political thinker and as a historian, addressing her ideas without condescension. For all his reservations, Guizot's translation of 1827 very quickly gave her an international reputation.

Nevertheless, there is still a need for a modernized text that is accessible to readers but follows the manuscript without the residual deletions and additions of earlier editors. And a growing number of readers will want something different, an edition that offers something like the reading experience of the small group of friends and family members who were allowed access to the manuscript. In carefully registering her revisions and corrections, the Oxford edition may not reveal a pure and unmediated personal voice, but it will certainly make it easier to understand the texture of Lucy Hutchinson's language and to follow the processes by which a narrative was formed out of highly discrete, varyingly gendered, blocks of material and given an urgent personal and ideological unity. And however garrulous or uncharacteristic the result may appear, at least readers will for the first time have the opportunity of forming their own judgements.

---

[46] Bodleian MS. Eng. hist. c. 487, p. 1355. Sections from this MS have been edited in Edmund Ludlow, *A Voyce from the Watch Tower. Part Five: 1660–1662*, ed. A. B. Worden, Camden Fourth Series 21 (London: Royal Historical Society, 1978), whose introduction provides a fascinating account of the kinds of vagaries that might have been encountered by the "Life" had it been printed at this time.

Open Business Meetings, MLA

Editing Ralegh's Poems
Historically

MICHAEL RUDICK

I 'VE TITLED THE BOOK "THE POEMS OF SIR WALTER RALEGH: A HIS-
torical Edition."[1] An edition is historical if it proposes to represent texts
that existed at some time in the past. So I must hope my subtitle sounds
neither redundant nor pretentious. I chose it because the edition has, at least
by implication, more than one story to tell. The usual story, a chronological
succession of poems written by Ralegh, wouldn't require the subtitle. But
another story — the narrative of the formation of a canon by agencies apart
from the author — is the historical process represented in this edition. Another is a narrative of textual change, not the adventitious changes that (as we
sometimes say) corrupt texts through transmission, but a more active and
deliberate process of change, or of variability, or of alternative construction.
This, too, is represented in the edition — in fact the edition is conceived of
as a textual history. It offers a kind of a narrative of how, over some seventy
years, Ralegh's contemporaries and his immediate posterity constructed him as
a poet. You may expect — if only because the Renaissance English Text
Society wouldn't sponsor anything else — a critical edition, to be judged by
critical standards. But it does ask readers to adjust, at least in some respects,
their expectations of what the poems of Sir Walter Ralegh might turn out to

---

[1] *The Poems of Sir Walter Ralegh: A Historical Edition*, ed. Michael Rudick, MRTS
209 (Tempe, AZ: MRTS for RETS, 1999).

be, if the norm is what Agnes Latham offered in her second edition printed in 1951.[2] We have now more poems and more documentation of Ralegh's poetry than were available to her, and most have thought that we needed more precision in editorial principles and more information on textual transmission than she chose to offer. I hope to have met the needs both of being up to date and of giving the fullest consideration to the editorial question. But the latter consideration has led me to what I will claim to be a reconception of what to present as Ralegh's poems. What lies behind this is my main topic.

Because I must be brief, I ask your indulgence of my frequent statement of certain claims without offering full arguments for them. I hope that you'll be able to find the evidence for them in the printed book.

The first problem is common knowledge among students of Ralegh: the uncertainty, or the disputed status, of his canon (both prose and verse). We have no extant authorized collection of his poems — I mean "authorized" in the received sense: texts of poems organized and prepared for readers' use more or less directly by the poet. Therefore, the canon and its texts must be recovered piecemeal, a process begun by William Oldys and Thomas Birch in the eighteenth century,[3] which took some peculiar turns in the early nineteenth, rectified by John Hannah later in that century,[4] and brought to the current state of knowledge by, principally, Latham and Pierre Lefranc in the twentieth century.[5] Authorized Ralegh texts are few: four commendatory poems for his friends' books and the verse translations of Latin poetry in *The History of the World*. These he published. Manuscript copies of three versions of a verse petition to Queen Anne, their dates uncertain, may lie at not too

---

[2] *The Poems of Sir Walter Ralegh*, ed. Agnes M. C. Latham (Cambridge, MA: Harvard Univ. Press, 1951; repr. 1962).

[3] William Oldys, "The Life of Sir Walter Raleigh," in *The History of the World . . . The Eleventh Edition* (London, 1736; repr. separately in 1740 and in Vol. 1 of Ralegh's *Works* [Oxford: Oxford Univ. Press, 1829]); Thomas Birch, *The Works of Sir Walter Ralegh, Kt.* (London, 1751).

[4] *Poems by Sir Henry Wotton, Sir Walter Raleigh, and Others*, ed. John Hannah (London: W. Pickering, 1845); *The Courtly Poets from Raleigh to Montrose*, ed. John Hannah (London: Bell & Daldy, 1870; repr. as *The Poems of Sir Walter Raleigh, Collected and Authenticated, with those of Sir Henry Wotton, and Other Courtly Poets from 1540 to 1640* [London: G. Bell & Sons, 1875; repr. 1891; reissued 1892]).

[5] Pierre Lefranc, *Sir Walter Ralegh écrivain* (Paris: Armand Colin, 1968), and his most important verse discovery, "Une nouvelle version de la 'Petition to Queen Anne' de Sir Walter Ralegh," *Annales de la faculté des lettres et sciences humaines de Nice* 34 (1978): 57–67. The most complete inventory of poems attributed to Ralegh is in Peter Beal, *Index of English Literary Manuscripts*, vols. 1 and 2 (London and New York: Mansell, Bowker, 1980–93).

far a remove from authorized copies, though this is complicated. And we have the nearly 600 lines of five "Cynthia" poems in Ralegh's own hand. But these are a special case: authorial they are, but are they authorized? What state of authorial finish the holographs represent remains speculative. Therefore, even in these instances of our being quite securely in proximity to the author, we can sometimes have doubts about what we're dealing with.

Beyond these, there are forty-seven poems — ignore for the time being how we will define a discrete poem — forty-seven poems known to carry attributions to Ralegh from the 1580s through about 1660. Here the disputes begin, and there's by now much secondary literature on the acceptability or unacceptability of many of these attributions. They come from non-authorial sources, almost all from verse miscellanies and comparable documents, often chronologically removed from Ralegh's lifetime. Twenty-three of these attributions (including some old Ralegh favorites like "The Pilgrimage") are in fact posthumous, recorded only in sources well after 1618, and in a number of these cases, the poems themselves, irrespective of attribution, are unknown before 1625. The reliability of miscellany attributions is a subject of debate. Compilers of printed anthologies are said to have a penchant for the loose use of names to conjure with, and manuscript miscellany collectors surely saw more value in a poem attributed to a notable than in the same poem by Anonymous. This can make documentary ascription seem capricious, but I think this is a mistake. Miscellany ascription may make more sense if we ask for the reason that lies behind the ascription. In recent years, some scholars have argued for more confidence in the reliability, both attributional and textual, of manuscript miscellanies; studies by Mary Hobbs and Henry Woudhuysen are examples, the former of collections from the 1630s and 1640s, the latter of, especially, two Elizabethan miscellanies — both categories important as sources of Ralegh ascriptions.[6] Few students of Ralegh, at least among those not content to accept the Latham canon uncritically, have been altogether confident to accept miscellany attributions without some other evidence to support them, usually internal evidence, whether biographical asso-

---

[6] Mary Hobbs, *Early Seventeenth-Century Verse Miscellany Manuscripts* (Aldershot: Ashgate, 1992); H. R. Woudhuysen, *Sir Philip Sidney and the Circulation of Manuscripts 1558–1640* (Oxford: Clarendon Press, 1996). Other valuable studies of verse miscellanies are Harold Love, *Scribal Publication in Seventeenth-Century England* (Oxford: Clarendon Press, 1993), and Arthur F. Marotti, *Manuscript, Print, and the English Renaissance Lyric* (Ithaca and London: Cornell Univ. Press, 1995). Steven W. May, *The Elizabethan Courtier Poets: The Poems and their Contexts* (Columbia, MO: Univ. of Missouri Press, 1991) draws much of its content from May's study of the extant Elizabethan miscellanies.

ciation or poetic manner. What I've found is a tendency to prefer the presumed internal evidence as the sole test of any miscellany's reliability, with this
result: a commentator can use or refuse documentary evidence as taste dic-
tates. I've also found a tendency toward circularity in the use of internal evidence: a set of characteristics is drawn from a body of verse no more certain
of attribution than the specific poem whose characteristics are under scrutiny.

To sum up a circumspect examination of the question of the canon: beyond the authorized poems, the holographs, and a none-too-firm consensus
on the canonicity of some other poems, disagreement can lead to agnosticism
on the one hand, or to an irreducible tendentiousness on the other. A "definitive" settlement of the canon — hence a "definitive" edition of Ralegh's
poems — seems impossible unless the disputants can agree to redefine "definitive" expectations. Whether they will or won't agree to do so remains to be
seen, but I ask consideration of my effort toward that redefinition, which is
based upon this question: what do the extant documents in fact allow us to
conclude about the Ralegh canon and the texts of that canon? I've chosen to
answer it in terms of material history, believing that the documentary context
— that is, the material context — of these poems offers a kind of textual
knowledge different from what we are accustomed to having in the case of
differently circumstanced poets. We don't deal with a scribal tradition that
might allow a stemmatic solution; this is not a genealogical problem. Neither
is it — at least not very often is it — a biographical problem. It is a problem
of the historical contexts of various kinds of non-authorial documents. Each
category, in some cases each specific document, permits a certain kind of inference, and these need to be differentiated when their historical reason for
being is appreciated. That done, what we find is that, while we are always in
touch with the name Walter Ralegh, we are not very often in touch with an
author Ralegh.

We owe our texts and our attributions to the impulses of collection, not
to authorial will and not to the institution of scribal transmission. This is not
to say that collection is a whimsical or capricious phenomenon. We're beginning to learn more about this aspect of literary culture in the Renaissance, and
we can venture a good many generalizations about the aims and habits of
those who collected poems and wrote them into manuscript miscellanies. The
difference in aim between scribal traditions and collections needs to be appreciated. This is too large a subject to be dealt with briefly, but I can outline the
principal feature of difference. When a poem's status is that of what we'd
today call a collector's item, its connection with an originary authorial moment, if not altogether effaced, is very much attenuated. Think of any antique
object — work of art or household utensil — that's put behind glass in a museum's collection or placed within an ensemble of objects in a home, and you

have something of the idea. The shape and use of the item are at the will of its new possessor; it's been removed from its original context of creation and use and adapted to a new context. So with poems. The collectors entitle themselves to a kind of proprietorship over the texts. Their appropriation enables, perhaps constitutes, their recontextualization. Something — the moment of authorial origination — is lost, but something is also gained: a new use, in some sense a new identity for the poem.

For the textual criticism of Ralegh, the consequence is a rather more dispersed notion of textual authority, if the word "authority" is at all proper to a situation in which an author plays no determinative role. Metaphors of chain and tree are appropriate to scribal traditions, which assume determinate linkage and continuity. They fail in this case, where discontinuity is the more frequent rule. We can admit that some relation of continuity, however attenuated, lies behind the scattered and variant texts. But that relationship, I would argue, can't be recovered, given the kinds of documents we have. I would further argue that there is indeed some sense of new creation involved in a collector's appropriating a poem. This is what creates the discontinuity in textual forms, and the discontinuity is worth paying attention to, both as a part of literary history and as a crucial determinant of the Ralegh canon and texts.

Therefore, the initiating questions of traditional canon and textual study may not always be the appropriate ones. Conventionally, we want to know which works and which words are authentic, that is, ascribable to the author's hand, and reciprocally, what methods and kinds of evidence are admissible in arguments to claim or disclaim authenticity. But these questions necessarily direct themselves to a poem's moment of origin, a moment in the poet's biography, and they entail a belief in the poem as a revelation of its author — an important assumption in Ralegh's case, because the biographical interest has more often than not motivated, even determined, the study of the poems. However, the biographical interest can be satisfied only by those relatively few poems whose texts are authorized or close to authorial, while all the rest come to us far removed, and deeply and variously altered, from their biographical moments of origin. This removal makes us in so many cases unsure even to whose biography the poems may once have been attached. In seeking to understand the conditions of sixteenth- and seventeenth-century miscellany collection, we find that the problem of canon and the problem of text are not separate questions to be dealt with in sequence, but are rather reciprocal within a single configuration.

My editorial decision — my navigation through tendentiousness and agnosticism — has been to try to let this phenomenon speak for itself. It's not inaccurate to call miscellany collection an institution. Especially in the second quarter of the seventeenth century, this institution created for itself a remarkably consistent picture of Ralegh as a poet, not, or at least not often, drawn from the life, but, in keeping with an agenda I think we can specify, a picture that is as close as we are likely to get to Ralegh the poet. It is in any case no more distortive a picture than that given by the nineteenth or the twentieth centuries. But in all these epochs, modern and early modern, we deal with a Ralegh much more socially constructed than we've wished to recognize. Pursue the history of editing Ralegh's poetry, from William Oldys to Agnes Latham or Walter Oakeshott, and you find the leitmotif to have been the problem of how to cope with loss.[7] A meager canon of reliably authenticated poems is somehow not a satisfactory representation of a major English hero. The nineteenth century, before Hannah's editions, had its way of redressing the presumed loss, and the twentieth has had its way. One way or another, more had to be found. If Hannah discredited his predecessors' additions to what could be documented, and thereby deprived the 1829 Oxford edition's canon of much of its bulk, then twentieth-century students would have to compensate for the leanness of Latham's first edition of 1929. This accounts for why so many of the poems she printed in the second edition are included on very thin documentary grounds, or no documentary grounds at all. The seventeenth century had its own motives for its construction of the Ralegh canon, but this wasn't one of compensating for an indeterminate body of work believed to have been lost. It was, instead, a wish to appropriate Ralegh's name and voice to sponsor its understanding of its own recent history. This is a process which, for prose works attributed to Ralegh, has been discussed in a recent book by Anna Beer.[8] My treatment of the poetry is in some ways complementary.

It's necessary to distinguish between the biographical canon and the historical canon. Beyond the authorial and the authenticable pieces, the former is and probably always will be subject to dispute. For the evidence on which to

---

[7] An example is Latham's remark, "[E]verything Ralegh did seems tainted by a curious impermanence . . . his poetry is lost" (*Poems*, xiv), but the symptom begins as early as Oldys's regret (in *Works*, 1: li–liii) for the loss of a sizable poem titled "Cynthia," inferred from Spenser's notices in *The Faerie Queene*. Thomas Warton, *The History of English Poetry* (London, 1781): 3: 438, is responsible for attributions to Ralegh of poems subscribed "Ignoto" in Elizabethan and Jacobean printed miscellanies, all of which were gathered in the 1829 *Works*. Walter Oakeshott, *The Queen and the Poet* (London: Faber & Faber, 1961), renewed a tendency toward speculative attributions.

[8] Anna R. Beer, *Sir Walter Ralegh and His Readers in the Seventeenth Century: Speaking to the People* (London and New York: Macmillan, 1997), esp. chaps. 4–6.

conduct the dispute, see *Poems* (ed. Rudick, xiii–lxxiv, 206–11). But the historical canon is determinate: fifty-nine poems, fourteen of them in variant versions, which come to us with Ralegh's name in one or more documents from 1576 through about 1660. This is, then, something of a hybrid: an author-centered edition in that it prints what can securely attributed to Ralegh and presents evidence for the likelihood of other attributions which aren't as secure; but also a historical edition (in some sense itself a miscellany) in that it includes all that comprises the canon socially constructed through the processes of collection and miscellany compilation. But it isn't divided into a section of authentic or probably authentic poems to begin, and then a section of apocrypha appended. My aim has been to place in the foreground the material history of these texts, and I've arranged them in groups determined by the kinds of documents that carry them, and arranged these groups in a rough chronological order. First is an Elizabethan canon in three categories: poems attributed to Ralegh in Elizabethan printed books, then poems attributed to him in Elizabethan manuscripts, then the "Cynthia" holograph poems. After that is a group of poems, all but one in manuscript, attributed to him between King James's accession and his own death in 1618, followed by the verse translations from *The History of the World*. Last are the twenty-three posthumous attributions, almost all from manuscript miscellanies of the 1630s and 1640s. In this last category, I try to group poems according to the phase of Ralegh's life or Ralegh's character to which their attributors imagined them to relate.

This is, as I've said, meant to place in the foreground a material textual history, an edition made perforce almost entirely from the point of view of reception rather than from the point of view of authorial intention. Yet that reception is hardly passive, because miscellany collection can often show us, as I've suggested, a creative face, an active engagement with texts quite different from that of scribal traditions. Scribes may fail to reproduce their copy, and they may take initiatives to alter it. But their assignment precludes what is of the essence in collection; they may not do what collectors could and did do: appropriate the texts to their own uses and dispositions. That fact has determined how I have presented the texts.

I made the point earlier that collection disperses authority. A collector's putative fidelity to an authorial original is only one possibility among several to be reckoned with in the assessment of a miscellany text, and fidelity to an original can be in any case irrelevant in a situation where poems as collector's items float free of their origins. Consequently, the search for a "true original copy" may be impertinent, and the effort to determine a collected text's authority rests not necessarily on the pattern of its variation from other extant copies, especially when all are themselves collected copies. The textual criticism of poems extant only in miscellanies isn't a new subject. Whether to

practise recension in order to derive a stemma or to practise controlled eclec-
ticism has been debated, but this debate is one over method; it ignores the
source of the problem, which is not methodological, but instead — may we
say? — ontological. I don't want to exaggerate here, because in textual matters
all generalization may be overgeneralization. Copyists, even collectors as copyists, however they conceive their task, can be careless, can make bad guesses,
can sometimes write down nonsense. Collation of variant texts may sometimes
enable judgment of readings likelier or less likely to be archetypal or authorial.
And sometimes miscellany texts fall into categories of relation based on shared
textual features, enabling rough genealogical inferences. But to govern judg-
ments by the concepts of authority or originality or descent is to substitute ab-
straction for material history. The historical modality of these texts is to exist
independently of authority and originality as traditionally conceived. Hence
my decision to reject what I would argue in this case to be an unhistorical
procedure, the construction of stemmata to arrive at something close to "true
original copies."

Therefore, the texts in this edition are constructed neither through recension nor through selection of variant readings from several copies. Each text
printed represents a copy preserved in some historical source, with a necessary
minimum of alterations in the interests of accessibility. That was the one hard
and fast rule for editorial procedure that I induced. Beyond that, because the
documentary contexts are diverse, each poem is a given case. Choice of copy-
texts and what to include in the apparatus depended on several factors, such
as the certainty or probability of Ralegh's authorship, the different forms a
poem may have assumed through its circulation, and the nature and number
of the sources that carry the poem in different forms. Several poems in the
historical canon are printed in more than one version, because they circulated
in fairly distinct forms, which may differ in content and structure, or in quite
distinct verbal texture. I believe these variant versions are best understood as
alternatives, not as a succession of genealogically linked developments of a
text, though it's sometimes possible to infer the sequence of a poem's reworkings. And sometimes only one of two or three discrete materializations of a
poem is connected with Ralegh. The phenomenon of plural versions is, of
course, not a new recognition, but coming to terms with its being of the essence of miscellany circulation seems to me important. French critics of trou-
badour and trouvère lyric did so some time ago, and we might adopt their
term, *mouvance*, after Paul Zumthor.[9] Plurality inheres even in those poems
whose copies don't vary enough to count as discrete versions, and I have

---

[9] P. Zumthor, *Essai de poétique médiévale* (Paris: Éditions du Seuil, 1972), 64–73.

organized the critical apparatus to represent this. Variants included are not meant to be a record of "corruption," nor are they to be used to infer a genealogy of textual states. Since a copy-text from a miscellany represents one collector's appropriation of the poem, the variants in the apparatus were chosen to illustrate those that make other appropriations of it distinct; therefore, I include — perhaps risking a charge of idiosyncrasy — variants which make a difference to sense or texture, and which give some indication of a copy's characteristics. Because, in these conditions of circulation, originality is a questionable concept, so, too, is the concept of "corruption." Certainly, copyists made mistakes of the kinds copyists are prone to, but mistakes of that kind are of no interest. I've found that miscellany texts rarely fail to make sense, and so virtually all marked variation not owing to the merest carelessness may be a clue to how some copyist engaged the text in the process of appropriating it. It's surely just when members of our guild complain that the painstakingly prepared critical apparatus is that part of the edition least likely to be read by its users. The one inducement I can offer is that mine is not an inventory of rejected readings. The apparatus invites the reader to consider alternatives to the copy-text, because these have their place in a material history that no single copy can represent adequately.

My last substantive point has to do with what isn't in this edition, specifically all those poems attributed to Ralegh in the last three hundred years which are unconnected with his name before 1660. This, I expect, is a controversial choice, because there are scholars who credit all, or at least some, of the more recent conjectural attributions, a string of consecutive poems in the Elizabethan anthology *The Phoenix Nest*, proposed by Hoyt Hudson in the 1930s and printed by Latham in her second edition.[10] Some time ago, I published my own argument explaining why these attributions shouldn't be credited.[11] The decision to omit them was based partially on that argument; I haven't changed my mind, even if I recognize the debate can go on. But I based the decision also on my wish to be consistent in making a historical edition. The historical period of choice is the 1570s through the 1650s. The Hudson conjectures didn't become history until our own century, and so are not part of the stories this edition proposes to tell. All conjectures of the eighteenth, nineteenth, and twentieth centuries are, I would argue, efforts to fashion a Ralegh who could, as a poet, live up to some confected image of him in the other departments of his life. This is no less true of the seventeenth century, though, as I've tried

---

[10] H. Hudson, review of Latham's first edition, *MLN* 45 (1930): 200–2, and Hudson, "Notes on the Ralegh Canon," *MLN* 46 (1931): 386–89.

[11] M. Rudick, "The 'Ralegh Group' in *The Phoenix Nest*," *SB* 24 (1971): 131–37.

to suggest, the motives behind the fashioning were different in the earlier epoch. I don't want to revise Stephen Greenblatt's account of Ralegh as a life-long *self-fashioner*.[12] But uncritical acceptance of the Latham canon, including, but not limited to, the Hudson conjectures, has had this effect: biographical critics haven't been able to discriminate between Ralegh's self-fashionings and the fashionings of him by other agencies, some at work in the earlier period, some in the later.

In all, then, my aim has been to present a material history of canon and texts, based upon what survives and limited to what the extant documentation, especially the kind of documentation, allows us to do. I found myself trying to follow Harold Love's recommendation to present texts and apparatus "as a means of interrogating the transmissional history," giving the "story" of a text's various contextualizations — although I don't believe any edition can give the whole story.[13] But I would say that this has not been a theoretical project in the sense of its illustrating a particular doctrine or approach to textual criticism. The result has been enabled by, and perhaps will find what acceptance it does within, the anti-Romantic or anti-idealist theoretical climate pioneered by McGann's *Critique* of 1983 and McKenzie's Panizzi Lectures of 1985.[14] These proposed a socially conditioned concept of textual authority and the historical reception of texts as factors to be reckoned with in the making of editions. Yet what I've done with Ralegh can't serve as a general model for editorial approach. Risking the charge of naïveté, I prefer to think that the history has determined the approach rather than vice versa. In the first place, we needn't believe that all authors' canons are as socially constructed as Ralegh's is, or that authorial texts are always as past hoping for as they are even for many poems in the biographical Ralegh canon. In the second place, historical editing can't, by the nature of its project, conform to a single model; the one chosen has to depend on the nature of the historical sources, and if these differ, then different models must coexist within one edition. The test of this edition, so I would think, is not its theoretical contribution, but rather what use is made of it — what kinds of historical understanding, what critical or interpretive possibilities are opened or provoked by the edition's presentation of the poems in their documentary contexts within the chosen historical period.

---

[12] S. Greenblatt, *Sir Walter Ralegh: The Renaissance Man and His Roles* (New Haven and London: Yale Univ. Press, 1973).

[13] Love, *Scribal Publication*, 350.

[14] Jerome McGann, *A Critique of Modern Textual Criticism* (Chicago: Univ. of Chicago Press, 1983); D. F. McKenzie, *Bibliography and the Sociology of Texts* (London: British Library, 1986; repr. Cambridge: Cambridge Univ. Press, 1999).

A Response to Michael Rudick

ARTHUR F. MAROTTI

T HIS A WONDERFUL TIME FOR TEXTUAL CRITICISM AND AN OPPOR-
tunity for textual critics to reach an interested audience far beyond the
old-fashioned disciplinary boundaries. We are aware of the possibilities
of both editing and unediting the Renaissance.[1] Late manuscript culture's per-
sistence through the first two and one-half centuries of the Gutenberg era has
left us fascinating documentary remains that scholars have begun to look at
afresh for evidence of literary practices different from those associated with
developed print culture. Authors and authorial intention have been decentered
from their position in the textual field. Thus Michael Rudick's historical edition of Ralegh is both timely and necessary.

When I was working on my book on the manuscript and print transmission of lyric poetry in the English Renaissance,[2] I used Rudick's University
of Chicago dissertation-edition of Ralegh's poetry[3] — not only because it was
a better critical edition of the verse than Agnes Latham's,[4] but also because it
laid bare more of the manuscript sources for Ralegh's verse and for the larger
body of poetry associated with his name. Rudick did this work under the

---

[1] See, for example, Leah S. Marcus, *Unediting the Renaissance: Shakespeare, Marlowe, Milton* (London and New York: Routledge, 1996).

[2] A. F. Marotti, *Manuscript, Print, and the English Renaissance Lyric* (Ithaca and London: Cornell Univ. Press, 1995).

[3] Michael Rudick, "The Poems of Sir Walter Ralegh, An Edition" (Ph.D. diss., University of Chicago, 1970).

[4] *The Poems of Sir Walter Ralegh*, ed. Agnes M. C. Latham (Cambridge, MA: Harvard Univ. Press, 1951).

magisterial direction of William Ringler, adhering to traditional methods of constructing a critical edition. It was clear to me, however, that the scientific means for authenticating authorship and settling on a certain canon of undisputed poems by Ralegh so reduced the field of texts associated with the Ralegh name that the effect was, in fact, to cut off the Ralegh canon from the very historical contingency that defined Ralegh as an author in the decades following his death and in the more modern reconstructions of the Raleghan texts. But the authentic Raleghan canon, in effect, never existed, or, at the least, existed only for a very restricted coterie readership. Outside of this sphere, historically specific processes worked to construct a succession of literary Raleghs and the literary history of Raleghan texts. Within a chronology running from the 1570s through the 1650s, Rudick has edited, through "a material history of canon and texts," the "historical Ralegh," that is, the one constructed by the circulation of texts associated with Ralegh's name and by the co-creative participation of reader–scribes who appropriated and modified the Raleghan texts they collected. This kind of author-figure is immanent, rather than transcendent. The traditional way of editing a poet according to the kind of textual idealism prevalent in twentieth-century textual scholarship has been to edit only poems we can see as "authentic," but also, perhaps, those "probably" and "possibly" by that author, filtering out as "corruptions" those non-authorial changes and misattributed pieces that entered into the textual history of his or her works in the media of manuscript and print. Such "author-centered" editing is, of course, both necessary and valuable, but it tends to suppress the more varied textual history of works associated with a particular author, thus losing touch with the actual socio-literary history of that larger body of work. Mainly because Rudick is working with a poet with whose name a very large number of texts by other writers and revisers were associated during his lifetime and in the fifty years after his death, he has wisely decided to edit "Ralegh" as a socially constructed entity, only part of which is constituted by the actual poems we are certain that Sir Walter Ralegh wrote. The historical presence and impact of this "Ralegh" are visible in his historical edition.

   Rejecting the traditional textual method of stemmatics as "unhistorical," Rudick "unedits" Ralegh in presenting each of the poems in his edition as a particular text found in a single source, rather than constructing an "ideal" or corruption-free text by means of genealogical detective work. Thus, as he says, he presents variant versions of poems as alternatives, valuable because they each circulated as historically important textual units. Furthermore, he invites those who would use the edition to make use of the textual apparatus to discern interestingly modified and supplemented versions of poems along the lines of their transmission histories. While acknowledging that scribes can make simple mistakes, Rudick does not dismiss as textual "corruptions," but values as socio-literary evidence, some of those changes introduced by people other than the original author.

People apparently could not resist altering and supplementing Raleghan texts. The classic example of this phenomenon is found in the transmission history of a poem such as "Farewell falce love, thou oracle of lies." As I have already noted elsewhere,[5] this text survives in eighteen-, twenty-four-, and thirty-line versions, the shortest surviving in only one manuscript, whereas the longest appeared, some thirteen years after Ralegh's death, in a printed book, Thomas Deloney's *Garland of Good Will* (1631), and it was reproduced later in the 1660 printed collection, *Le Prince d'Amour* (1660). If the 18-line version of the poem is authentically Ralegh's, then both the 24- and 30-line versions (the former of which also appeared in a printed book) were probably the product of other pens down the line of manuscript transmission before they were taken up for print publication. Although such literary appropriation doesn't suit the normal workings of a highly developed print culture, in which the roles of literary producer and literary receiver are more sharply separated, the phenomenon is characteristic of manuscript culture.

Of course, as Anna Beer's recent book on Ralegh's prose also demonstrates,[6] there were sometimes strong political motives for modifying and supplementing Raleghan texts as well as for taking texts composed by other authors and ascribing them to Ralegh. Especially from the Jacobean era through that of the Civil Wars and Interregnum, Ralegh's identity as a politically oppositional figure was developed in English culture, determining not only how his works were read, but also which works were associated with his name. He is a kind of limit case for the politics of textuality.

Since Ralegh is virtually the last major poet of the early modern period to be edited according to the standards of modern textual scholarship, I expect Rudick's work to have a great impact on the field and to become the new standard edition of Ralegh. But, even more importantly, I expect it to get a lot of positive attention as a more socially-based edition. I hope it leads other editors and specialists in the field to appreciate his kind of historical, socio-centric editing. As he is the first to admit, this approach works better for some authors than for others — and Ralegh is an obvious choice for such treatment. But one could imagine trying the method on a poet such as John

---

[5] Marotti, *Manuscript, Print,* 145–46.

[6] Anna Beer, *Sir Walter Ralegh and His Readers in the Seventeenth-Century: Speaking to the People* (Basingstoke, Hampshire, and London: Macmillan, and New York: St. Martin's Press, 1997).

Donne — whose verse is being presented in the ongoing Variorum edition[7] in a way that lays bare the extraordinarily rich documentary history of the texts, but whose manuscript evidence is still, for the most part, used in a textually idealistic way. The documentary mess of the Raleghan texts invited the change of perspective Rudick adopted after his dissertation-edition of Ralegh. But other editors editing other authors could well profit from such a reconceptualization of their enterprise.

---

[7] *The Variorium Edition of the Poetry of John Donne*, under the general editorship of Gary A. Stringer, has already yielded two volumes: Volume 6, *The Anniversaries and the Epicedes and Obsequies* (Bloomington and Indianapolis: Indiana Univ. Press, 1995), and Volume 8: *The Epigrams, Epithalamions, Epitaphs, Inscriptions, and Miscellaneous Poems* (Bloomington and Indianapolis: Indiana Univ. Press, 1995).

The Ethics of
Post-Mortem Editing

SUZANNE GOSSETT

WHEN JOSEPHINE ROBERTS AND MARY BETH ROSE APPLIED FOR an NEH grant in 1988 to support Roberts's proposed edition of Lady Mary Wroth's *Urania*, they promised the funding agency that there would be two "vetters" on the project, Janel Mueller of the University of Chicago and myself.[1] The precise language describing our role was that we would "serve as consultants to Professor Roberts about editorial problems and procedures for the duration of the project"; further, we were to "examine the final text of the holograph manuscript and collaborate on the introductions." We were pleased to be involved. We had a double commitment and connection, both to the dissemination of this important early modern text by a woman and to the Renaissance English Text Society, which was prepared to devote resources of time, money, and scholarly expertise to publishing the edition.

In the next few years we would see Jo during her trips to Chicago and

---

[1] This paper was delivered at the RETS session of the 33rd International Conference on Medieval Studies in Kalamazoo, Michigan, in April 1998, while *The Second Part of the Countess of Montgomery's Urania* was being prepared. A later version, incorporating further thoughts about, and complications of, the project and called "The Ethics of Post-Mortem Editing, or, What Constitutes Collaboration?" was delivered at the Society for Textual Scholarship in New York City in April, 1999.

discuss problems surfacing as work proceeded. These varied, of course, depending upon whether she was working on the printed volume of 1621 or, later, on the unique holograph continuation housed in the Newberry Library.[2] Some of our duties for the first volume included determining editorial procedures, reading sample notes, and discussing what needed to go into the introduction. For the manuscript volume Jo required a different kind of assistance: Lady Mary's hand is very difficult; certain parts of the manuscript have suffered extensive bleed-through, making it even harder to decipher; and Lady Mary's concept of punctuation was not ours. We worked with Jo on establishing the boundaries of intervention for a text she wished to publish in old spelling but with modernized punctuation. We did not feel that we were able or expected to check every letter of the text, and Speed Hill suggested we contact the Center for Scholarly Editions for their guidelines in similar cases. The CSE, it turns out, mandates that ten percent of a manuscript be checked letter for letter; Janel and I agreed that *each* of us would check ten percent, and we would in addition both attempt to assist Jo with the most badly damaged pages, those presenting the greatest difficulty. Therefore, something between twenty and twenty-five percent of the manuscript transcription would have a final, letter-by-letter, check. We felt good about our level of participation, and Jo also seemed satisfied with the combination of help and simple admiration that we were able to offer.

All of that changed in August of 1996 when Jo was killed. Suddenly the phrase about "the duration of the project" seemed uncannily prescient. Yet all the reasons why a *Urania* edition was called for still obtained, and there was added a strong desire to honor Jo's memory by completing volume two.[3] After all, the 1995 edition of the 1621 printed volume — copies of which do exist in rare book rooms in the United States and in England — had originally been an afterthought to the original, more urgent proposal to edit the text of the otherwise unavailable Newberry manuscript. Nevertheless, it took a while for the situation to sink in. Not only was Jo gone, but the RETS Council was making it clear that they considered Janel and me the obvious people to change roles, from vetters to joint editors. It is our experiences in the last year and a half that I would like to talk about today.

---

[2] *The First Part of the Countess of Montgomery's Urania*, by Lady Mary Wroth, ed. Josephine A. Roberts, was published as MRTS 140 by Medieval and Renaissance Texts and Studies, Binghamton, NY, for the Renaissance English Text Society in 1995.

[3] See now *The Second Part of the Countess of Montgomery's Urania*, by Lady Mary Wroth, ed. Josephine A. Roberts and completed by Suzanne Gossett and Janel Mueller, MRTS 211 (Tempe, AZ: MRTS for RETS, 1999).

The problems we faced were both personal and professional (see now *Second Part*, xi–xiv). One of the first was dealing with the family, so suddenly bereft of wife and mother. Understandably enough, it took quite a while — almost a year — for Jim Gaines, Jo's husband, to sort through and gather together the materials she had left. When these arrived, they included boxes of notes, paper files, and a disk containing a series of *Urania* files from Jo's hard drive. The paper materials were of varying usefulness; they ranged from a packet from the paleography seminar that Jo had attended at the Folger, to historical information about locations in London and in the geographical world of the *Urania*, to the actual beta radiography photographs of the watermarks in the Newberry manuscript. I'll talk about the disk in a moment. Included also was a projected table of contents that we could use as a finding list. It appeared that Jo had completed the text, the commentary notes, and the lists of substantive and non-substantive variants. She had *not* drafted the textual introduction; the critical introduction, which she anticipated dividing into five sections; or the indices, of which she proposed four: characters in part two, places in part two, first lines of poems in part two, and an index of subjects in parts one *and* two.

It fell to me to print out the diskfiles in which Jo had kept her work. As I did so, my heart sank a little. The pages of text were in WordPerfect, which I use, and everything seemed fine there. But as soon as I began to print out the annotations and textual notes, I noticed that their numbering increasingly diverged from the numbering on the pages of text. It appeared to me — it still appears to me — that some of these files must have been penultimate rather than the very last version on which Jo worked. And I suspect that it is files of the text itself which are penultimate, because in several cases Jo had a textual note which did not correlate to the version of the text that we were sent. For example, at one point (1.4) she says she has changed "paire, all" to "paine. All," but the text we received still reads "paire"; and at another point (321.6) her note indicates she has changed "the" to "then," but the text still reads "the." But we were loath to bother Jim again, and, given all the searching he had done, we suspected that later versions simply didn't exist. Thus, we felt we had no choice but to use what we had.

The presence of the discrepancy, however, sent us back to the Newberry, to understand the exact nature and status of the text we had received. Busily I began to compare Jo's pages to the manuscript. It was when I found an unquestionable error — the omission of a word — that I began to think structurally about the situation we were in. Compare the position of a general editor dealing with an individual editor. The individual editor — say Suzanne Gossett — sends in her proposed text, say of a Middleton play called *A Fair Quarrel*. The general editor — say Gary Taylor — reads it and raises concerns of varying kinds, from issues affecting the wording of the lines to the nature, length, or scope of the introduction or notes. The individual editor responds in a variety of appropriate ways, perhaps accepting textual corrections, arguing for her own wishes and desires regarding the introduction, and adjusting the notes to bring them in line with an editorial house style. The manuscript goes back and forth a few times, and, when the general editor is satisfied, it is published. There is no ethical difficulty, because both parties understand and accept their roles.

But what is the position of the replacement for an individual editor who is no longer present to explain her work and defend her decisions where more than one approach might be possible? How do we balance our respect for Josephine Roberts's work and her enormous knowledge of Lady Mary Wroth and the *Urania* text, with or against our concern for future audiences and our desire to uphold our own scholarly standards? What shall we do when we find errors? When we disagree about matters of style? Must we adhere to the proposed sections of the critical introduction, several of which have rather cryptic titles?

Faced by an impending RETS Council meeting in December 1997, Janel Mueller and I conferred about the proposed contents of the second volume. Neither of us, I should point out, is a Wroth scholar: normally I do not even work on prose or on women's writing, and Janel, who does, was busy completing an edition of the works of Queen Elizabeth with Mary Beth Rose and Leah Marcus. I had a moment of great relief when Janel firmly announced, first to me and then to the Council, that we would not write a critical introduction, certainly not the one that Jo foresaw. With typical intellectual clarity Janel pointed out that while editions may last seventy-five or a hundred years, critical introductions tend to be outdated within their own decade; without Jo's knowledge of Wroth and the *Urania*, we do not want to enshrine our analysis in the standard edition. This decision, once made, allowed us to reconsider, and distinguish between, the sections Jo proposed. Three we immediately dismissed: "The Empires of the East and West," "Baynard's Castle," and "Music." One and three presumably were to be Jo's analysis of the thematic or historical importance of these elements of the romance; we can't know what she had in mind, although intimations are to be found in her introduction to the 1995 edition of volume one. Baynard's Castle was the Herberts' London home; a 1640 letter to Wroth from George Manners, seventh Earl of Rutland, in which he refers to "a manuscript you shewed me in your study att Banerds Castell" has been interpreted by Gary Waller to suggest that at least part of the *Urania* was written there.[4] But the building has been

---

[4] *The Poems of Lady Mary Wroth*, ed. Josephine A. Roberts (Baton Rouge: Louisiana State Univ. Press, 1983), 29; Gary Waller, *The Sidney Family Romance: Mary Wroth,*

destroyed, and all the notes in the folder Jo kept on this topic lead to dead ends. Of the other two sections, "The Relationships of Parts One and Two" and "The Reception of the Work," Jo herself has written, in the introduction to *The Poems of Lady Mary Wroth*, the introduction to part one, and occasional essays, almost all that we will be able to recount. The relationship between the parts as well as the geopolitics of the text are now covered in *Second Part*, xxviii–xxxiv, "Altered Narrative Directions in Part Two." Reception, as well as Wroth's personal life and movements during the period of composition, figure in *Second Part*, xxiii–xxv, "History of the Manuscript."

On the other hand, we do feel obliged to provide a textual introduction. Because what we know as "the" *Urania* is textually so divided, and the printed volume differs so much from the manuscript, the introduction to the first volume will not sufficiently serve the reader's needs. This decision was made easier as it became obvious that in the current circumstances we must do what we had originally declined to do, that is, check the entire transcription letter by letter. Having found places where we do not agree with Jo's readings, we cannot in good conscience publish the text without going over it entirely. Furthermore, because the identifiers of textual notes — page and line numbers, in Jo's system — did not align with her text, we would have to go over almost every line in any case.

At this point someone — I think it may have been Arthur Kinney — had a wonderful idea. We have been very fortunate in our dealings with Medieval and Renaissance Texts and Studies, which was at SUNY Binghamton under Mario De Cesare when it published volume one, and is now at the Arizona State University under Bob Bjork. After some extremely cooperative discussion and negotiation, we sent Karen Lemiski, the production manager at MRTS, our disks, that is, copies of Jo's files. Dr. Lemiski converted them into the materials MRTS will use to publish the book and sent us back working — even beautiful — page proofs. On these proofs we made our corrections, and to these proofs, and their page and line numbers, we keyed the commentary, textual notes, and indices.

Ah, yes, indices. If you have used volume one, and if you don't have a photographic, super-capacious memory, you too have been grateful that the index of characters cheerfully reminds the reader that Antissius 1 is "son of the King of Romania 29, marries Lucenia, who bears a son, also named Antissius, 32–33, banished by command of his step-mother 51–53 ..." etc. We immediately decided that the indices of characters, places, and first lines are essential, and we were very fortunate in persuading a finishing graduate student

---

William Herbert, and the Early Modern Construction of Gender (Detroit: Wayne State Univ. Press, 1993), 128.

at Loyola to undertake this task. Micheline White, who was about to become an assistant professor at Carleton University in Ottawa, is an expert on Renaissance women's writings — you may read her article on Anne Lock in *ELR*[5] — and while indexing is partly mechanical, we were also glad to have Micheline's thoughtful consultation on the project. But we have regretfully decided that we will not, indeed cannot, undertake the comprehensive subject index to parts one and two that Jo promised in her acknowledgments to the first volume. Such an index, she said, would "allow scholars to locate references to Jacobean social practices, court culture, and women's concerns mentioned throughout Wroth's work" (ix). We do not feel qualified to second-guess just what practices, culture, and women's concerns might have figured here. (Indices of characters, places, and first lines of poems in Part Two are now found in *Second Part*, 555–76.)

Having decided on structure, we moved on to issues of style, both scholarly and critical (see now *Second Part*, xl–xliv). Jo had decided upon, and defended, an edition of part two in old spelling with modern punctuation. One major motivating factor was the reader's convenience and potential appreciation of Lady Mary's fiction: read without paragraphs, periods, or indications of direct address, the *Urania* seems much more remote and inaccessible than it in fact is. Yet this type of edition is a peculiar scholarly hybrid, a compromise not to everyone's liking. At the RETS Council, with Jo gone, some members chose to protest it anew; but they were rapidly squelched. No one is going to intervene on such a fundamental stylistic decision at this point; among other things it would mean entirely redoing all of Jo's text. And while I was a bit surprised to find conservative Josephine Roberts doing just what Gary Taylor does, formulating her own emendations in old spelling, it also seems best to leave alone the places where she had inserted "yett" rather than "yet."

One question before us now is just how much we *should* intervene in stylistic matters, or, to put it another way, just what constitutes style, what substance? For example: Jo's commentary notes were very lengthy, constituting little essays. To the line, "her librarie was ther, and the most sumptiuous in the world for a woeman to have," Jo had a two-page note about the collections of aristocratic Englishwomen, including those of Lady Frances Egerton, Countess of Bridgewater; Mary Sidney; Anne Clifford; and Susan Herbert, with a long additional paragraph about the women collectors mentioned in Sears Jayne's catalogue and further details from Julian Sharman's 1889 *The Library of Mary Queen of Scots*. I have served on RETS general editing commit-

---

[5] Micheline White, "Renaissance Englishwomen and Religious Translations: The Case of Anne Lock's *Of the Markes of the Children of God* (1590)," *ELR* 29 (1999): 375–400.

tees before, and the fundamental rule has been that if information is available in standard sources it need not be included in these notes. Thus, Jo's notes will almost certainly be cut, as they would have been had she been alive. In fact, I predict that they will be cut *less* than usual, out of a sense of deference and respect.

On the other hand, small matters of style will be left alone. It is all very well to say we will modernize the punctuation: there is more than one way to do that. Jo was — to my taste — fussy with commas, parentheses, and hyphens. Since I am currently preparing an edition of *Bartholomew Fair*, a play with an endless number of potentially hyphenated words, from pig woman to puppet play, I am sensitive on this issue and have learned from comparing English and American sources from the *OED* to Webster that there is no agreed-upon norm.[6] I personally would opt for Chicago style, which uses as few hyphens as possible; Jo chose a more heavily punctuated, to my ears more "old-fashioned" style.

The commas are an even bigger challenge, as there are three styles at issue: Lady Mary's, Jo Roberts's, and whatever norm the replacement editors adhere to. Here is an example: Lady Mary writes, of a silent traitor, "little could they get out of him, till seeing the tortures brought he thus spake." Roberts made it "little could they get out of him till, seeing the tortures brought, he thus spake." Is that better? She has clearly demarcated a participial phrase, but I think there is more logic to Lady Mary's division, which treats the separate phrase as a modifier of time and circumstance.

The textual notes have presented a particular problem. We received from Jo's husband a file of substantive emendations and two separate, overlapping files of non-substantive variants, with different numbers of notes and different numbers on the notes. Simple multiplication suggested to us that Jo may have changed her criteria for non-substantive notes because keeping up the rate of the fullest file, which went only through the first ten folios, she would have generated a 300-page file of non-substantive variants. As I began to work with these files I realized that the differences would be obscure to a reader, and the separation would hinder an understanding of the text's history. Let me give you a fairly simple example. As Pamphilia marries, the text will say, "she had three bride knights, when one had binn fitter to have bin the right bride groome." In the divided system, we learn from the *non-substantive* notes that both "have" and "right bride" are inserted; in the *substantive* notes we learn that after canceling both "the" and "her" Wroth settled on "the" before

<hr>

[6] Ben Jonson, *Bartholomew Fair*, ed. Suzanne Gossett (Manchester: Manchester Univ. Press, 2000).

"right." Here's a worse one: speaking of an angry man, the text we received reads, "his collerick voice was knowne better than his milde was, which made the booke seller past all patience" (290; 35–36). From two separate *non-sub-stantive* notes we learn that "better" and "which" were each inserted in a different ink. The substantive notes tell us that "knowne" is the editor's decision, replacing "better, <kn> knowne," and that "milde was" was followed by an ink blot that may have cancelled "was" in a different ink. The reader, in other words, would have to consult two different lists, both in the back of the volume, to work out the process of writing. Therefore, courtesy of the computer skills of Ian Mueller, we have combined the two lists, and when we have something like the last example, there will be combined notes, e.g. "knowne better" will have the note, "ed.; better <kn> knowne +better+ (ins. in different ink)," and since it is clear to us that "was" *was* cancelled, a second note will read "mild, which] milde <was> +which+ (ins. in different ink)."

You notice from that cancelled "was" that we are prepared to intervene, in effect to disagree with Jo. I have been working out in just which categories we will do this, as I consider that the most fundamental ethical issue. My first category is clear error, of which the simplest are those few places where we have found an omitted word. But when Jo read "siding" and I read "sieling," and the sentence describes how Parselius rested with "the Canopie of heaven for his lodging *blank*" I am willing to change her "siding" to "sieling." Different reading of a letter can change seeming to seeing, prince to prime, putting to pulling. A few similar errors — and Jo had very few — are inevitable in a text this long.

Another category is emendation. Several times Jo emended because, I believe, she misread the syntax. Here's an example: Jo proposed, "All (ore any thing) now hee had lost, her being [maried] but new gyves to his imprisoned soule . . ." I think that the comma goes after "her," and the sentence, without the addition of "married," makes sense reading, "All (or anything) now he had lost her, being but new gyves to his imprisoned soule. . . ." Since this would *restore* Lady Mary's original, I'll intervene. Similarly, Jo can emend for overcorrectness: she changed the phrase "none should come armed into his court, ore within ten mile of it" to ten *miles*, but the *OED* tells us that while the use of the singular form with a plural numeral is "now only vulgar or dialectical," previously it was permissible colloquially. Compare Henry ordering Falstaff "Not to come near our person by ten mile" (*2 H IV*, 5.5.65). Similarly, Jo changed "he that owed this place before" to "he that owned this place before," but as Onions tells us, owe = possess was the original meaning, and it is almost as frequent in Shakespeare as the modern meaning, with examples like *King John*, "That blood which ow'd the breadth of all this isle" (4.2.99) or *Othello*, "What a full fortune does the thicklips owe" (1.1.65).

Finally, we will have to decide what to do about ambiguity, places where there are choices even about inserted indications of direct discourse. Jo had a youth report that his braggart lord said, "I am an Erle, and one of the anti-entest, but" (hee aledging that to often and harshly) "a meaner lord," sayd hee, "had never read of an Erle in the creation." I think this should be " 'I am an earle, and one of the antientest,' but hee aledging that to often and harshly a meaner lord sayd he had never read of an Erle in the creation." And I haven't ever begun to tell you about our uncertainties about those assertions of "different ink," "different hand," "later." This summer we will be facing these issues, as well as the textual introduction, watermarks, and all the other sections necessary to complete the edition by our self-imposed deadline, October 1998.

§

Postscript: We, like Steven Greenblatt, began with the desire to speak with the dead. How could we otherwise know just what Jo had in mind? But without this possibility, we have had to proceed as best we could. Earlier this week, for the first time in about a year, there was a message for me to call Jim Gaines. I admit that I was very apprehensive: what could he want? what could he have found? And it turns out that he is moving house and indeed has found something. Apparently these are paper files of notes, perhaps for the introduction, which we will be happy to use if possible — I have not yet seen them. But as I picked up the phone I thought, if he has found the disks with the last version, we can't use them; we can't ask the press to regenerate the page proofs, we can't redo all the checking that's already been done. And I suppose what that means is that at this point the *Urania* project is in the hands of the living, and we must do what we can and what appears best to us, to RETS, to MRTS, while keeping in mind that the edition is still, definitively, Jo Roberts's.

Notes on *Editing*
The Verse Miscellany of
Constance Aston Fowler:
A Diplomatic Edition

DEBORAH ALDRICH-WATSON

TEN YEARS AGO, WHEN I SOMEWHAT NAIVELY UNDERTOOK A DIP-
matic edition of Constance Aston Fowler's verse miscellany, I had
never before done any kind of textual editing, and my experience
with sixteenth- and seventeenth-century manuscripts was limited to the week
I had so far spent at the Huntington Library. Hoping to find contemporary
marginal comments on seventeenth-century copies of John Donne's lyrics, I
was paging through every printed and manuscript miscellany and commonplace book the library owned. When I came upon HM904, I was immediately entranced. While it contained a number of echoes of Donne's poetry, what
captivated me was the obvious care someone had taken of the book, the effort
that had gone into neatly copying the poems and elaborately decorating many
of them with fancy borders, and the integrity of the manuscript: sections of
pages had been torn out here and there, but for the most part even my first
cursory reading showed that it had been very carefully written and preserved.
Although I could easily discern at least two distinct hands and although there
were sections of blank pages, it was unlike a number of other bound manuscripts I had looked at in that it did not seem fragmented. It did not appear to
have been passed on to miscellaneous writers, with different purposes for the
book. Furthermore, it contained only poetry (no recipes, prose observations,

or school exercises); it seemed to have been compiled during a specific period of time without later additions; and a woman had owned it and fashioned it.

This woman, Constance Aston Fowler, was the youngest daughter of Walter Aston, twice Spanish ambassador during the reigns of James I and Charles I. Between roughly 1634 and 1640 she copied poems by family members and by poets contemporaneous with and preceding her, as well as several she may have composed herself. Her book, a leather-bound volume, designated HM904 in the Huntington Library's manuscript collection, contains sixty-five poems, forty-nine of which are in Constance Fowler's hand, fifteen (I argue) in her sister Gertrude's hand, and one plus a part of another in their father Walter's hand.

Although scholars interested in early modern manuscript culture and the circulation of manuscripts among men and women, like Arthur Marotti and Margaret Ezell, have recently taken note of HM904,[1] when I first looked at it in 1990 it had received little critical attention: B. H. Newdigate in two 1942 *TLS* essays had argued that the book was not the commonplace book of William Habington, as had been previously thought, but of Constance Fowler; forty years later Jenijoy La Belle became interested enough in the manuscript to index it and write an essay on Herbert Aston's love poetry, but stopped short of editing the manuscript.

As I began the project of editing it, I could understand why La Belle had not undertaken the task, and very early on I had doubts myself about the value of editing a volume of poems many of which had been previously printed elsewhere, in the individual poets' works or in editions of sixteenth- or early seventeenth-century lyrics. Why produce a printed edition of poems that had been published elsewhere and were available in multiple texts and manuscripts? Why, for example, look at Fowler's version of a Herrick poem, given the variety of editions available in any academic library? Some of my doubts, I see now, were due to my inexperience: I was approaching the manuscript from the perspective of producing a new edition of the poems in Fowler's book, which includes well-known poems by the Catholic poet Robert Southwell, Henry King's "The Exequy," lyrics by Richard Fanshawe and Owen Feltham — not all widely known or read poets but still ones for whom good modern editions are available. Even Herbert Aston's love poems — probably the best amateur poetry in the miscellany — had appeared in La

---

[1] A. F. Marotti, *Manuscript, Print, and the English Renaissance Lyric* (Ithaca: Cornell Univ. Press, 1995), 49–50; M. Ezell, "The Myth of Judith Shakespeare: Creating the Canon of Women's Literature," *New Literary History* 21 (1990): 579–92, here 589.

Belle's 1980 essay, "A True Love's Knot: The Letters of Constance Fowler and the Poems of Herbert Aston."[2] What was the point?

Producing a diplomatic edition would seem to answer those questions. Maybe many of these poems had been printed elsewhere, but in HM904 they were in a unique form — exactly the way a young seventeenth-century woman had copied them, down to the ink blots, stray marks, crossouts, and erratic capitalizations. Furthermore, as I compared Fowler's versions with printed editions of poems and studied the manuscript histories of these poems, I realized that HM904 could provide valuable information about the circulation of poems in manuscript, whether or not printed editions were available in Fowler's time. Indeed, F. M. McKay notes the remarkable textual similarities between MS. Bodleian Eng. poet. b.5 (a mid-seventeenth-century Oxford manuscript that I will discuss later, which shares many poems with HM904), and the contemporary manuscripts (as opposed to the printed editions) of Southwell's poetry. He adds, "Could more instances such as that provided by Eng. poet. b.5 be found, one might be able to establish that, although by 1650 there had been twenty editions of Southwell's poetry, it was still circulating in manuscript."[3] HM904, which I believe was a source for the Bodleian manuscript, may provide a vital link in the history of the circulation of Southwell's manuscript poems as well as that of several other canonical poets.

Henry King's "The Exequy," probably circulating only in manuscript at this time, offers a parallel example. La Belle lists "interesting variants" between the Huntington manuscript version of the poem and that in Margaret Crum's 1965 edition of King's poems, pointing out that in two cases, the end rhyme is more perfect in HM904 than in Crum's text (HAM 549–50). Constance Aston Fowler, her family, and her circle were avid readers and literary collectors. Is it possible that the manuscripts to which they had access were more accurate than others modern editors have relied on? Or that the Aston–Fowler coterie had such close contacts with the poets themselves that the HM904 copies are more reliable than other contemporary manuscripts? This was certainly the case with the poet Richard Fanshawe, who traveled to the Aston family estate at Tixall and wrote at least two poems for Constance and her sister Gertrude — "A dreame" and "Celia hath for a brothers absence sworne."[4] Future editors of Southwell, King, Ben Jonson, Fanshawe, Thomas

---

[2] *Journal of English and Germanic Philology* 29 (1980): 13–31.

[3] F. M. McKay, "A Seventeenth-Century Collection of Religious Poetry: Bodleian Manuscript Eng. poet. b.5," *The Bodleian Library Record* 8 (1970): 187.

[4] Poems 59 and 61 in *The Verse Miscellany of Constance Aston Fowler: A Diplomatic Edition*, ed. Deborah Aldrich-Watson (Tempe, AZ: MRTS for RETS, 2000).

Randolph, and Robert Herrick, to list a few, would do well to consult HM904 for manuscript variants.

Other poets besides Fanshawe visited Tixall and wrote poems for specific occasions important to the Aston–Fowler circle. Helpfully for the modern reader, Fowler often attributed the poems she copied, and more times than not she did so accurately. Poem 65, "The Constant Lovers," bears the initials R. T., for the poet Thomas Randolph (1605–35), who, typically, was associated with the Aston–Fowler family circle. Constance's close friend Lady Dorothy Shirley, the widow of a staunch Catholic, married William Stafford, a Protestant, whom Thomas Randolph knew through his association with William's uncle.

When Randolph contracted smallpox in 1634, he lived first with his father and then with his friend William Stafford and his new wife, Lady Dorothy Shirley, daughter of the second Earl of Essex and Sir Philip Sidney's widow, Frances Walsingham Sidney. The courtship between Shirley and Stafford had "weathered a period of storm," as Newdigate put it (1.204), because the Catholic Shirleys, and probably the Astons also, opposed Lady Dorothy's marriage to the Protestant Stafford (Newdigate 2.216). As Newdigate quite appropriately points out, the initials MWS and LDS at the beginning of Randolph's pastoral indicate that his subject was the courtship of William Stafford and Lady Dorothy Shirley (1.204), written from the perspective of their recent marriage, probably in the early spring of 1634. Randolph died in 1635, and this was probably the last poem he wrote. (For those who are concerned about such things, G. C. Moore Smith in 1927 believed that Randolph's poem on the marriage of Richard Love, dated January 1634, was probably his last.)[5] Although not on the order of discovering a new Shakespeare poem, this bit of literary history supplements Randolph studies and perhaps more importantly adds to our growing awareness of early modern social and cultural practices.

Likewise, Fowler probably had Aurelian Townshend, another minor seventeenth-century poet, in mind when she concluded Poem 38, "on the Death of the Duke of Bucchingham," with the large, bold, ornate initials Mr. A. T., although Cedric Brown does not include this poem in his 1983 edition of the poet (The Poems and Masques of Auerlian Townshend [Reading: Whiteknight, 1983]). George Villiers, Duke of Buckingham during the first years of Charles I's reign, was extremely unpopular with the English, for his political power and decisions as well as his Catholic leanings. After his assassination in 1628

---

[5] G. C. Moore Smith, Thomas Randolph, Warton Lecture on English Poetry (London: Oxford Univ. Press, 1927), 30–31.

many poems were written celebrating his death, whereas extant poems praising the dead duke, as the Huntington manuscript poem does, are rare. If this laudatory elegy does prove to be one of Townshend's, it would be one of only a few of its kind attributable to a canonical poet.

Beyond its significance for textual studies and ascription, what I've come to value most about the manuscript are the coterie nature of the collection and, related to that, the familial connections explicit or hidden in practically every poem Fowler copied. Of the forty-nine secular poems in HM904, thirty-six are certainly or almost certainly by or about family members and friends; three others, in addition to two religious poems, may have been composed by Constance; and for only ten could I find no connection to the Aston, Fowler, or Thimelby families.

The familial nature of the volume is evident in the first poem, "Verses presented with a beautious picture to celestinae." Walter Aston, Constance's father, perhaps composed this poem (he was a translator and, as Dennis Kay has shown, a minor poet).[6] But whether Walter Aston himself wrote the poem, he certainly copied it into the gift book as a dedicatory tribute to his newly married fourteen-year-old daughter. La Belle believes the hand of this poem is Constance's, but the differences are such that I wasn't convinced this scrawled poem was Constance's work. After searching documents from the Aston, Fowler, Thimelby, Stafford, and Shirley families, I finally read Walter Aston's commonplace book in the Stafford public records office. The hand in the commonplace book, which he kept during his first ambassadorship to Spain, and the hand of the first poem are clearly the same. If, as I believe, Walter Aston presented this book to his daughter on the occasion of her marriage, before he left again for Spain, the poem is a graceful and apt tribute to Constance. The poem is Catholic in tone — Walter had either already converted to Catholicism or was on the verge of formally doing so; several in his family also professed Catholicism — and describes "Celestina," a name that in other poems is associated with Constance, as a "virgin wife," quite appropriately, since her marriage to Walter Fowler, her fifteen-year-old neighbor, had probably not been consummated. The poem is hastily scribbled but appropriately initiates what Constance would turn into a poetic family album.

And the familial nature of the manuscript is immediately evident even to a casual reader of Fowler's poems: as La Belle notes, "In some ways the anthology becomes like a personal journal — implicitly revealing Constance's attitudes towards the authors or their subjects" (HAM 545). La Belle in this

---

[6] D. Kay, "Poems by Sir Walter Aston, and a Date for the Donne/Goodyer Verse Epistle 'Alternis Vicibus'," *Review of English Studies* 37 (1986): 198–207.

comment is referring primarily to those poems written by members of Fowler's extended family, of which there are many — a translation as well as the dedicatory poem by her father, poems by her brother Herbert Aston, her best friend and future sister-in-law Katherine Thimelby, her brothers-in-law William Pershall and Henry Thimelby, and her good friend Dorothy Shirley and her husband William Stafford.

In copying such poems, Constance was following family tradition: as Arthur Clifford's *Tixall Poetry*[7] attests, the Fowlers, Astons, and Thimelbys composed poems for every conceivable family occasion. Constance's desire to celebrate her family extends, however, beyond the poems by or even about her family members. Some poems in HM904 divulge their connection to Fowler's family only upon close examination (and, admittedly, some speculation about Constance Fowler's methods). Two examples will illustrate how I believe her mind worked in collecting these poems.

Fowler's reasons for copying Ben Jonson's "An Elegie on the lady Iane Paulet marchionesse of winchester" (1607–31) (*Miscellany*, 42) are only somewhat opaque. In 1622 Jane Savage married John Paulet, the fifth marquis of Winchester. When her sister, Lady Elizabeth Savage, married Sir John Thimelby of Irnham, Jane became the sister-in-law of Katherine Thimelby (later Katherine Thimelby Aston). Although probably neither Constance nor Katherine knew Lady Jane well (she died when Constance was about ten), Constance's loyalty to and love for her friend were such that this poem became a part of her family volume,[8] much as we today might clip out a newspaper obituary of our best friend's sister.

That Jonson wrote this poem about Lady Jane probably caused Constance to include an anonymous elegy on Jonson's own death, and another poem initialed *B I*; this poem, titled elsewhere "My Midnight Meditation," was actually written by Henry King, but Constance believed that she was including another poem by her best friend's sister-in-law's elegist. (This same kind of mistaken attribution undoubtedly caused Constance to include a poem dubiously attributed to Suckling, which she clearly believed was written by "M. H. T.," her brother-in-law Mr. Henry Thimelby.)

Although Constance Fowler's letters are shockingly devoid of political news or commentary, she clearly loyally followed her father's political career, and the second example of poems connected to her family involve her father's Spanish ambassadorship. No doubt Fowler included the previously mentioned elegy to Buckingham in her collection because her father had come to know

---

[7] Edinburgh: John Ballantyne and Co., 1813.

[8] Constance might well have copied this poem from a manuscript rather than a printed version, given the interesting textual variations.

the Duke during the failed marriage negotiations between the future Charles I and the Spanish Infanta. A letter from the Duke to Walter Aston attests to some friendliness between the two. On that basis, Constance copies two poems that she may have believed Robert Herrick wrote and includes them in her book because he had been chaplain to Buckingham on his expedition to the Isle of Ré in 1627. Walter Aston may in fact have known him. Fowler probably included "When by sad fate" (*Miscellany*, 63) for a similar reason: its poet, Owen Felltham, besides being one of the group of seventeenth-century Catholic-leaning poets, including William Habington, Richard Fanshawe, and Thomas Randolph, all associated with the Astons, also wrote "*On the Duke of Buckingham slain by Felton, the 23. Aug.* 1628," which is another rare compliment to the dead Duke. Were Fowler not able to get a copy of Feltham's laudatory elegy on Buckingham, she might have copied "When by sad fate" as an acknowledgement of Feltham's political (and religious) sympathies.

As La Belle discovered in the early 1980s, Constance cared deeply about her book. As late as 1656, probably long after she had stopped adding poems to her collection, Constance Fowler returned to her book to scratch through at the end of five poems the initials of her brother-in-law William Pershall, who had disgraced himself financially and had in 1656 brought a land suit against Constance's brother, the second Lord Aston (HAM 551). It's not a stretch, then, to conceive of her going out of her way to copy poems with positive, though distant, connections to her father.

In this overview of the kinds of poems Fowler included in her book and of their careful and deliberate selection, I have omitted discussion of one significant group of poems, the sixteen religious, generally Catholic, poems and ballads often found as well in sixteenth-century manuscripts, and usually copied in the hand second in frequency to Fowler's. La Belle declares definitively that this second hand is that of Constance's older sister Gertrude Aston (Thimelby). Early on in working with the manuscript, I accepted La Belle's attribution as reliable and set about to track down the other examples of Gertrude's handwriting for my own comparison. I have been able to find none that are without a doubt Gertrude's. She certainly wrote poems herself: Arthur Clifford with good reason attributes several to her in his 1813 volume *Tixall Poetry*, though apparently the documents or scraps of paper on which he found the originals are long lost.

However, one afternoon while looking through a Bodleian manuscript for textual variants between several pairs of religious poems common to both manuscripts, I found the hand I had been looking for. Although, again, nothing connected this hand in the Bodleian manuscript with Gertrude Aston Thimelby, the poems in both manuscripts had obviously been copied by the same person, and furthermore, the Bodleian Library manuscript — Eng. poet.

b.5 — had obviously been copied from the Constance Fowler manuscript.[9]
F. M. McKay describes Eng. poet b.5 as a recusant manuscript probably com-
piled by Thomas Fairfax, a Warwickshire yeoman, who, in 1656, refused the
Oath of Abjuration renouncing Catholicism ("Seventeenth-Century Collec-
tion," 189). The manuscript contains the birth, baptismal, and death record of
Fairfax's son in 1654.

Thirty-six pages before this record, at the end of the duplicate poems, is
written, "finis, thus ends ye. /. of Anna Alcoxs Songes sent frõ Alveston at
Christmas last 1651 written by herselfe" (fol. 51).[10] McKay believes "the
six-year-old Anna" sent Fairfax the poems (191). Although a precocious child
could conceivably have copied and sent these poems, it seems unlikely. And it
is even less unlikely that she had copied them originally in Constance's book.

A number of clues indicate that the Bodleian poems were copied from the
Huntington manuscript. For example, a variant and rare spelling of "eisell," or
vinegar (28, l. 47), as "Isall" appears in both manuscripts. In addition, a copying error in HM904 produced the line, "In Egypt seauen yeares I we stayd";
in the Bodleian manuscript, the line is written exactly as it appears in HM904,
only with the phrase "I we" deliberately crossed out and replaced with "we."
These along with the remarkable similarities in spelling and punctuation lead
to the conclusion that Gertrude (if, indeed, the second hand in HM904 is
hers) either spent some time in Warwickshire or that Anna Alcocks had access
to HM904, possibly when she was visiting the Fowler family at St. Thomas
Priory, where Constance and her husband lived. In either case, if McKay's age
for Anna is correct, dating is still problematic. I have, unfortunately, been
unable to find further information on Anna Alcocks. A John Alcock (1651–
1704), who took the alias Gage (probably his mother's maiden name) on en-
tering St. Omer's, had two brothers and two sisters (Foley 5.949n), one of
whom might have been Anna. The third Walter Aston married Catherine
Gage, and so there may have been some familial connection among the Astons, Gages, and Alcocks.

It is, of course, possible that as in so many commonplace books and poetic
miscellanies of the seventeenth century, a visitor to Tixall, perhaps a priest
with a penchant for old Catholic ballads and Robert Southwell's poetry,
picked up Constance's book, added his own selection of poems, and copied
these into another book, which he then carried to Warwickshire. In some
ways, that is the simpler theory. But given what I've come to know of Constance Fowler and her affection for and attention to her book, this frankly

---

[9] The poems that appear in both manuscripts are numbered 9–12, 27–33 in the
RETS edition of Fowler's poetry.

[10] Alveston is in Warwickshire, about four miles north of Stratford-upon-Avon.

seems less likely than that she allowed her sister — part of her immediate family and a close companion — to copy into her book (at least initially) some of Gertrude's favorite poems. I specify *initially* because there are no religious poems after Poem 33 (fol. 46 of the manuscript). The second hand also disappears for thirty-two poems, to reappear only in "A Pastorall Egloune on the death of Lawra": the final poem in the volume and an elegy written on Lady Dorothy Shirley's death.

The possibility of an extraneous hand in HM904, one not intimately related to Constance Fowler or her family, may make logical sense in the context of seventeenth-century miscellanies and commonplace books, many of which are collections in several hands. Also, it could be that a priest or male visitor would be more likely to have traveled the forty miles between Stafford and Alveston carrying a book than would a young woman. Certainly an upper-class woman like Constance might have lost track of a juvenile book in the midst of running a household and bearing children — at least twelve in Constance's case. Then we simply have two "volumes" of poems — familial and religious — interspersed between the covers of one book. However, this scenario doesn't fit the character of the woman who copied the majority of the poems. Quite simply, Constance cared too much about her "book," as she fondly calls it in a letter to her brother Herbert, to have relinquished control of it to anyone but a trusted family member. Her concern for the book was not transitory (remember, she blotted William Pershall's initials as late as 1656), and the book ends with an elegy in the second hand on Lady Shirley's death. Would a priest (or any other copier of religious poetry without ties to the Aston-Fowler circle) be interested in copying this poem? Gertrude, who was a friend of Lady Dorothy's and later in her life became a nun, seems the most evident choice.

This collection of copied poems, then, far from needing justification, contributes a great amount to our understanding of manuscript circulation, especially among women, of amateur family poetry as well as of canonical poems. If after completing the edition I retained any fears over the relevance of publishing HM904, they were quickly put to rest during the last month, when I received two separate e-mails expressing interest in further research on Constance Fowler and her coterie. I was also gratified recently to find Gertrude Aston Thimelby's poetry printed in the just published seventeenth-century anthology, *Female and Male Voices in Early Modern England*.[11] It would seem that this edition is coming at a most important time in the study of early modern literature.

---

[11] Ed. Betty S. Travitsky and Anne Lake Prescott (New York: Columbia Univ. Press, 2000), 158–59.

The Medieval Congress at Kalamazoo

Working with a Complex Document: The Southwell–Sibthorpe Commonplace Book

JEAN KLENE

I. Assumptions

A T FIRST GLANCE, I THOUGHT, EDITING FOLGER MS. V.B.198 should be a relatively simple and straightforward task, for much of the writing is in clear italic hands. Moreover, the whole volume contains only seventy-four folios, some of which are blank. Providing a context for Lady Anne Southwell did not seem to be too difficult either, for she was first married to Thomas Southwell, the nephew of the well-known Jesuit martyr and poet, Robert Southwell. An experienced editor glanced at the volume and agreed.[1] The next years showed me how wrong I was in most of my assumptions. Discovering that seven men in the late sixteenth century were named Thomas Southwell, for starters, did not bode well. But other issues relating to Folger V.b.198 posed even greater problems: first, the question of the authorship and/or responsibility for the entries. A number of factors

---

[1] I would like to thank the Renaissance English Text Society for printing *The Southwell–Sibthorpe Commonplace Book*, MRTS 147 (Tempe, AZ: MRTS, 1997), for it is hard to imagine that a commercial press would consider an edition with so many enigmatic aspects. Secondly, I would like to thank the editors, President Arthur Kinney, Lynn Kent, the late Josephine Roberts, and Laetitia Yeandle for their helpful challenges and recommendations, and their patience in working with me.

suggested that Lady Anne Southwell was largely responsible for the composition and insertion of most of the items in the Folger manuscript. Either her hand, her name, or a reference to her appears seventy-three times on the folios, as indicated in Appendix I of the edition. Although two of the long decalogue poems in the Folger manuscript do not have her hand or name on their pages, the expanded poems are attributed to her in another manuscript, British Library MS. Lansdowne 740 (better known for its many poems by John Donne). Because the many colorful examples of sins in the two poems provide Brueghelian vignettes of a cultural milieu, they make up Appendix II in the edition. Aspects of style and mood also recur often enough to sound the strong creative voice of a feisty and independent woman. Captain Henry Sibthorpe's voice, by contrast, speaks in a mentoring, cautioning, and panegyrical way, mainly about the woman he loves.

II. The Scribal Hands

While most of the writing is in clear italic hands, the angular, non-cursive writing of Lady Southwell herself is often undecipherable. Could she have been a left-handed person using a right-handed pen, for she makes thick downstrokes without the usual diamond-shaped tops and bottoms? More puzzling is the way different letters are formed with the same downstrokes and a slight variation. An "r" can be a "u" or a "v"; a "t" an "e"; and an "m" a "w." The spelling she uses in the pages of her drafts for poems tantalizes the eye (fols. 44v–46r & 57r–58v), for she seems to write as she hears words, omitting silent letters, especially when consonants are juxtaposed. The word "ignorance," for example, becomes "innorance." Sometimes reading lines out loud suggests what a word is meant to be; at other times a biblical context suggests the word she was attempting. Other idiosyncrasies are discussed briefly in the introduction. I hope that people who know theology and other disciplines much better than I do will have other ideas about some of the lines. I welcome their input, recognizing how much I benefitted when Donne scholar Janel Mueller generously confirmed some of the echoes from Donne that I had suspected and suggested others.

There is also much to be said about the various skillful hands of Southwell's second husband, Captain Henry Sibthorpe. The speedy secretary hand on fol. 73, apparently writing a draft for fol. 74, differs radically from the careful italic hand of fol. 74, where the line-lengths shape a kind of pillar honoring Sibthorpe's deceased wife. Other hands seem to be those of various household servants, like Samuel Rowson, who signs receipts for the payments of the rent and also writes much of the volume.

III. Dates

The watermarks, predominantly those of Nicholas Lebe of the 1580s, date the folios before 1600, except for the final two, which are early seventeenth-century. The earliest dates in the manuscript, 1587–88 (fols. 5–6 and 62–64) come from John Sibthorpe's entries for payments to soldiers fighting in the Netherlands. The title page of the volume includes the next date in chronological order: "The workes of the Lady Ann Sothwell:. / Decemb: 2° 1626°" and suggests that her second husband, Captain Henry Sibthorpe, probably gave the volume of folios to Lady Southwell around the time of their marriage in 1626.

Some of the poems in the Folger volume must have been written before that date, however. The three stanzas on fol. 42v, for example, which praise "that prynce that governs bryttan now," point to King James I in mentioning "his books" and his forgiving nature — even to those who wanted to kill him. Because James was more famous for his books than Charles was, the "prynce that governs bryttan now" was probably the former. Furthermore, the lines "Whose godlike mynde hath sent from his blest breath / pardon of lyfe to those that sought his death" probably refer to the Gunpowder Plot of 1605.

Another poem which must have been written before 1626 is on folio 27. I believe that the rhymed couplets are Captain Sibthorpe's expression of desire for the "rich" and "rare . . . iewell," which I take to be Lady Anne Southwell. He must have written the poem while her first husband was still alive, for the speaker bemoans the "putt-betweens" that must be removed before he and the loved one can enjoy each other. The paper on which the poem was written had been folded several times so that it had torn on a crease and been repaired and later pasted on one of the original folios. It is impossible to be certain whether the inserting was done by Lady Southwell alone, both husband and wife together, or husband alone after his wife's death.

Examining the folios in their various sizes shows that some seemed to be a part of the original volume and others to have been tipped in on a guard, that is, inserted into the book. Some of the long decalogue poems make up gatherings of folios similarly tipped in, like fols. 35–44. They contain Precept 3, "Thou shalt not take the name of god in vayne," and Precept 4, "Thou shalt keepe holy the saboth daye," poems which also appear in an expanded version in British Library MS. Lansdowne 740. Because the stanzas about James I are on these folios, it is not surprising that they would have been written before 1626 and then inserted into the volume as husband and wife compiled it. Other single works pasted on a folio were also inserted, like the two letters on fols. 3 and 4. Data regarding which leaves were inserted into the volume and which are original appear in Appendix I of the edition, along with other information about the physical volume.

IV. Textual Uncertainties

Textual uncertainties abound. Sometimes where a poem begins and/or ends is unclear, as the ending of the meditation against stealing is (fol. 57). Folio 25 at first seemed puzzling also; is it three poems or one of three stanzas? Besides the content, which seems to have resonance with Herbert's kind of wordplay and sense of paradox, paleographic reasons also point to one poem only. Although the stanzas are different in their line-lengths, all three stanzas are close together with no lines of closure separating them, as lines sometimes separate sonnets on other folios. Nor do all three stanzas together fill the page; rather they are in the upper half of it, and the bottom half is blank. The work needs more study, especially because of its resonances with Herbert.

The cropping of some folios which took place when the volume was rebound in the nineteenth century makes the tops and the right-hand sides of some compositions difficult to read. Readers can guess at many words, but others are more enigmatic, like the top line of the translation of Psalm 25 written "to ye first Earle of Castlehauen" on fol. 7, where line one reads, "Written by the Lady A[nne] B-----------." The cropping of the tops of the letters makes "Anne" an uncertainty, the next word an educated guess, and the third word a highly conjectural guess. The first cropped word could also be "Amie," but the second cannot be "Southwell" because the bottom of the first letter is that of a "B." The rest of the letters could make up the bottoms of "Blunt," which was the married name of the first earl of Castlehaven's daughter, Anne Blunt. The descending loop in the next cropped word could be "daughter," for which there is sufficient space. If the words do name Castlehaven's daughter, then the addressee of the poem must be the first earl of Castlehaven, rather than the more notorious second earl.

The occasional alternative readings make me think that Lady Anne often used the volume somewhat like a workbook. In the poem against adultery, for example, she first writes a rather domestic analogy for the inseparable union of man and wife: "as the soft skin that in an eggshell lyes / our indevyduall loving harts shall cleaue" (fol. 50v, ll. 188–189). Above line 188, she added a few words to create another comparison, "as is the opticke arterie to the ies." (Could she have seen the anatomical drawings of Da Vinci?) Both analogies seem visceral in their expression of an indivisible unity. Alternate readings like this indicate that Southwell did not expect to have the page printed, but used it to work out her ideas.

Various letters and words in the hand of Lady Southwell appear throughout the manuscript; some make sense as an insertion or a reference to a line, but others still puzzle me. Numbers for the stanzas are often written over more than once and are out of order. Next to one stanza, she herself writes, "this must cum next to the sense of last" (fol. 42v), suggesting a revising effort, but one she never completed. Why she never erased, or at least crossed out, the "mount" about an inch from l. 256 and the "nt" off l. 258 in Precept 4 (fol. 41r) baffles me. Earlier, a totally different stanza was written on another small sheet and finished the lines with the pen running off the oblong paper onto the main folio so that we have "mount" and "nt" all by themselves about an inch to the right of a stanza — with no connection whatever to the two lines. She must have subsequently put the small overleaf, as it is now, over a different stanza, 24 lines above, but without adding the "mount" or the letters "nt," both of which are necessary to complete two lines. I added them in brackets with an explanation in the Textual Notes.

In another puzzling instance, on fol. 32r Southwell writes one line of a stanza and leaves the four straight lines after that empty. Apparently she was not sufficiently interested in the composition to return and complete the stanza or to cross out the one finished line. Occasionally she does seem to trudge through topics gleaned from the rhetoric books just to fill out stanzas, especially in the decalogue poems. Without her usual passionate involvement, she seems to lose interest.

V. Titles

Finally, what to title such a document also puzzled me.[2] Because one reader raised the question of whether the volume is really a commonplace book, I will address that question briefly. The volume is clearly a miscellany, but is "commonplace book" not a more accurate title? In an address to the Bibliographical Society of Virginia, Edwin Wolf describes commonplace books as those which "include within their covers, in full or excerpted, such items as poems, songs, witty sayings, legal precedents, homilies, maxims, medical

---

[2] Since giving this paper, I have realized that I should have addressed the question of Southwell's name. Technically, she would be Anne, Lady Southwell, after the June 1626 death of Sir Thomas Southwell (according to the death certificate in British Library Additional Ms. 4820, fol. 98v), and I have occasionally but hesitantly called her this. My editor from the New Dictionary of National Biography recently changed all uses of her name to "Anne Sibthorpe." Neither form, however, appears in the Folger or the British Library manuscripts. The lady signs her own name as "Anne Southwell" (fol. 2) and others also refer to her as "Anne Southwell" and "Lady Anne Southwell" or those initials. Historians of the seventeenth and eighteenth centuries who mention her also refer to her as "Lady Anne Southwell" or "Lady Southwell." Tablets (taken from lines on fols. 73 and 74) hanging on the back wall of St. Mary's Church in Acton since her death also say "Lady Anne Southwell"; one is still there and another is in the possession of the local historian, Thomas Harper Smith.

nostrums and kitchen recipes."³ Folger V.b.198 contains all but the medical nostrums and recipes.

Peter Beal describes the contents of commonplace books in much the same way, mentioning their "loose" quality and citing "usefulness" as the key word. Compilers copied excerpts to have them as ready references.⁴ Southwell explicitly tells us she wants to use certain works. About the mini-bestiary, for example, she says, "I haveing survayed the booke⁵ haue for my ow[ne] memorye sett downe some perticulers that I best affect" (fol. 68r–v). The study of the "perticulers" could be a fascinating one, especially from a psychological point of view. Ideas from the apophthegms on fol. 69r also appear in her poems. Reflections on affliction perhaps stem from no. 25, for example. The word "affliction" itself is one of the most frequently recurring ones in the Folger volume. Wise sayings by John Fox and Henry King she probably had copied because she admired both men. Although there is no evidence except that of her witty and frequently "folksy" style, I suspect that she was having fun when she composed this one: "A glutton digs his owne grave with his own teeth." In writing various elegies, she often uses lines from the popular formula, "Like to a lampe wherin the light is ded" (fol. 9). Other listings are practical items, like a list of the sources of invention, that is, Aristotle's "5 predicables and 10 predicaments" (fol. 5v); receipts for rent paid (fols. 71r–72v); theological commentary (fols. 66v and 67r); a list of the books owned by her and her second husband (fols. 64v–66r); and inventories of household goods or personal clothing which, according to the headings above the lists on fols. 59 and 61, were moved from her home in Clerkenwell in 1631 to the tenements she rented in Acton.

The uniqueness of the document and its privateness (until years later when Sibthorpe proudly shared it?), other hallmarks of the commonplace book, also led me to believe that it should be so titled. Perhaps I should have called it "Southwell's Miscellany," for that would have been a much more user-friendly

---

³ Edwin Wolfe, *The Textual Importance of Manuscript Commonplace Books of 1620–1660*, An Address before the Bibliographical Society of the University of Virginia (Charlottesville, VA: Bibliographical Society of the Univ. of Virginia, 1949), 265–75.

⁴ Peter Beal, " 'Notions in Garrison': The Seventeenth-Century Commonplace Book," in *New Ways of Looking at Old Texts: Papers of the Renaissance English Text Society, 1985–1991*, ed. W. Speed Hill (Binghamton, NY: Medieval & Renaissance Texts & Studies in conjunction with the Renaissance English Text Society, 1993), 131–47.

⁵ "A booke of the nature of foure footed bests" [sic]. See *The Historie of foure-Footed Beastes, collected out of all the Volumes of Conradvs Gesner . . . by Edward Topsell* (London, 1607) and *The History of Serpents* (London, 1608).

title. I confess that I myself occasionally call it that. Yet, without Captain Henry Sibthorpe, it would not exist. He took an active role in its creation and also composed some of the pieces. While his poetry often consists of predictable rhymed couplets, the active support he gave his wife seems noteworthy.

Reflecting on the volume rebound in the nineteenth century helps us review its history. First owned by John Sibthorpe, it began life as a book of financial records. John probably gave the many folios to Captain Henry Sibthorpe, who gave them to Lady Southwell around the time of their wedding (though he probably copied some of the poems for her at an earlier date). With Henry's encouragement, she used the folios to have scribes record her own compositions, works by others which she liked, and items of a more practical nature.

Lady Southwell and her second husband worked on some of the pages together, judging from his comments in the margins. In the poem forbidding adultery, for example, he criticizes her over-use of a rhyme by writing "wyf / lyfe to ofte" in the margin. She then has the rhyme changed to the more subservient sounding "beauty / duty." But Henry's admonition, like the law in Duke Vincentio's Vienna, becomes as "much in mock as mark," for she uses the second rhyme even more often than the first one. One of the changes of the first rhyme to the second is in Anne's own angular hand, illustrating that, while the poem was being composed, their interaction — playful or otherwise — is undeniable.

As a whole, the volume seems to become the commonplace book where she stores what Beal calls "notions in garrison" in giving a title to his essay on commonplace books. Saying that no two such books are alike, Beal also describes the "loose" quality of such collections, an adjective which also applies to the disparate works in Folger MS. V.b.198.

The last evolution of the volume began, I suspect, with the insertion of fols. 73 and 74, when the work turned into a kind of memorial which Sibthorpe created to honor his wife. He probably also added other pieces to the volume. One can make informed guesses about his additions, but it is impossible to be certain without more evidence and reflection. The letter to the demoted Falkland had been folded into small squares probably many years before it was pasted onto fol. 4, and it may have been added to show his wife's importance by the importance of the one to whom she wrote. One of the few things about which we can be certain is that Sibthorpe would have to have added the last of the titles in the booklist on folios 64–66 at a later date, because some of the books were not published until the 1660s. Folger V.b.198 is a fascinating collection of disparate works that two people compiled, Lady Southwell more in the first years of the volume and Captain Henry Sibthorpe more in the later years of the creation of the extant document.

Towards a Textual History of the *1680 Folio* The History of the Life, Reign, and Death of Edward II *(attributed to Elizabeth Cary, Lady Falkland): Understanding the Collateral 1680 Octavo* The History of the Most Unfortunate Prince

JESSE G. SWAN

S EVERAL ISSUES KEEP THE MOTHER OF THE CELEBRATED LORD FALK-
land, the revered recusant, and the first woman to write an original play
in English from the further distinction of being the first woman to write
a modern, "politic" history in English.[1] One central issue — the source of

---

[1] The celebrated Lord Falkland is Lucius Cary, second Viscount Falkland (1610–
43). The two nineteenth-century publications of Elizabeth Cary's biography, authored
primarily by Lucy Cary, one of Elizabeth's four Catholic daughters, one by Richard
Simpson, *The Lady Falkland: Her Life* (London: Catholic Publishing & Bookselling
Co., 1861), the other by Lady Georgiana Fullerton, *The Life of Elisabeth Lady Falkland
1585–1639* (London: Burns and Oates, 1883), are published because the biography is

many of the problems in attribution and the topic of this paper — is the relationship of the first two printed editions of the history of Edward II thought by some, including myself, to be authored by Elizabeth Tanfield Cary, Viscountess Falkland (1585–1639). Both published in 1680, the first two editions are easily distinguished by format, title, authorial attribution, publisher, and length. The longer of the two, a folio, bears the title and attribution, both on the title page and in *The Term Catalogues*, of *The History of the Life, Reign, and Death of Edward II. King of England, and Lord of Ireland. With the Rise and Fall of His Great Favourites, Gaveston and the Spencers. Written by E. F. in the year 1627. And Printed verbatim from the Original* and is published by Charles Harper, Samuel Crouch, and Thomas Fox.[2] The title page employs its layout and varying cases, typefaces, and even use of ink to ornament and to accentuate, as in the initials identifying the author, which are printed in red to contrast sharply with the black ink of the page, but the substance of the title is the same as in *The Term Catalogues* for Michaelmas or November 1679. The shorter of the two is an octavo and bears the title and attribution, again both on the title page and in *The Term Catalogues*, of *The History of the Most Unfortunate Prince King Edward II. With Choice Political Observations on Him and His Unhappy Favourites, Gaveston & Spencer: Containing Several Rare Passages of Those Times, Not Found in Other Historians. Found among the Papers of, and (Supposed To Be) Writ by the Right Honourable Henry Viscount Faulkland, Sometime Lord Deputy of Ireland* and is sold by John Playford. Like the folio, the octavo employs its layout and varying cases and typefaces to ornament and to accentuate, but the substance of the title is produced as by *The Term Catalogues* for Hilary or February 1680. Both folio and octavo bear on the title pages a 1680 publication date. Further distinguishing these two publications are the very different prefaces. The folio provides a short note from "The Publisher To the Reader" and a shorter note headed "The Author's Preface To the Reader," the latter

---

felt to reveal the life of a model recusant, an "example offered to the imitation of all who suffer for justice'[s] sake" (Fullerton, *Life*, viii). See Heather Wolfe, *Elizabeth Cary, Lady Falkland, Life and Letters*, MRTS 230 (Cambridge, U.K., and Tempe, AZ: Renaissance Texts from Manuscripts and Arizona Center for Medieval and Renaissance Studies, 2001); and Jesse G. Swan, "A Woman's Life as Ancillary Text: The Printed Texts of the Biography of Elizabeth Tanfield Cary," *JRMMRA* 18 (2000 for 1997): 211–36, as well as the essay by Wolfe in this volume. For the designation of "politic" history and its genesis in English in Cary's period, see F. J. Levy, *Tudor Historical Thought* (San Marino, CA: The Huntington Library, 1967).

[2] The 1680 folio and *The Term Catalogues*, ed. Edward Arber (London: Privately Printed, 1903), differ in points of typeface, capitalization, and spelling (e.g., "favorites" in Arber for "favourites" in the folio), but not in substantive matters. The same is true of the octavo (e.g., "Falkland" in Arber for "Faulkland" in the octavo).

signed "E. F." The octavo provides a much longer note entitled "The Preface." These are the basic material facts that have reasonably led scholars into
certain disputes over the textual history and attribution of the two 1680 witnesses of Cary's history of Edward II.

The fundamental flaw in the bibliographical consideration of the two 1680
editions comes from the scholar to whom we owe the modern realization of
the proper authorial attribution, Donald A. Stauffer. As one might expect
from the author of *English Biography before 1700*,[3] Stauffer's aim, in an essay
included in a Festschrift on dramatic literature celebrating Thomas Marc Par-
rott,[4] was "to demonstrate, in one individual case, the deep influence of
drama upon historical biography" ("Passion," 291). Stauffer does not intend
to establish the bibliographical relations of the two editions. However, in arguing that the relation between English drama and biography was, in the early
seventeenth century, unidirectional — drama shaping biography, but biography not shaping the drama — Stauffer established the filial relation of the
octavo *The History of the Most Unfortunate Prince* to the folio *The History of the
Life*. Stauffer establishes the filial relation inadvertently: in proceeding throughout the essay by a "technique of mystification," as he concedes he does, his
admittedly unsubstantiated assumption that the octavo edition "was a shortened redaction" of the folio becomes a required and, more significantly, an
unimportant circumstance to the larger literary issue of the formation of English biography from English drama ("Passion," 291, 295). Because the assertion
that the octavo edition derived from the published folio edition has been so
integral to arguments about the folio's textual history and the attribution of
authorship, and because such a filial relation is wrong, as I will show, I quote
the entire note Stauffer provides to permit his claim:

> Who did this shortening I cannot determine. The titlepage of the 1680
> octavo suggests that this short version is Falkland's [i.e., Henry Cary,
> Viscount Falkland's] work. Falkland died in 1633. But a tendency in
> this octavo version to simplify the language and to omit archaisms
> might support the theory that the original Falkland manuscript was
> published in folio in 1680, and that upon this edition the printers of
> the octavo edition, who are not the printers of the folio, based their
> shortened biography. There is, of course, no positive proof that the

---

[3] Cambridge, MA: Harvard Univ. Press, 1930.

[4] Stauffer's essay is entitled "A Deep and Sad Passion." The Festschrift is *The Par-
rott Presentation Volume*, ed. H. Craig (Princeton: Princeton Univ. Press, 1935; repr.
New York: Russell & Russell), 289–314.

short edition is not the original text, of which the longer account is a
poetic elaboration. This, however, seems unlikely.

("Passion," 295, n. 7)

Though he does not note the fact, the appearance in *The Term Catalogues* of
the folio three months before the appearance of the octavo could support such
a relation, as could the feeling that the octavo's preface underscores the text's
"relevance to present occasions" of 1680.[5] However, as Edward Arber noted,
many factors, including "the size of the book," could delay the actual publication of a volume listed: "Evidently, books were often inserted in this List
from what we should now call a Proof Title Page, in advance of actual publication of the book" (Arber, *Term Catalogues*, 1.11). Given the folio's format
and title page date of 1680, this seems to be the case. The fact that the octavo's preface points up parallels to circumstances of the 1680s, as I will demonstrate, indicates, not that the edition's main text is from the period, but that
the preface is.

The important but misleading assumption in Stauffer's essay is that the octavo was derived from the published folio. In part, Stauffer wants to knock
Samuel Johnson for reprinting, with William Oldys in *The Harleian Miscellany*,
the octavo, while "they overlooked a book more rare and more curious [i.e.,
the folio], published the same year, of which their own [i.e., the octavo] was
a shortened redaction" ("Passion," 295). But more constructively for his overall purpose, Stauffer wants to get to Elizabeth Cary. Through a quasi-mystical
combination of mostly astute, if not always appreciative, associations, Stauffer
brings his essay to a surprising conclusion: the deep and sad passion of the
folio's preface, which is offered as the motivation for writing the history of
Edward II — "To out-run those weary hours of a deep and sad Passion, my
melancholy Pen fell accidentally on this Historical Relation" the folio preface
opens[6] — "would be hers" and not Henry's (314). The last paragraph of
Stauffer's essay, then, comes back to his erroneous bibliographical relationship
of octavo and folio on which to found its telling attitudes about books, lives,
authorship, gender, historical periods, and literature. This time, though, more
than before, he conflates the two editions:

---

[5] Barbara Lewalski, *Writing Women in Jacobean England* (Cambridge, MA: Harvard
Univ. Press, 1993), quoted from 317. Lewalski finds that the preface is like the body
of the edition: following Stauffer, Lewalski declares that "the abridgement was clearly
devised to comment on the Exclusion Crisis (1679–1681)" (317).

[6] "The Author's Preface To the Reader," *The History of the Life, Reign, and Death
of Edward II*, A2v.

> Last of all, the editors who published the life [of Edward II], with no
> case to prove or theory to uphold, state that it was found among Lord
> Falkland's papers and publish the dedication signed with the unidenti-
> fied letters "E.F." Falkland's name was Henry. If this work be hers,
> then the long line of noble and notable female authors of England must
> be pushed back beyond Aphra Behn and the Matchless Orinda, not
> without honor, to include Lady Elizabeth Falkland, whose mature and
> melancholy "History of the Life, Reign, and Death of Edward II," am-
> phibious, hermaphroditic, marks the wedding, under the Stuarts, of
> prose and verse, of biography and the drama. (314)

The octavo title page states that its text was found among Henry's papers; the
folio says nothing of the sort. The folio title page identifies its author as "E.
F." and provides the signed preface from "E. F."; the octavo offers the speculation of Henry both on the title page and in the preface. Clearly the body of
the texts of the editions are related, but the editions are also clearly separate
and must be kept separate to arrive at a proper accounting of each edition's
textual history. Stauffer inadvertently inaugurated the conflation of bibliographical evidence that has persisted and caused as much confusion as it has
approbation.[7] The rest of the present essay partially redresses this problem by
explaining the pre-publication history of the 1680 octavo so as to suggest that
it is a collateral, and not a filial, edition of the 1680 folio.

Although the post-publication textual history of the octavo plays a integral
role in the obfuscation for modern readers of the original 1680 publication, an
obfuscation I detail elsewhere,[8] the pre-publication history is clarified by the
realization that the author of the octavo's preface is also the publisher. Most
modern commentators have taken John Playford as the publisher of the octavo, and some have thought he was also the author of the preface.[9] But Playford was the retailer of the volume, not the agent who prepared or caused the
volume to be printed and put forward to the public. Even the title page and
the entry in *The Term Catalogues* note this: the copies printed "are sold by

---

[7] See *Bibliographical Note*, below.

[8] My full textual history is promised to Heather Wolfe for a collection of new
scholarship on Elizabeth Cary, and my edition of both 1680 editions of Cary's history
is forthcoming in the series The Early Modern Englishwoman: Contemporary Editions, ed. Betty S. Travitsky and Anne Lake Prescott, from Ashgate Press. In them I
attend to the complete pre- and post-publication history of the octavo and folio,
among other matters.

[9] Of the commentators, none has questioned John Playford's status as publisher of
the octavo.

John Playford."[10] Playford was a noted dealer in music books, not political pamphlets. Two of his usual printers, and the printers of the octavo, were Ann Godbid and her partner John Playford the younger.[11] These printers are not said to have printed the volume "for" Playford, as is common when the seller acts in some measure as a publisher, a condition that obtains with the 1680 folio edition. We must look farther afield to learn who authored the preface and who caused the volume to be published.

Remarkably, the search does not have to be far off, since Anthony à Wood knew who authored the preface, as he reports in his notice of Henry Cary, Viscount Falkland, in *Athenae Oxonienses*.[12] Concerning the "supposed" authorship of *The History of the Most Unfortunate Prince*, Wood writes: "Which book being found among the papers of the said Henry visc. Falkland, was published therefore as his, when the press was open for all such books that could make any thing against the then government, with a preface to the reader patch'd up from very inconsiderable authors, by sir Ja. H. as is supposed" (566). This identification could give validity to the DNB's notice of the preface's attribution to Sir James Harrington, but the regicide dies in exile in 1680, and he would be presumably in sympathy more with the body of the history than the substance of the preface.[13]

---

[10] Wing accurately notes this distinction as well: Donald Wing, ed., *Short-Title Catalogue of Books Printed in England, Scotland, Ireland, Wales and British America, and of English Books Printed in other Countries 1641–1700*, 2nd rev. ed. (New York: Index Committee of the Modern Language Association, 1972), Wing F314. Some critics, such as D. R. Woolf, wanting Playford to be the publisher, simply transform the information from the title page, *The Term Catalogues*, and Wing to say "for." See Woolf, "True Date and Authorship," 450, n.3 (see *Bibliographical Note*, below).

[11] Henry R. Plomer, *A Dictionary of the Booksellers and Printers Who Were at Work in England, Scotland and Ireland from 1641–1667* (1907; repr. London: The Bibliographical Society, 1968), 148.

[12] (London: Rivington, 1813; repr. New York: Johnson Reprint, 1967), 2: 565–72.

[13] *Dictionary of National Biography*, 3: 1150. The DNB entry for James Harrington explains that people conflate James and Sir James. Considering the content of the preface, James Harrington, author of *Oceana*, would be a more likely candidate than Sir James, but he was an esquire, not a knight or baronet. Sir James Harrington, the regicide (1607–80), authored and had published two books, one, *Horae consecratae*, coming out two years after his death. The *Biographia Britannica* (London: W. Innys, et al., 1747–66) identifies Sir James Harrington as the author of the preface, but it conflates and confuses various James Harringtons as much as does Sir James's eighteenth-century biographer, Mark Noble, in *The Lives of the English Regicides*, 2 vols. (London: John Stockdale, 1798), 302–5, who gives Sir James publications, but not the octavo preface. Also see Ian Grimble, *The Harington Family* (New York: St. Martin's Press, 1957).

Such speculation, though, is not necessary, since reading on in Wood we learn who Sir Ja. H. is. A few columns after casually referring to the author of the octavo preface, Wood relates the story of Henry Cary, fourth Viscount Falkland (1634–63), selling his father's considerable library at Great Tew. Wood writes: "The next [Viscount] was Henry, not educated in academical learning, but so exceeding wild and extravagant, that he sold his father's incomparable library for a horse and a mare, as I have been informed by sir J. H. who married his widow" (Wood, *Athenae Oxonienses*, 571). The man who married Henry's widow, Rachel Hungerford Cary, was Sir James Hayes, most noted for serving as Prince Rupert's secretary, ensuring the early success of the Hudson's Bay Company, and attending to Queen Mary II as a privy councilor.[14] Hayes was not much respected by Wood, though he was of enough note to be recognizable by his initials and to require a notice of his death, belated as the notice was.[15] The combination of an apparent common knowledge of the author of the octavo's preface,[16] an immediate recognition of the author through initials, a definite animosity or disdain for the author, and a sense of unimportance concerning the author of a patched-up preface culled from inconsiderable authorities came, by the middle of the eighteenth century, when the octavo was edited again for inclusion in *The Harleian Miscellany*, to obscure almost to oblivion what was perfectly clear at the end of the seventeenth century: that the author of the preface to an octavo history of Edward II was Sir James Hayes, stepfather of the sitting Lord Falkland,

---

[14] For Hayes, see Douglas MacKay, *The Honourable Company: A History of the Hudson's Bay Company* (Indianapolis: Bobbs–Merrill, 1936); Paul Chrisler Phillips, *The Fur Trade* (Norman: Univ. of Oklahoma Press, 1961); E. E. Rich, *Hudson's Bay Company*, vol. 1 (New York: Macmillan, 1960); and, especially, Peter C. Newman, *Company of Adventurers*, vol. 1 (Markham, Ontario: Viking, 1985). The Hayes River is named for this Sir James Hayes.

[15] Wood's notice of Hayes's death is in *Wood's Life and Times*, by Andrew Clark (Oxford: Oxford Historical Society, 1891), 3: 426: For 04 July 1693, "T., Dr. [Arthur] Charlet told me that Sir James Hay has been dead a month." Narcissus Luttrell, *A Brief Historical Relation of State Affairs from September 1678 to April 1714* (Oxford: Oxford Univ. Press, 1857), 3: 28, reports Hayes's death under "Saturday, 4th Feb.," as "Sir James Hayes, who married the countesse dowager of Falkland, died on Thursday last at Kensington."

[16] Besides the evidence from Wood on the common knowledge of Hayes as the author of the preface, Arber notes that "It would also seem that the authorship of any licensed publication was rarely unknown to the Trade; even if it were unknown by the public" (*Term Catalogue*, 1: 11). Wood's sense of common knowledge would not necessarily mean common to all literate persons, but to the "Trade" and other such persons, such as Wood.

Anthony Cary (1656–1694), and that he was also the person responsible for having the octavo, with its preface, published.

Knowing about Hayes, two questions arise: how or why could he have believed that Henry and not Elizabeth authored the manuscript that he caused to be printed and retailed? and why would he publish the manuscript when he did as he did? Hayes would not know who wrote the manuscript he came upon in his wife's house, because those who would have known the authorship were dead.[17] Rachel's first husband, Henry, fourth Viscount, would not have cared to learn from his father, Lucius, second Viscount, or from his mother, the identity of the author of what would have been to him an insignificant manuscript, one of probably too many in the house for his taste. His parents, though, certainly knew who wrote the manuscript, but it is precisely because the authorship was so clear and obvious to them that it never occurred to them to write the author's name on it. That Hayes could know that it was among the first Viscount's papers would be clear from the other papers stored with the manuscript. These rather quotidian conditions account for how Hayes could believe that the document was authored by Henry, the first Viscount, and the conditions surrounding his publication of it complement these to explain why he wanted the author to be the first Viscount.

The period in which Hayes published the octavo, that is, the period between 1678 and 1681, was, of course, the period of the Exclusion Crisis.[18] Being a man of considerable ability and involvements and being Prince Ru-

---

[17] Exactly when Hayes and Rachel Hungerford Cary married is not known, but it is certainly during the fifth Viscount's minority, since Hayes took control of the Falkland estate of which his wife was executor. The wills of Lettice Cary, second Viscountess, with its many codicils, of Hayes, and of Anthony Cary, fifth Viscount, suggest the movement of fortunes. See John Gough Nichols, ed., *The Herald and Genealogist* (London: J. G. Nichols and R. C. Nichols Printers to the Society of Antiquaries, 1866), 3: 132–33, 135–39. Also reproduced in *The Herald and Genealogist* notice is an entry in Evelyn's diary remarking on the fact that Anthony "had the good luck to marry a very good fortune" (3: 136), which would be necessary if his patrimony had effectively been diverted by his stepfather. Hayes leaves Anthony no material inheritance, but does leave him the state of mourning: "In token of respect to Lord Falkland, son of my dear wife, and his lady, to whom I hold myself much obliged, I leave them mourning, and wd have asked his lordship to have been ex'or, but considered he had so much business to look after" (3: 137–38).

[18] Although some discount construing the period as one of a crisis over the exclusion of the Duke of York from the throne (e.g., Ronald Hutton, *Charles the Second: King of England, Scotland and Ireland* [Oxford: Oxford Univ. Press, 1990], 396), many continue to see the period substantially definable by the most incendiary demands of the three parliaments of the period. Especially see Mark Knights, *Politics and Opinion in Crisis, 1678–81* (Cambridge: Cambridge Univ. Press, 1994).

pert's primary secretary (Newman, *Company of Adventurers*, 1: 334), Hayes naturally was involved in the turmoil. However, because Hayes was an entrepreneurial sort of man with royal and noble connections, and because he was so very self-interested, it is not accurate to understand his actions as Whig or Tory during the crisis or any other period of his life or service.[19] Rather, it is better to understand Hayes's actions in terms of his personal, financial, and immediate circumstances and desires. It is during this period, a period in which Hayes writes the Earl of Tweeddale that he is "very much afray'd of great troubles at hand,"[20] that he brings to the press the manuscript of *The History of the Most Unfortunate Prince*, a narrative that is uncompromising in portraying a dissolute and consequently ineffectual and tyrannical king, a king who "unties the Links of Duty and Allegiance" by his passionate, petulant, and unreasonable actions.[21] Although Hayes wanted Charles II to allow the Parliament to meet,[22] and although he probably favored some version of the exclusion sentiment, these views do not appear to have entirely motivated his publication of the manuscript. What does impel him to publication is his surprising and humiliating dismissal from his post on the Commission of Peace.[23] Hayes was "left out of the commission"[24] in early January 1679/ 80, and the octavo edition is advertised in *The Term Catalogues* for Hilary or February 1679/80.

Hayes's intentions in publishing the manuscript are suggested less by either the preface or the history individually, and more by the content of his preface and its relation to the content of the history. All of Hayes's references in the preface were royalists, one extremely so, as was his desired author. Besides being royalists of varying degrees, the two most important of the four references — Sir Richard Baker and Sir Winston Churchill, from whom Hayes quotes extensively — particularly reveal Hayes's work and intentions. Hayes

---

[19] Hayes's self-interest and self-aggrandizement was acutely noted during the last years of his service as Deputy Governor of the Hudson's Bay Company. Objecting to the many large disbursements from company funds by Hayes to Hayes and labeled simply "miscellaneous" in accounting statements, other shareholders found themselves without recourse as Hayes simply repaired to his mansion in Kent, Great Bedgebury, refusing all calls. See Newman, *Company of Adventurers*, 1: 335.

[20] Quoted in Knights, *Politics and Opinion*, 3.

[21] Quoted from *The History of the Most Unfortunate Prince*, 75.

[22] Knights, *Politics and Opinion*, 271, n.

[23] See Woods, *Life and Times*, 2: 476; Luttrell, *Brief Historical Relation of State Affairs*, I: 37; Knights, *Politics and Opinion*, 260. Knights calls the reformation of the Commission of Peace a "purge."

[24] Wood, *Life and Times*, 2: 476.

cites Baker because Baker was the historian country gentlemen appreciated —
despite his low academic reputation.[25] Churchill was cited not only because
he was an ardent royalist who nonetheless criticized monarchical policy, but
also because Hayes wanted to ingratiate himself with John Churchill, the
future Duke of Marlborough, who was Sir Winston Churchill's son and a rising star of the Stuart court. A few years after the octavo's publication, Hayes,
as Deputy Governor of the Hudson's Bay Company, was able to persuade
John Churchill to assume the position of third Governor of the company
upon James's resignation as the second Governor to assume the throne.[26] Ac-
cordingly, Hayes's "inconsiderable authors," as Wood terms them, serve to
appeal to the court party, while the history's criticism of a government, like
the Stuart court's, serves to appeal to a mercantile and, perhaps, country party.
Hayes's sources serve to assert an identity as a country gentleman (Baker) who
appreciates the court (Churchill). By prefacing the history as he did, and by
ascribing the authorship as he did, Hayes intended to maintain "a healthy and
mutually productive liaison among the Court, the Company, and the City."[27]

This desire to balance contending interests is further manifested by the
relationship between the preface and the narrative of the history of Edward II.
In the octavo the history is relentless in its focus on Edward as a bad, justly
executed king.[28] To compensate for such a potentially treasonable narrative,

---

[25] See Thomas Blount, *Animadversions upon Sir Richard Baker's Chronicle and its
Continuation*, 1672; DNB under Baker; and, of course, Wood concerning the quality
of Hayes's authors, as already quoted.

[26] See Newman, *Company of Adventurers*, 1: 103.

[27] Quote from Newman, *Company of Adventurers*, 1: 334. Hayes's merit as Rupert's
secretary and as shareholder and Deputy Governor of the Hudson's Bay Company was
primarily his talent for constructing documents. See Newman, *Company of Adventurers*,
80, 82.

[28] A few scholars have recognized the harshness of the octavo's history. For instance, besides those who see the octavo as written or reshaped in the heated days
close to the publication date, Krontiris, *Oppositional Voices*, and Travitsky, "The *Feme
Covert* in Elizabeth Cary's *Mariam*," quote from the octavo, which both believe to be
authored by Cary (Travitsky correctly believing, contrary to Stauffer and most others,
that the octavo's manuscript was written before the more elaborate folio manuscript
was; see *Bibliographical Note*, below), when particularly succinct and harsh text is required. Further, M. C. Bradbrook, though writing of the folio version, notes that
Cary's history of Edward II "is more courageous, and more *seditious*, than is recognized" (my emphasis); see Bradbrook's review of *The Paradise of Women*, ed. Betty
Travitsky, in *Tulsa Studies in Women's Literature* 1 (1982): 93. Although puzzling from
the start, since she bases her interpretation on the claim that it "does not depend on
Cary's authorship" of either edition of the history of Edward II, only that her interpretation depends upon "the feminist interest and investment in Cary having written it

Hayes, in the preface, concentrates on vilifying and condemning the perpetrators of Edward's murder and on evoking pity for the victimized king. Both
long quotes in the preface — from Baker and from Churchill — provide the
balance. The perpetrators — the "Actors and Abettors" — are besmeared by
the preface's narration of their cruelty and their wicked cunning.[29] Such a
preface compensates for the unrelentingly critical history, and such compen-
sation constitutes a balance between at least two dangerously hostile parties at
a particularly contentious moment. Venting his frustration in the name of the
first Viscount Falkland and with the octavo history of Edward II, Hayes criticizes the court that has humiliated him, while, by authoring the preface as
every relevant person knew he had, he shows that he is ready to forge, and
capable of forging, a new and profitable, if compromised, relationship.

The conditions of publication for the octavo *The History of the Most Unfortunate Prince* resolve many problems with the textual history of the folio *The
History of the Life, Reign, and Death of Edward II*. The octavo is not a shortened
redaction of the published folio, but an entirely separate edition. Further,
those who have perceived a definite Exclusion Crisis presence in the work
have been right inasmuch as it was highly localized and personalized motives
that produced the preface and the print publication of the octavo. However,
these facts have little to nothing to do with the folio publication. Further, the
conditions of the octavo's publication and its collateral relation to the folio do
not, in themselves, fully corroborate the attribution to Elizabeth Cary, even if
the conditions relieve several previous burdens and provide other material
links. By correcting a central, highly misleading misapprehension of the bibliographical record, the relationship of the folio *The History of the Life, Reign,
and Death of Edward II* and the octavo *The History of the Most Unfortunate
Prince*, the present essay means simply to contribute to the larger goal of writing both a full textual history of the history of Edward II, in all its states and
forms, and a materially substantiated argument, from such a textual history, for
attributing the history of Edward II to Elizabeth Cary. My full textual history

---

[i.e., the folio version]" (281), even though the "text [i.e., the folio history] is ex-
ceptional in offering as it does a female perspective on turbulent historical events"
(289–90), Dympna Callaghan, in "The Terms of Gender: 'Gay' and 'Feminist' Edward
II," in *Feminist Readings of Early Modern Culture: Emerging Subjects*, ed. Valerie Traub,
M. Lindsay Kaplan, and Dympna Callaghan (Cambridge: Cambridge Univ. Press,
1996), 275–301, also finds, in the folio version, a seditious, if "moral project — the
outright condemnation of Edward and justification of this wife's [Edward's Queen,
Isabel's] treason" (291). As seditious as the folio version may appear, it is a softened
version of the octavo.

   [29] Quoted from octavo preface, A3v.

of both the octavo and folio editions, including their relation to the two extant manuscripts from the 1620s, builds from this essay's corrections to yield
at least as solid an attribution of authorship to Elizabeth Cary as we have for
attributing to her the play, *The Tragedie of Mariam, The Faire Queene of Iewry.*

Bibliographical Note

In relating the folio and the octavo bibliographically, those who have followed Stauffer
include Elaine V. Beilin, *Redeeming Eve: Women Writers of the English Renaissance*
(Princeton: Princeton Univ. Press, 1987); Virginia Brackett, " 'Sharp Necessities',"
Women and Language 19 (1996): 7–18; Isobel Grundy, Reply to D. R. Woolf, "Falk-
land's *History of . . . King Edward II," The Bodleian Library Record* 13 (1988): 82–83;
Tina Krontiris, *Oppositional Voices: Women as Writers and Translators of Literature in the
English Renaissance* (London: Routledge, 1992), developed from the more circumspect
"Style and Gender in Elizabeth Cary's *Edward II*," in *The Renaissance Englishwoman in
Print: Counterbalancing the Canon,* ed. Anne M. Haselkorn and Betty S. Travitsky (Amherst: Univ. of Massachusetts Press, 1990), 137–53; Randall Martin, ed., *Women Writ-
ers in Renaissance England* (London: Longman, 1997); Joan Parks, "Elizabeth Cary's Domestic History," in *Other Voices, Other Views: Expanding the Canon in English Renaissance Studies,* ed. Helen Ostovich, Mary V. Silcox, Graham Roebuck (Newark, DE:
Univ. of Delaware Press, 1999), 176–92; Louise Schleiner, "Lady Falkland's Reentry
into Writing: Anglo-Catholic Consensual Discourse and Her *Edward II* as Historical
Fiction," in *The Witness of Times: Manifestations of Ideology in Seventeenth Century England,* ed. Katherine Z. Kellor and Gerald J. Schiffhorst (Pittsburgh: Duquesne Univ.
Press, 1994), 201–17, 284–88; Schleiner, *Tudor and Stuart Women Writers* (Blooming-
ton: Indiana Univ. Press, 1994); Meredith Skura, "Elizabeth Cary and Edward II:
What Do Women Want to Write?" *Renaissance Drama* 27 (1996): 79–104; Kim Wal-
ker, *Women Writers of the English Renaissance* (New York: Twayne, 1996); and Stephanie Wright, "The Canonization of Elizabeth Cary," in *Voicing Women: Gender and
Sexuality in Early Modern Writing,* ed. Kate Chedgzoy, Melanie Hansen, and Suzanne
Trill (Pittsburgh: Duquesne Univ. Press, 1997), 55–68.

Most of these follow also, most importantly, Barbara Kiefer Lewalski, *Writing
Women in Jacobean England* (Cambridge, MA: Harvard Univ. Press, 1993). That the oc-
tavo is an "abridgement" of the folio is an unquestioned axiom in Lewalski's appendix
on "Elizabeth, Lady Falkland, and the Authorship of *Edward II*," reifying for recent literary studies the inadvertent misapprehension by Stauffer in 1935. In "Elizabeth Cary's
Edward II: Advice to Women at the Court of Charles I," in *Women, Writing, and the
Reproduction of Culture in Tudor and Stuart Britain,* ed. Mary E. Burke et al. (Syracuse,
NY: Syracuse Univ. Press, 2000), 157–73, Karen Nelson implicitly endorses the view
that the octavo is a shortened redaction of the published folio: she bases her comments
upon the folio edition and cites mostly those commentators who exclude the octavo

from consideration, including Kim Walker, who is cited as "Kim Hall" (157, nn. 2, 3) and quoted as declaring that "the 'changes in the octavo *History* suggest its return to the traditions of masculine biography' (143)" (157, n. 3). Diane Purkiss, *Renaissance Women: The Plays of Elizabeth Cary, The Poems of Aemilia Lanyer* (London: William Pickering, 1994), mentions the problem of the relation of the octavo and folio, but does not treat it, other than by implicitly dismissing the octavo in preference for the folio (see esp. xxv). Jonathan Goldberg, *Desiring Women Writing: English Renaissance Examples* (Stanford: Stanford Univ. Press, 1997), and Barry Weller and Margaret W. Ferguson, eds., *Elizabeth Cary the Lady Falkland The Tragedy of Mariam the Fair Queen of Jewry with The Lady Falkland Her Life by One of Her Daughters* (Berkeley: Univ. of California Press, 1994), mention or review the bibliographical and textual problems of the *Edward II* without declaring on them, though Goldberg mentions the issues in a coda to his chapter on *Mariam* so as to offer further cogent literary evidence for taking the folio to be authored by Cary, evidence in accord with his reading of *Mariam* and figuration of Cary.

First following Lewalski, *Writing Women*, and Donald W. Foster, "Resurrecting the Author: Elizabeth Tanfield Cary," in *Privileging Gender in Early Modern England*, ed. Jean R. Brink, Sixteenth Century Essays and Studies 23 (Kirksville, MO: Sixteenth Century Journal Publishers, 1993), 141–73, Gwynne Kennedy, in "Reform or Rebellion?: The Limits of Female Authority in Elizabeth Cary's *The History of the Life, Reign, and Death of Edward II*," in *Political Rhetoric, Power, and Renaissance Women*, ed. Carole Levin and Patricia A. Sullivan (Albany: SUNY Press, 1995), 205–22, and then following Jesse G. Swan, "Elizabeth Cary's *The History of the Life, Reign, and Death of Edward II*: A Critical Edition" (Ph.D. diss., Arizona State University, 1993), in *Just Anger: Representing Women's Anger in Early Modern England* (Carbondale: Southern Illinois Univ. Press, 2000), agrees, quite rationally and reasonably, with the viability of the theories that the octavo was either written by someone else (Foster) or that it was a shortened redaction of the published folio (Lewalski, *Writing Women*, and Swan, "Cary's *History*," both following Stauffer). My Renaissance English Text Society presentation on the relationship between the octavo and folio and this essay documenting that presentation is meant, in part, to correct my own dissertation's argument about the bibliographical record on this point using my subsequent research findings, findings funded, in part, by an Eastern New Mexico University Faculty Research Grant, for which I am grateful.

Independently of Stauffer or any other commentator, D. R. Woolf, "The True Date and Authorship of Henry, Viscount Falkland's *History of the Life, Reign, and Death of King Edward II*," *The Bodleian Library Record* 12 (1988): 440–52, argues that the folio "is almost certainly a piece of propaganda, occasioned by the Exclusion Crisis of 1679–81 and published almost immediately after it was written, not rescued from an older Caroline manuscript for the existence of which there is no evidence" (440; n.b.). But two manuscripts from the mid-1620s bear unmistakable witness to the develop-

ment of the history of Edward II in the early years of Charles I's reign (see Fitzwilliam
Museum, MS. 361, and Northamptonshire Public Record Office, Finch Hatton MS.
1). Woolf naturally benefits from dismissing the octavo as "clearly extracted from <A>
[i.e., the folio], not the other way around," even though, as he notes, the folio "does
not make the same assertion" of authorship as the octavo does, as one would expect
("True Date and Authorship," 442).

Finally, sensing that the octavo is an early version of the elaborated folio and that
both are by Cary (Foster has the octavo as an earlier version of the folio as well, but
he has the octavo authored by someone other than Cary, probably her husband, and
that Cary elaborated upon it for the text that becomes the folio), Betty S. Travitsky
has maintained an interest in the octavo that others have failed to appreciate: "The
Feme Covert in Elizabeth Cary's *Mariam*," in *Ambiguous Realities*, ed. Carole Levin and
Jennie Watson (Detroit: Wayne State Univ. Press, 1987), 184–96, and, provocatively,
in *The Paradise of Women: Writings by Englishwomen of the Renaissance* (Westport, CT:
Greenwood Press, 1981; repr. New York: Columbia Univ. Press, 1989), 209–19.

Although many people contribute to everything I manage to do, and although
none is responsible for my errors, here I would particularly like to thank for
kind assistance, while I read at the Houghton Library, Hugh Amory, and,
while I read at the British Library, Michael Crump.

The Ulster Plantation and
the Colonial Archive[1]

MARK NETZLOFF

I N A DOCUMENT ENTITLED "GENERALL HEADS OF THINGS IN THE
Office of Papers, July 29, 1618," Sir Thomas Wilson, the Keeper of Records under James I, catalogued the archival records and diplomatic correspondence he had been organizing at Whitehall since 1612 as the State Paper
Office. Among twelve geographically-arranged sections, Wilson noted that the
largest set of holdings was to be found among the "Hibernia" papers, 120
books of documents related to the English administration of its Irish colonies
from 1560 to 1612.[2] Wilson's efforts to organize the State Papers soon gained
the attention of the highest officials at Whitehall, even prompting an official
visit to the office by King James himself. In a letter to James I dated March
10, 1619, Wilson reminded his monarch of this earlier visit, recollecting the

---

[1] This essay is an abbreviated version of an article that first appeared under the title
"Forgetting the Ulster Plantation: John Speed's *The Theatre of the Empire of Great
Britain* (1611) and the Colonial Archive," *Journal of Medieval and Early Modern Studies*
31 (2001): 313–48. I would like to thank Duke University Press for permission to re-
publish material from this article. A longer reworking of this essay can be found in
Mark Netzloff, *England's Internal Colonies: Class, Capital, and the Literature of Early Modern English Colonialism* (New York: Palgrave/St. Martin's Press, 2003).

[2] "Sir Thomas Wilsons generall heads of things in the Office of the Papers. July
29, 1618," Public Record Office, SP 45/20/ fols. 62–66; other copies of this document include: British Library, Additional MS. 48008; Yelverton MS. 8 fols. 3–6; a
copy, c. 1803, found in Stowe MS. 548 fols. 2–7; *CSP, Ire., 1603–1606*, xx–xxi.

king's reaction of wonder at the size and scope of the archival collection, including James's exclamation of surprise that "wee had more a dooe, wth Ireland than wth all ye world besides."[3]

As James I toured Sir Thomas Wilson's State Paper Office, the "marvels" of the archive represented a startling and innovative intersection of writing and power. But the power of the archive was predicated on the relative anonymity of its contributors, and ultimately, the invisibility of its workings.[4] The archive, in its incongruous blend of meticulous documentation alongside a necessary disappearance from memory, provided a key technology in the textual production and institutional maintenance of the project that concerned the majority of its records — the expropriation of over three million acres and the displacement of a population of six counties that was known, and then forgotten, as the Ulster plantation.[5] Despite the pervasive and visceral currency of several key events in seventeenth-century Ulster, the Ulster plantation resists mythologization.[6] In part, this resistance to narrative may result from

---

[3] Public Record Office, SP 45/20/fol. 73; *CSP, Ire., 1603–1606*, xxi.

[4] The State Paper Office, founded in 1578 as a library for the Privy Council and Secretary of State, was reorganized under James I, who advanced Sir Thomas Wilson to a permanent position as Keeper of Records in order that "he would make it the rarest office of that quality in Christendom" (W. Noel Sainsbury, ed., "Calendar of Documents relating to the History of the State Paper Office to the year 1800," *Annual Report of the Deputy Keeper of the Public Records* [London, 1869], 229). Despite James's intentions, and perhaps because of its necessary secrecy, Wilson's frequent petitions attest to the neglect his office received. The State Papers remained in a state of disarray until the formation of the Public Record Office began in 1838: see F. Smith Fussner, *The Historical Revolution: English Historical Writing and Thought, 1580–1640* (New York: Routledge and K. Paul, 1962), 77 and 92, and John Kenyon, *The History Men: The Historical Profession in England since the Renaissance* (London: Weidenfeld and Nicolson, 1983), 89–92.

[5] The most detailed account of the Ulster plantation remains George Hill's *An Historical Account of the Plantation in Ulster at the Commencement of the Seventeenth Century, 1608–1620* (1877; repr. Shannon: Irish Univ. Press, 1970). Useful general accounts also include Aidan Clarke, "Pacification, Plantation, and the Catholic Question, 1603–23," in T. W. Moody et al., eds., *A New History of Ireland, Volume 3: Early Modern Ireland, 1534–1691* (Oxford: Clarendon Press, 1984), 187–232 [hereafter referred to as Moody]; Philip Robinson, *The Plantation of Ulster* (Dublin and New York: St. Martin's Press, 1984); Richard Bagwell, *Ireland under the Stuarts*, vol. 1 (1908; repr. London: Holland Press, 1963); Jonathan Bardon, *A History of Ulster* (Belfast: Blackstaff Press, 1992), 115–47; Brendan Fitzpatrick, *Seventeenth-Century Ireland: The War of Religions* (Dublin: Gill and Macmillan, 1988), 5–35.

[6] On the use of historical memory to consolidate class relations and a racialized separation of communities within Northern Ireland, see Tom Nairn, "Northern Ireland: Relic or Portent?," in *The Break-Up of Britain: Crisis and Neo-Nationalism*

the nature of the state-sponsored construction and administration of the plantation, which, unlike other colonies, consequently seems to lack myths of origin, initial settlement, and survival.[7] J. G. A. Pocock has noted the connection between English state formation and the centralization of archives in London, corollary processes that allow a monopolization of narrative and representational power.[8] Unlike the other major plantation effort in early modern Ireland, the Munster plantation, Ulster also lacked a resident poet like Edmund Spenser both to commemorate it and urge its to reform.[9] This lack of a canon of "literary" texts associated with the Ulster plantation helps to explain why literary studies of English colonialism — even those dealing with Ireland — have generally omitted any consideration of Ulster.[10]

The Ulster plantation instead becomes textually located in a documentary form of writing that helps transform the role of historical memory in the production of knowledge. Wilson's archive and the early colonial era represent an emerging history of documents, record-keeping, and the forms of knowledge

---

(London: NLB, 1977), 216–55, and Theodore W. Allen, *The Invention of the White Race, Volume One: Racial Oppression and Social Control* (London and New York: Verso, 1994), 115–35.

[7] The Ulster plantation remains omitted from many state-sponsored narratives of Ulster history. For example, the Ulster Museum, the self-described "national museum for Northern Ireland" located in South Belfast, barely touches on the events of the early plantation era: for a discussion, see Richard Kirkland, *Literature and Culture in Northern Ireland Since 1965: Moments of Danger* (London and New York: Longman, 1996), 1–3.

[8] J. G. A. Pocock, "British History: A Plea for a New Subject," *Journal of Modern History* 47 (1975): 601–28, here 611.

[9] On Munster, see Michael MacCarthy–Morrogh, *The Munster Plantation: English Migration to Southern Ireland 1583–1641* (Oxford: Oxford Univ. Press, 1986). My argument emphasizes the distinctiveness of the Ulster plantation from Munster and other projects due to its initial Jacobean context, and therefore its central place in both early formulations of British imperialism and the construction of Wilson's state archive. Despite the Jacobean resettlement of Munster following the Nine Years' War, MacCarthy–Morrogh finds that Munster was relegated to secondary importance in the wake of the Ulster plantation (144).

[10] Despite the voluminous scholarship on Spenser and Ireland, only two essays examine Spenser's influence on English colonialism in the seventeenth century: Nicholas Canny, "Identity Formation in Ireland: The Emergence of the Anglo–Irish," in Nicholas Canny and Anthony Pagden, eds., *Colonial Identity in the Atlantic World, 1500–1800* (Princeton: Princeton Univ. Press, 1987), 159–212, and Willy Maley, "How Milton and Some Contemporaries Read Spenser's *View*," in Brendan Bradshaw, Andrew Hadfield, and Willy Maley, eds., *Representing Ireland: Literature and the Origins of Conflict, 1534–1660* (Cambridge: Cambridge Univ. Press, 1993), 191–208.

and forgetting specific to its institutional operations. The document, as Foucault has argued, "is not the fortunate tool of a history that is primarily and fundamentally memory."[11] Rather than serving as an inert repository of the past, the mass of documentation accumulating in the archive serves the administrative, bureaucratic needs of the present moment; it embodies the constructedness of the writing of history and demonstrates a discontinuous relation to the past. The archive does not merely accumulate documents and produce knowledge; it also exercises forms of selection and erasure.[12] The documentary form of writing allows the process of plantation to be transformed into an inert repository of documents, as power relations are effaced and restructured into an ordered "quarry of facts."[13] The Ulster plantation thus produces a system of knowledge based on a disjunctive relation to historical objects, a knowledge based on loss and forgetting that finds its articulation through the technologies of history writing and cartography, and the site of its accumulation and disappearance within the contentious site of the archive and the conflicts waged over its accessibility and control.

The paradoxical discursive formation and forgetting of the Ulster plantation enabled through Sir Thomas Wilson's State Paper Office is paralleled by a similar process of simultaneous documentation and displacement found in the most pervasive cartographical image of Ulster in the early modern period, John Speed's map of Ulster from *The Theatre of the Empire of Great Britain* (1611).[14] Speed's cartographical atlas presented the first completed set of

---

[11] Michel Foucault, *The Archaeology of Knowledge and the Discourse on Language*, trans. A. M. Sheridan Smith (New York: Pantheon, 1972), 7. My discussion of how emergent forms of knowledge production displace an emphasis on historical memory is influenced by Frances A. Yates, *The Art of Memory* (Chicago: Univ. of Chicago Press, 1966), esp. 368–89.

[12] For a similar argument, see Michel-Rolph Trouillot, *Silencing the Past: Power and the Production of History* (Boston: Beacon Press, 1995), 52.

[13] My discussion is indebted to Dominick LaCapra, *Rethinking Intellectual History: Texts, Contexts, Language* (Ithaca and London: Cornell Univ. Press, 1983), 31, and Gayatri Chakravorty Spivak, "The Rani of Sirmur," in Francis Barker et al., eds., *Europe and its Others*, 2 vols. (Colchester: Univ. of Essex Press, 1985), 1: 128–51, here 130. On the nineteenth-century archive and knowledge production, see Thomas Richards, *The Imperial Archive: Knowledge and the Fantasy of Empire* (London: Verso, 1993).

[14] Although I follow conventional usage by giving the date of Speed's texts as 1611, the title pages of Books III and IV of the *Theatre* are dated 1612, when Speed's texts were finally published, while Speed's maps of Ireland were engraved in 1610: see R. A. Skelton, *County Atlases of the British Isles, 1579–1850* (1970; repr. Folkstone, Kent: Dawson, 1978), 31–33.

county maps for regions of England, Wales, Scotland, and Ireland, a visual representation of James I's multinational empire of Great Britain.[15] Despite the spatial incorporation of Ireland into James's empire, Speed's map of Ulster is unable to fix Ulster at any precise spatial or temporal location. The most puzzling aspect of Speed's map of Ulster lies in the fact that, although engraved in 1610, its details do not reflect any awareness of the Jacobean Ulster plantation. Instead, Speed anachronistically attributes much of Ulster to regional Irish chiefs, demarcating the land along the lines of sixteenth-century divisions that reflect Ulster's earlier status as a region largely resistant to English colonial infiltration. There were empirical reasons for Speed's inability to map contemporary Ulster, as there was no authoritative map that he could use as a model.[16] Two Elizabethan cartographers, Richard Bartlett and John Browne, were in fact killed as they attempted to survey Ulster.[17] As John Davies rather dryly recorded, the Gaelic Irish of Ulster "would not have their country discovered."[18]

---

[15] For discussions of Speed's contributions to cartography, see J. H. Andrews, *Shapes of Ireland: Maps and their Makers, 1564–1839* (Dublin: Geography Publications, 1997), 89–117; E. G. R. Taylor, *Late Tudor and Early Stuart Geography, 1583–1650* (London: Methuen, 1934), 49–51; R. V. Tooley, *Maps and Map-Makers*, 6th ed. (London: Batsford, 1978), 52, 68–70, 84, 92–93. On Speed and Renaissance historiography, see D. R. Woolf, *The Idea of History in Early Stuart England* (Toronto: Univ. of Toronto Press, 1990), 64–72; Stan A. E. Mendyk, *Speculum Britanniae: Regional Study, Antiquarianism, and Science in Britain to 1700* (Toronto: Univ. of Toronto Press, 1989), 78–81; F. J. Levy, *Tudor Historical Thought* (San Marino, CA: The Huntington Library, 1967), 196–99; T. D. Kendrick, *British Antiquity* (1950; repr. New York: Barnes and Noble, 1970), 124–25, 164–65.

[16] Earlier published images of Ulster included the maps of Ireland by Gerard Mercator (1564) and Baptista Boazio (1599); in both of these maps, Ulster was given few details, especially in the interior of central Ulster, leaving the province as an empty territory that resembled early depictions of the interior of North America (see Andrews, *Shapes of Ireland*, chaps. 2–3). Speed's main sources were Camden's *Britannia* (1586), a later Mercator map, *Ultoniae orientalis pars* (1595), and most significant, the manuscript maps by Francis Jobson, who was commissioned to survey central Ulster in 1590–91 following O'Neill's surrender at the end of the Desmond Rebellion of 1584–89 (Andrews, *Shapes of Ireland*, 103, 107, 109). For discussions of the Irish maps that preceded Speed's, see Bernhard Klein, "Partial Views: Shakespeare and the Map of Ireland," *Early Modern Literary Studies* 4 (1998): 1–17, and Mercedes Maroto Camino, " 'Methinks I see an Evil Lurk Unespied': Visualizing Conquest in Spenser's *A View of the Present State of Ireland*," *Spenser Studies* 12 (1998): 169–94.

[17] Andrews, *Shapes of Ireland*, 89, 103; Hawkyard, *Counties of Britain*, 269. On Bartlett's maps of Ulster, see G. A. Hayes-McCoy, *Ulster and other Irish Maps, c. 1600* (Dublin: Irish Manuscripts Commission, 1964).

[18] *CSP, Ire., 1608–1610*, 280.

Speed's map memorializes a social hierarchy that had been effectively displaced from Ulster by 1610. The Earls of Tyrone, Tyrconnell, and Maguire, to whom is attributed much of western and central Ulster, had fled to the continent in 1607, opening up much of the region for confiscation and redistribution. They had left Ulster not to escape imminent military conquest, but to avoid the more subtle forms of control that the English colonial government of Lord Deputy Sir Arthur Chichester and Attorney-General Sir John Davies had devised to eliminate remaining sources of Gaelic Irish authority, particularly through manipulation of the parliamentary franchise, the justice system, and land tenure. Chichester and Davies were subsequently able to imprison or execute several lesser Gaelic Irish leaders, including Sir Cahir O'Doherty, to whom Speed attributes the northern peninsula of Inishowen, and Sir Donal O'Cahan, whose lands in Coleraine were confiscated and granted to the city of London in 1608 and formed much of the territory of the Londonderry plantation.[19] As Speed prepared his map of Ulster for publication in 1610, the six escheated counties had been surveyed, redistributed, and already settled by Protestant English and Scottish undertakers. When the reorganization of land in Ulster was completed in 1610, the same year that Speed's map was engraved, Irish landowners of all ranks — Gaelic Irish and Catholic Anglo-Irish alike — held only 20 percent of land in Ulster.[20]

---

[19] On the London companies' plantation, see T. W. Moody, *The Londonderry Plantation, 1609–1641: The City of London and the Plantation in Ulster* (Belfast: Mullan, 1939), and James Stevens Curl, *The Londonderry Plantation, 1609–1914* (Chichester, Sussex: Phillimore, 1986); documents related to the plantation are reprinted in T. W. Moody and J. G. Simms, eds., *The Bishopric of Derry and the Irish Society of London*, 2 vols. (Dublin: Irish Manuscripts Commission, 1968), and *Londonderry and the London Companies, 1609–1629. Being a survey and other documents submitted to King Charles I by Sir Thomas Phillips* (Belfast: H. M. Stationery Office, 1928).

[20] Moody, *A New History of Ireland*, 3: 202; Robinson, *The Plantation of Ulster*, 75–77; for a list of Irish grantees, see Robinson, *Plantation*, Appendices 3 and 4 (199–201). A total of 280 Irish landowners were granted estates; 26 of these individuals received 1,000 acres or more, estates comparable in size to those granted to English and Scottish undertakers. But these lands were most often not in grantees' home districts, allowing the English government to resettle O'Donnells and O'Neills far from Tyrconnell and Tyrone. Many of these leases also expired with the death of the grantee, allowing for future legal expropriation of additional territory (Robinson, *Plantation*, 75–77). This latter practice demonstrates an early example of what came to be known as the "Ulster custom," restrictions in Catholic leasing that abetted the geographic segregation of the province (Allen, *The Invention of the White Race*, 1: 121–24, 129–33).

Speed's map of Ulster defies an analysis of early modern cartography that locates mapping as a technology that helps ensure a more efficient political control over a region through an increasingly detailed surveying of the land.[21] In his omission of the Ulster plantation from visual representation, Speed's map attests to how early modern maps constitute power not only through their technical claims to increasing accuracy and "scientific" objectivity.[22] Maps also possess power through the forms of knowledge they produce, and, it should be added, through the knowledges which are not produced as a result of a map's silences and gaps.[23] Some of these cartographical silences may result from deliberate policy and reflect how maps and surveys are important components in often-contentious networks of power. But the shocking absence of the Ulster plantation from Speed's map raises a more profound question regarding the limits of a map's knowledge: in other words, how could Speed or any contemporary surveyor have represented such a profound and recent process of displacement as that constituted by the Ulster plantation?[24]

The epistemic limits expressed by Speed's map of Ulster also point to the important role played by the Ulster plantation in a process of capital formation in early modern "Britain." The withholding of cartographical information regarding the Ulster plantation reveals the important commercial advantages

---

[21] See J. H. Andrews, *Plantation Acres: An Historical Study of the Irish Land Surveyor and his Maps* (Belfast: Ulster Historical Foundation); for discussions of practices of surveying in England, see Andrew McRae, *God Speed the Plough: The Representation of Agrarian England, 1500–1660* (Cambridge: Cambridge Univ. Press, 1996), 169–97, and Garrett A. Sullivan, Jr., *The Drama of Landscape: Land, Property, and Social Relations on the Early Modern Stage* (Stanford: Stanford Univ. Press, 1998).

[22] On the "scientific" claims of cartography, see Howard Marchitello, *Narrative and Meaning in Early Modern England* (Cambridge: Cambridge Univ. Press, 1997), 77. Bernhard Klein analyzes how the increasingly scientific claims of early modern surveying helped to transform land to "a marketable commodity" and remove it from the realm of social relations and "popular memory" in "The Lie of the Land: English Surveyors, Irish Rebels and *The Faerie Queene*," *Irish University Review* 26 (1996): 211.

[23] See J. B. Harley, "Silences and Secrecy: The Hidden Agenda of Cartography in Early Modern Europe," *Imago Mundi* 40 (1988): 57–76.

[24] Hill, *Plantation in Ulster*, ii. As evidence of the difficulties faced in calculating the size of the Ulster land confiscation, other estimates provide conflicting information, including a 1611 document that gives the size of the plantation as 511,465 acres, a figure mistakenly followed by later historians: see J. S. Brewer and William Bullen, eds., *Calendar of the Carew Manuscripts, preserved in the Archiepiscopal Library at Lambeth* (1873; repr. Nendeln, Liechtenstein: Kraus Reprint, 1974), xxxii and 235. Contemporary historians who underestimate the size of the Ulster plantation ironically mimic the practice of early modern English surveyors: the survey of 1609, for example, gave the size of Co. Tyrone (806,650 acres) as 98,187 acres (Bagwell, *Ireland under the Stuarts*, 75).

sought by both state officials and private investors. J. B. Harley speculates that
the practices of secrecy endemic to the history of cartography bear a parallel
with the activities of monopoly capitalism, the ensuring of commercial advan-
tage through exclusive rights to cartographical knowledge.[25] But the process
of capital formation itself is predicated on an absence from representation,
whether in the form of an erasure of human subjects as their labor is ab-
stracted, or the disappearance of the money-form as it is converted into capital.[26] Deleuze and Guattari extend this comparison: a process of capital formation, such as that witnessed in the Ulster plantation, "that divides the earth
as an object and subjects men to the new imperial inscription," is best seen as
"a movement of deterritorialization."[27] Speed's map of Ulster testifies to how
New English authority in Ulster under Chichester and Davies is, in a sense,
unrepresentable, as its power operates through its absence from representation
and ability to efface the effects of the process of its domination.

To offset the deterritorialization on which the Ulster plantation is predicated, the project is instead made analogous with a process that accumulates
knowledge and documents. Equally important to the dissemination of meticulous records and "knowledge" of Ulster, though, is control over the access
and interpretation of this information. It was Sir Thomas Wilson, in his role
as Keeper of Records of the State Paper Office, who was instrumental in preserving the institutional secrecy of the Ulster plantation. When Wilson assumed the position of Keeper of Records in 1612, his oath of office stipulated:

> yo^u shall carefullie and faithfullie keepe secret and conceale from y^e
> knowlege of others eyther by writting or relacon all such things therein
> contayned as shalbe fitt eyther for reason of state or otherwise for his
> Maties seruice to be concealed and keepe secrett . . .[28]

Wilson's official duties illustrate how cartography and history writing are employed to help ensure monarchical state authority, as these technologies are
among the state secrets that must be concealed from all but authorized officials.[29] Similar to Richard Rambuss's analysis of the importance of Spenser's

---

[25] Harley, "Silences and Secrecy," 61.

[26] For a discussion of this point, see Gilles Deleuze and Félix Guattari, *Anti-
Oedipus: Capitalism and Schizophrenia* (Minneapolis: Univ. of Minnesota Press, 1983),
225.

[27] Deleuze and Guattari, *Anti-Oedipus*, 195.

[28] Public Record Office, SP 14/94/ fol. 192.

[29] It may be helpful to think of cartography as what Anthony Giddens terms an
"authoritative resource," a mechanism intended for "the retention and control of

"secret career" as a colonial official in Ireland, Wilson's role as secretary entails an authority over institutional secrecy through his bureaucratic identity as the official in control of the circulation and access to "secret" documents.[30] Appropriately, Wilson was recommended to his post as Keeper of Records after having previously served as chief secretary to Sir Robert Cecil, the Earl of Salisbury, James I's primary architect of the Ulster plantation.[31] It would have

---

information or knowledge" which constitutes itself through practices of notation and documentation: see *A Contemporary Critique of Historical Materialism, Vol. 1: Power, Property and the State* (Berkeley: Univ. of California Press, 1981), 94. For other discussions of early modern European state apparatuses and control over the dissemination of geographical knowledge, see Harley, "Silences and Secrecy," 57–76, and Harley, "Maps, Knowledge, and Power," in Denis Cosgrove and Stephen Daniels, eds., *The Iconography of Landscape* (Cambridge: Cambridge Univ. Press, 1988), 277–312; Chandra Mukerji, "A New World-Picture: Maps as Capital Goods for the Modern World System," in *From Graven Images: Patterns of Modern Materialism* (New York: Columbia Univ. Press, 1983), 79–130; Peter Barber, "England II: Monarchs, Ministers, and Maps, 1550–1625," in David Buisserret, ed., *Monarchs, Ministers, and Maps: The Emergence of Cartography as a Tool of Government in Early Modern Europe* (Chicago: Univ. of Chicago Press, 1992), 57–98.

[30] Richard Rambuss, *Spenser's Secret Career* (Cambridge: Cambridge Univ. Press, 1993). As an example of how cartographical information often constituted the secret knowledge bequeathed to a secretary, Robert Beale (1541–1601), a clerk to the Privy Council, noted in his "A Treatise of the Office of a Councellor and Principall Secretarie to her Ma[jes]tie": "A Secretarie must likewise have the booke of Ortelius['s] Mapps, a booke of the Mappes of England, . . . and a good descripc[i]on of the Realm of Irelande, a note of the Noblemen and surnames English or Irish of their Septs, Enraghes, Galloglasses, Kerns and followers, and if anie other plotts or maps come to his handes, let them be kept safelie" (Conyers Read, *Mr Secretary Walsingham and the Policy of Queen Elizabeth* [Oxford: Clarendon Press, 1925] 1: 428–29). For a discussion of Beale's treatise, see Swen Voekel, " 'Upon the Suddaine View': State, Civil Society and Surveillance in Early Modern England," *Early Modern Literary Studies* 4 (1998): 1–29.

[31] *CSP, Ire., 1606–1608*, cxxi. Wilson had entered Salisbury's service, c. 1605–6, and was later appointed as Keeper of the State Papers shortly after Salisbury's death in 1612; one of his first duties entailed helping to transfer Salisbury's papers to the State Paper Office. Perhaps because Salisbury's papers outnumbered the documents previously held in the Office of Papers, Wilson seems to have regarded his tenure as Salisbury's secretary and Keeper of Records as a continuous period of service; in a 1615 letter to James I, for example, Wilson complained of having spent "more than 10 painful years" helping to "have reduced them into that due order and form, that your majesty and most of the Lords have seen and approved" (qtd. in Fussner, *The Historical Revolution,* 77). On Wilson, see A. F. Pollard's entry in *The Dictionary of National Biography,* vol. 21; *Annual Report of the Deputy Keeper,* 212–23; R. B. Wernham, "The Public Records in the Sixteenth and Seventeenth Centuries," in Levi Fox, ed., *English Historical*

been Wilson, then, who had earlier directed correspondence between Salisbury and his commissioners in Ireland during the crucial years of 1608–1610.[32]

As Wilson's oath of office demonstrates, the power of documents — whether histories, maps, or surveys — results not from their accuracy of detail, but from their legally-mandated ability to deceive, or more specifically, to control what may enter and disappear from the level of discourse and documentation. Similarly, Speed's map of Ulster demonstrates how early modern cartography is concerned less with questions of detail or accuracy than with the forms of knowledge produced, and sometimes elided, from the invention of imperial self-representation.[33] Among the dedicatory poems, Sir John Davies combines his roles as poet and colonial official, commending Speed for his "anatomizing" of Ireland: "In euery Member, Artire [sic], Nerue, and Veine, / Thou by thine Arte dost so Anatomize, / That all may see each parcell without paine" (sig. ¶ 2). Despite this praise, Speed's maps already had been superseded by official surveys in each of the previous two years, surveys conducted under Davies's auspices.[34] These surveys formed the basis of John Norden's detailed map of the new property holdings of Protestant undertakers in Ulster, also completed in 1610. But like most plantation-era maps and surveys of Ulster, Norden's was unpublished, its manuscript circulation sharply curtailed.[35]

Scholarship in the Sixteenth and Seventeenth Centuries (London: Oxford Univ. Press, 1956), 21–22.

[32] Wilson had a more literal investment in the success of the Ulster plantation during this period, having petitioned along with his brother for a grant of 2,000 acres in 1618; this potential income is most likely what prompted Wilson to write a treatise on the military rule of Ireland that same year (*CSP, Ire., 1615–1625,* 202). Wilson had earlier written two important texts dealing with Ireland: "On the state of England A.D. 1600, with a description of this country and of Ireland" [c. 1601] helped Wilson secure the patronage of the Cecils and James I (F. J. Fisher, ed., *Camden Miscellany* 16 [1936]: v–vii); "Booke on the State of Ireland" [c. 1599] contains a pastoral dialogue between "Peregryn" and "Silvyn," figures named after Edmund Spenser's sons Peregrine and Sylvanus. Although the latter manuscript may possibly have been written by Henry Cuffe, secretary to the Earl of Essex, Wilson claims authorship of it within his other treatise (*CSP, Ire., 1598–1599,* 505 ff.; "On the state of England," 18). Wilson also intended to write a chronicle history of Ireland from 1584 to 1619, a project he never accomplished (*Annual Report of the Deputy Keeper,* 217 and 231; *CSP, Domestic, 1623–1625,* 555).

[33] For a further discussion of early modern maps' gaps in knowledge, see Harley, "Silences and Secrecy," 57–76.

[34] On the 1609 survey, see J. H. Andrews, "Maps of the Escheated Counties of Ulster, 1609–10," *Proceedings of the Royal Irish Academy* 74 (1974): 133–70.

[35] British Library, Cotton Augustus, MS. I.ii.44. Norden's map is reproduced in

Why then does Davies praise Speed's obviously inaccurate, if not anachronistic, "anatomizing" of Ireland? Davies's desire to control and even absent the Ulster plantation from visual representation may result from the need to promote investment in the project while limiting the power and autonomy of prospective undertakers and their financial backers. As Davies's poem indicates, Speed's map is intended for the domestic consumption of an elite English audience who will "see each parcell without paine," in other words, survey the lands of Ulster, and perhaps gain interest in colonial investment, but do so without having to endure the risks of personal travel.[36] Speed's map thus conforms to the image of Ulster found in promotional texts such as Thomas Blenerhassett's *A Direction for the Plantation of Ulster* (1610), wherein Ulster is depicted as a depopulated and unclaimed territory requiring English intervention and investment.[37] The popularity of Speed's maps with an elite English audience is attested to by the fact that George Carew, President of Munster from 1600 to 1602 and an avid collector of Irish maps and manuscripts, is known to have decorated the walls of his study with Speed's maps of the Irish provinces.[38] As an indication of their symbolic capital, the display of these objects is used to advertise an Englishman's knowledge of "state secrets," even though these maps reflect little detail of the process of plantation.

Analecta Hibernica 8 (1938): 298. The maps resulting from Sir Josias Bodley's initial 1609 survey were presented to Salisbury and later deposited in Wilson's Office of Papers; their dissemination was so tightly controlled that they were not located and identified until 1860. Andrews speculates that alongside the set sent to Salisbury and later reproduced by Norden, another version of the 1609 survey was sent back to Ireland to assist in administering the plantation (Andrews, "Maps of the Escheated Counties of Ulster, 1609–10," 159, 163–64).

[36] For other examples attesting to the increasing popularity of maps and atlases among elite "armchair travelers," see Victor Morgan, "The Cartographic Image of 'the Country' in Early Modern England," *Transactions of the Royal Historical Society*, ser. 5, 29 (1979): 144–47, and Barber, "England II," in Buisserret, ed., *Monarchs, Ministers, and Maps*, 43, 58–84.

[37] In his pamphlet's most famous passage, Blenerhassett casts the feminized figure of "depopulated Ulster" as a damsel in distress, recently freed from "the vsurping tyrannie of Traytors," and proposes that the exportation of England's surplus population will ameliorate the condition of Ulster, where "there remayneth nothing but ruynes and desolatio[n]" (sig. A2).

[38] Andrews, *Shapes of Ireland*, 113. Carew had seen the Ulster plantation first hand, having been appointed by James to lead a commission to check on initial settlement in 1610–11 (Hill, *Plantation in Ulster*, 447). On Carew's map collection, see William O'Sullivan, "George Carew's Irish Maps," *Long Room* 26–27 (1983): 15–25; on his collecting habits, see Brewer and Bullen, eds., *Calendar of the Carew Manuscripts*, vii–xlix.

The dissemination and reception of Speed's Irish maps also reveal the political struggle engaged in by those competing for position in the Ulster plantation. In his prefatory poem to Speed's *Theatre*, Davies recognizes the importance of official control over the dissemination of geographical knowledge, praising Speed even though he himself had access to additional survey maps which helped him to redistribute land in Ulster.[39] The English colonial government, in fact, often used the inaccuracy of earlier surveys — including those conducted under its own authority — as a justification to invalidate, and thereby claim as its own, titles held by Irish landowners.[40] Officials also used this practice, the discovery of "concealed lands," as a way periodically to adjust the land holdings of Protestant New English undertakers.[41] The absence of a standard survey of property in Ulster allowed Davies to alter the parliamentary franchise, which helped ensure the first Protestant majority in the Irish Parliament of 1613.[42] In all of these examples, the mechanisms of colonial authority operate not only through their invisibility and absence from representation, but also from a general lack of referentiality.

This recognition may help us to understand why Davies may then praise Speed's "anatomizing" of Ireland despite — or perhaps because of — its lack of recognition of the Ulster plantation. This omission had little to do with the recent date of the Ulster plantation in 1610. When Speed subsequently revised his collection in 1627, he retained his Irish maps. Speed's original Irish maps

---

[39] Moody, *A New History of Ireland*, 3: 197.

[40] This practice helped to transfer half the county of Fermanagh from the Maguires to undertakers in 1605 (Bardon, *History of Ulster*, 116).

[41] William Farmer, a supporter of Chichester's administration, complained that surveys had underestimated the size of escheated properties, allowing for uncontrolled social mobility among undertakers, and recommended that James invalidate these tenures and confiscate the land recently planted by English settlers: see "A Chronicle of Lord Chichester's Government of Ireland" [c. 1615] in Thomas Lodge, ed., *Desiderata Curiosa Hibernica: Or a Select Collection of State Papers*, 2 vols. (London, 1772), 1: 249, 266–67.

[42] In the 1613 Parliament, Ulster put forward 38 of the added 84 seats to the lower house; only one of the province's 64 seats was represented by a Catholic. For details, see Moody, *A New History of Ireland*, 3: 210–19; Bagwell, *Ireland under the Stuarts*, 108–38; Falls, *Birth of Ulster*, 203–10. James M. Smith discusses the importance of this parliament in the context of relations between Old and New English communities in "Effaced History: Facing the Colonial Contexts of Ben Jonson's *Irish Masque at Court*," *ELH* 65 (1998): 297–321. Francis G. James, in *Lords of the Ascendancy: The Irish House of Lords and its Members, 1600–1800* (Dublin: Irish Academic Press, 1995), finds a surprising degree of accommodation among Gaelic Irish and Old English elites to the Protestant Ascendancy.

were also reproduced in posthumous editions of Speed's *Theatre*.[43] Even as
late as 1673, the English map-maker Richard Blome based his Irish maps on
Speed's for the collection *Britannia*, while other publishers retained Speed's
maps throughout the eighteenth century.[44] It is significant that Blome chose
Speed's maps as his model, rather than the Down Survey conducted by William Petty during the Cromwellian invasion; Petty's mapping of Ireland, a
five-year effort completed in 1657 which mobilized 1,000 workers, was not
even published until 1685.[45] For the first 75 years of its institutional lifetime,
the Ulster plantation did not cartographically exist.

While the accumulation of materials in the archive of Wilson's State Paper
Office reflects its instrumental role in the functioning of state power, the gaps
and silences of Speed's map of Ulster demonstrate how this process of formation necessarily entails a forced erasure of institutional and cultural memory.
The Ulster plantation's disappearance from the map and archival record reveals
the violence on which colonial practices and capitalist production originate
themselves. But the insistent need to erase Ulster from cartographical location
and historical narrative ultimately shows that this violence is not an action located in the past, but a set of forces renewed and reactivated in the present.
The subsequent elision of the Ulster plantation from the narrativized memo-
ries of communities illustrates how the violence of colonialism has been

---

[43] Speed's *Theatre* was republished several times in the seventeenth century: 1616,
1623, 1627, 1632, 1646, 1650 (with four editions from 1651–54), 1665, and 1676;
beginning in 1627, the *Theatre* was published together with Speed's *Prospect*. In addition, a Latin version of the *Theatre* was published in 1616, 1621, and 1646. As evidence of the increasing popularity of Speed's maps, they were also re-engraved in a
more accessible and cheaper octavo ("pocketbook") format and published under the
title *England, Wales, and Ireland Described* in 1627, 1632, 1646, 1662, 1665, 1666,
1668, and 1676; with the exception of 1666, editions from 1646 forward were published together with an octavo version of Speed's *Prospect*: see R. A. Skelton, *County
Atlases of the British Isles, 1579–1850*, 30–44 and *passim*; R. V. Tooley, "John Speed:
A Personal View," *Map Collector* 1 (1977): 1–9; Rodney W. Shirley, *Early Printed Maps
of the British Isles: A Bibliography, 1477–1650* (London: Holland Press, 1980), 102.

[44] Andrews, *Shapes of Ireland*, 114; Tooley, *Maps and Map-Makers*, 80, 93. For
examples of other late seventeenth and eighteenth-century atlases based on Speed, see
Rodney W. Shirley, *Printed Maps of the British Isles, 1650–1750* (London: Map Collector Publications, 1988).

[45] Tooley, *Maps and Map-Makers*, 93. Petty's text, *Hiberniae delineatio* (1685), has
been reproduced with an introduction by J. H. Andrews (Shannon, Ire., 1969). For a
discussion of Petty, see Andrews, *Shapes of Ireland*, 118–52, and Mary Poovey, *History
of the Modern Fact* (Chicago: Univ. of Chicago Press, 1998), 120–38.

rearticulated by mutually contradictory mythologies of the besieged community and its others.[46]

One intention of this essay has been to explain how forms of knowledge
production — history writing, documentation, cartography — were instrumental to early modern colonial practices in Ireland. This intersection is demonstrated by the surprising number of archival collections produced out of the
Ulster plantation, including the product of Wilson's State Paper Office, the
Public Record Office, as well as several collections comprised of the papers of
officials involved in the Ulster project, including Davies, Chichester, Sir
George Carew, Sir Robert Cecil, and Sir Robert Cotton.[47] Yet the "archive," to use Foucault's sense of the term from *The Archaeology of Knowledge*,
consists of more than a repository of documents or the institutions devoted to
their preservation.[48] The material archive of documents is produced by an
epistemic "archive" that defines acceptable methods of enquiry and types of
evidence, the rules and criteria necessary to validate historiography's objective
processes and totalizing conclusions.

The archive, in Foucault's definition, additionally constitutes the site of this
power's limits, the necessary blind spots of historical memory. The archive
may thus positively establish the discursive parameters of historical enquiry.
Any search for unities and origins is thwarted through the archive's own contradictory tactics of accumulation and disappearance. And it is through this
failure that a space is opened up for historical inquiry. The archive, Foucault
argues, "deprives us of our continuities; it dissipates that temporal identity in
which we are pleased to look at ourselves when we wish to exorcise the dis-
continuities of history."[49] Through its memorial of the historical discontinui-
ties of the Ulster plantation, the archive provides a shared colonial history of
displacement and exploitation for present-day communities, a counter-memo-
ry that offsets both a memory of loss and mourning — the Flight of the Earls
— and a narrative of violence and ascendancy — the victory of the Orange-

---

[46] John Montague's poetic sequence *The Rough Field* (1972) exemplifies a recent
attempt to critique these competing mythologizations of Ulster history. Montague, for
example, juxtaposes the nostalgic conjurations of Catholic Gaelic Ireland with the
(ab)use of history by Protestant writers, even including extracts from Chichester,
Davies, and Spenser in his text (5th ed. [Winston-Salem: Wake Forest Univ. Press,
1989]).

[47] For a list of collections, see *CSP, Ire., 1603–1606*, xxxi–cix.

[48] Foucault, *The Archaeology of Knowledge*, 129.

[49] Foucault, *The Archaeology of Knowledge*, 131.

men.[50] In this project, as Paul Ricoeur once commented, "this exercise of memory is here an exercise in *telling otherwise*"; the archive, the site of these narratives' construction, can thus provide "a space for the confrontation between opposing testimonies."[51] Remembering how the Ulster plantation was forgotten, ultimately, not only enables a critique of colonial discourse and the production of knowledge in the archive. This critical practice functions as well to intervene in the present ways that communities know of themselves and act politically.

---

[50] For a general discussion of the role of cultural memory in contemporary Northern Ireland, see Kirkland, *Literature and Culture in Northern Ireland Since 1965.*

[51] "Memory and Forgetting" and "Imagination, Testimony and Trust: a Dialogue with Paul Ricoeur," in Richard Kearney and Mark Dooley, eds., *Questioning Ethics: Contemporary Debates in Philosophy* (London and New York: Routledge, 1999), 9, 16. Kerwin Lee Klein surveys and critiques the use of memory as a term of analysis in "On the Emergence of Memory in Historical Discourse," *Representations* 69 (2000): 127–50.

Renaissance English Text Society

Officers and Council

President, Arthur F. Kinney, University of Massachusetts at Amherst
Vice-President, A. R. Braunmuller, University of California, Los Angeles
Secretary, Carolyn Kent, New York, N.Y.
Treasurer, Robert E. Bjork, Arizona Center for Medieval and Renaissance Studies
Membership Secretary, William Gentrup, Arizona Center for Medieval and Renaissance Studies
Past President, W. Speed Hill, Lehman College and The Graduate Center, City University of New York
Past Publisher, Mario A. Di Cesare, Fairview, North Carolina

Margaret Ezell, Texas A&M University
Susan Felch, Calvin College
Roy Catesby Flannagan, University of South Carolina, Beaufort
David Freeman, Memorial University, Newfoundland
Suzanne Gossett, Loyola University of Chicago
Elizabeth Hageman, University of New Hampshire
Margaret Hannay, Siena College
John King, Ohio State University
Ian Lancashire, University of Toronto
Leah Marcus, Vanderbilt University
Arthur F. Marotti, Wayne State University
Steven May, Georgetown College
G. W. Pigman III, California Institute of Technology
Germaine Warkentin, Victoria College in the University of Toronto
George Walton Williams, Duke University

Liaisons

The Renaissance English Text Society was established to publish literary texts, chiefly nondramatic, of the period 1475–1660. Dues are $35.00 per annum ($25.00, graduate students; life membership is available at $500.00). Members receive the text published for each year of membership. The Society sponsors panels at such annual meetings as those of the Modern Language Association, the Renaissance Society of America, and the Medieval Congress at Kalamazoo.

General inquiries and proposals for editions should be addressed to the president, Arthur Kinney, Massachusetts Center for Renaissance Studies, PO Box 2300, Amherst, Mass., 01004, USA. Inquiries about membership should be addressed to William Gentrup, Membership Secretary, Arizona Center for Medieval and Renaissance Studies, Arizona State University, Box 872301, Tempe, Ariz., 85287–2301.

Copies of volumes X–XII may be purchased from Associated University Presses, 440 Forsgate Drive, Cranbury, N.J., 08512. Members may order copies of earlier volumes still in print or of later volumes from XIII, at special member prices, from the Treasurer.

FIRST SERIES

VOL. I. *Merie Tales of the Mad Men of Gotam* by A. B., edited by Stanley J. Kahrl, and *The History of Tom Thumbe* by R. I., edited by Curt F. Buhler, 1965. (o.p.)

VOL. II. Thomas Watson's Latin *Amyntas*, edited by Walter F. Staton, Jr., and Abraham Fraunce's translation *The Lamentations of Amyntas*, edited by Franklin M. Dickey, 1967.

SECOND SERIES

VOL. III. *The dyaloge called Funus*, A Translation of Erasmus's Colloquy (1534), and *A very pleasaunt & fruitful Diologe called The Epicure*, Gerrard's Translation of Erasmus's Colloquy (1545), edited by Robert R. Allen, 1969.

VOL. IV. *Leicester's Ghost* by Thomas Rogers, edited by Franklin B. Williams, Jr., 1972.

THIRD SERIES

VOLS. V–VI. *A Collection of Emblemes, Ancient and Moderne*, by George Wither, with an introduction by Rosemary Freeman and bibliographical notes by Charles S. Hensley, 1975. (o.p.)

FOURTH SERIES

VOLS. VII–VIII. *Tom a' Lincolne* by R. I., edited by Richard S. M. Hirsch, 1978.

FIFTH SERIES

VOL. IX. *Metrical Visions* by George Cavendish, edited by A. S. G. Edwards, 1980.

SIXTH SERIES

VOL. X. *Two Early Renaissance Bird Poems*, edited by Malcolm Andrew, 1984.

VOL. XI. *Argalus and Parthenia* by Francis Quarles, edited by David Freeman, 1986.

VOL. XII. Cicero's *De Officiis*, trans. Nicholas Grimald, edited by Gerald O'Gorman, 1987.

VOL. XIII. *The Silkewormes and their Flies* by Thomas Moffet (1599), edited with introduction and commentary by Victor Houliston, 1988.

SEVENTH SERIES

VOL. XIV. John Bale, *The Vocacyon of Johan Bale*, edited by Peter Happé and John N. King, 1989.

VOL. XV. *The Nondramatic Works of John Ford*, edited by L. E. Stock, Gilles D. Monsarrat, Judith M. Kennedy, and Dennis Danielson, with the assistance of Marta Straznicky, 1990.

SPECIAL PUBLICATION. *New Ways of Looking at Old Texts: Papers of the Renaissance English Text Society, 1985–1991*, edited by W. Speed Hill, 1993. (Sent gratis to all 1991 members.)

VOL. XVI. *George Herbert, The Temple: A Diplomatic Edition of the Bodleian Manuscript (Tanner 307)*, edited by Mario A. Di Cesare, 1991.

VOL. XVII. Lady Mary Wroth, *The First Part of the Countess of Montgomery's Urania*, edited by Josephine Roberts. 1992.

VOL. XVIII. Richard Beacon, *Solon His Follie*, edited by Clare Carroll and Vincent Carey. 1993.

VOL. XIX. An Collins, *Divine Songs and Meditacions*, edited by Sidney Gottlieb. 1994.

VOL. XX. *The Southwell-Sibthorpe Commonplace Book: Folger MS V.b.198*, edited by Sr. Jean Klene. 1995.

SPECIAL PUBLICATION. *New Ways of Looking at Old Texts II: Papers of the Renaissance English Text Society, 1992–1996*, edited by W. Speed Hill, 1998. (Sent gratis to all 1996 members.)

VOL. XXI. *The Collected Works of Anne Vaughan Lock*, edited by Susan M. Felch. 1996.

VOL. XXII. Thomas May, *The Reigne of King Henry the Second Written in Seauen Books*, edited by Götz Schmitz. 1997.

VOL. XXIII. *The Poems of Sir Walter Ralegh: A Historical Edition*, edited by Michael Rudick. 1998.

VOL. XXIV. Lady Mary Wroth, *The Second Part of the Countess of Montgomery's Urania*, edited by Josephine Roberts; completed by Suzanne Gossett and Janel Mueller. 1999.

VOL. XXV. *The Verse Miscellany of Constance Aston Fowler: A Diplomatic Edition*, by Deborah Aldrich-Watson. 2000.

VOL. XXVI. *An Edition of Luke Shepherd's Satires*, by Janice Devereux. 2001.

VOL. XXVII. *Philip Stubbes: The Anatomie of Abuses*, edited by Margaret Jane Kidnie. 2002.

VOL. XXVIII. *Cousins in Love: The Letters of Lydia DuGard, 1665–1672, with a new edition of* The Marriages of Cousin Germans *by Samuel DuGard*, edited by Nancy Taylor. 2003.

VOL. XXIX. *The Commonplace Book of Sir John Strangways (1645–1666)*, edited by Thomas G. Olsen. 2004.

SPECIAL PUBLICATION. *New Ways of Looking at Old Texts III: Papers of the Renaissance English Text Society, 1997–2001*, edited by W. Speed Hill, 2004. (Sent gratis to all 2001 members.)

MRTS

MEDIEVAL AND RENAISSANCE TEXTS AND STUDIES
is the major publising program of the
Arizona Center for Medieval and Renaissance Studies
at Arizona State University, Tempe, Arizona.

MRTS emphasizes books that are needed ----
editions, translations, and major research tools ----
but also welcomes monographs and
collections of essays on focused themes.

MRTS aims to publish the highest quality scholarship
in attractive and durable format at modest cost.